ONE BOLD DEED OF
OPEN TREASON

In memory of
Dr Charles E. Curry

ONE BOLD DEED OF OPEN TREASON

The Berlin Diary of Roger Casement,
1914–1916

Edited by

ANGUS MITCHELL

MERRION
PRESS

Published in 2016 by
Merrion Press
8 Chapel Lane
Sallins
Co. Kildare

© 2016 National Library of Ireland
Introduction © Angus Mitchell 2016

British Library Cataloguing in Publication Data
An entry can be found on request

978-1-78537-056-4- (paper)
978-1-78537-057-1- (cloth)
978-1-78537-058-8-(PDF)
978-1-78537-059-5-(Epub)
978-1-78537-060-1-(Kindle)

Library of Congress Cataloging in Publication Data
An entry can be found on request

CONTENTS

MAPS

ACKNOWLEDGEMENTS

A photocopy of Casement's Berlin Diary has been in my possession for almost two decades. It was initially supplied to me by the former Keeper of Manuscripts at the National Library of Ireland, Gerard Lyne. The entire staff of that great institution are deserving of gratitude for my endless demands on their time. In particular, I must thank Colette O'Flaherty, Tom Desmond and James Harte.

Images were supplied by three principal collections. My thanks to the National Portrait Gallery, London; Günter Scheidemann at the Politisches Archiv des Auswärtigen Amts in Berlin; and Villanova University, where Michael Foight was of great assistance.

Film historian Ron van Dopperen provided valuable support in tracking down images and filling me in on Albert K. Dawson, who filmed and photographed Casement in Berlin in April 1915. His colleague Cooper Graham found and restored the image used on the cover.

Sections from this diary were published in *Field Day Review* 8 (2012) and it was with the initial support of Stephen Rea and Seamus Deane that I decided to undertake this work on Casement's months in Germany.

Conor Graham at Merrion Press was supportive of the edition from our initial discussion of the idea during the History Festival of Ireland held at Huntington Castle in Clonegal in June 2014. Lisa Hyde steered the book through to completion, although I never had the pleasure of meeting her in person.

In Limerick, my thanks to Tom Toomey Des Ryan and Anthony O'Brien and the on-going work of *The Old Limerick Journal*. Over the years, my Saturday morning meetings at the Milk Market with Brian P. Murphy have been a constant source of vital information and discussion.

At home, I must thank with all my heart Caoilfhionn, who was endlessly patient with my demands and was always ready to read through drafts of work and offer her thoughts and wisdom.

PART 1
INTRODUCTION

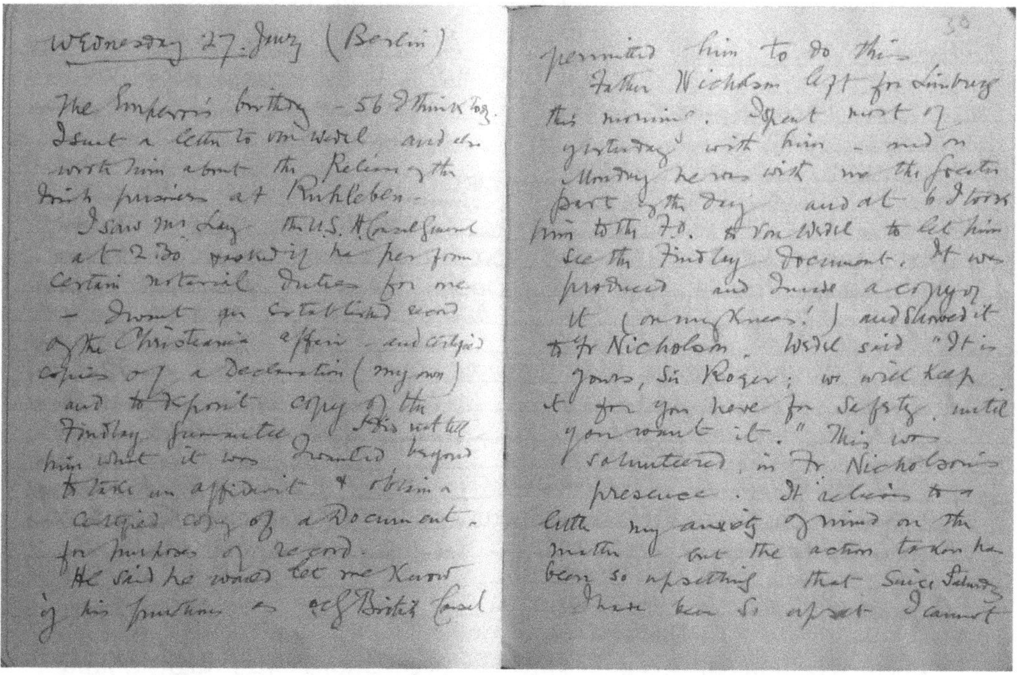
Wednesday 27. Jany (Berlin)

The Emperor's birthday - 56 I think to-day.
I sent a letter to von Wedel and also
wrote him about the Release of the
Irish prisoners at Ruhleben.
I saw Mr Ley the U.S. [illegible] Consul General
at 2.30 & asked if he [illegible] for
certain notarial duties for me
- I want an established record
of the Christiania affair - and certified
copies of a declaration (my own)
and to deposit copy of the
Findlay guarantee. I did not tell
him what it was I wanted beyond
to take an affidavit & obtain a
certified copy of a Document -
for purposes of record.
He said he would let me know
if his position as acting British Consul

permitted him to do this.
Father Nicholson left for Limburg
this morning. I spent most of
yesterday with him - and on
Monday he was with me the greater
part of the day and at 6 I took
him to the F.O. to von Wedel to let him
see the Findlay Document. It was
produced and I made a copy of
it (on my knees!) and showed it
to Fr Nicholson. Wedel said "It is
yours, Sir Roger; we will keep
it for you here for safety until
you want it." This was
volunteered in Fr. Nicholson's
presence. It relieves [illegible]
little my anxiety of mind on the
matter but the action taken has
been so upsetting that since Saturday
I have been so upset I cannot

The war diary maintained by Roger Casement during his eighteen months in Imperial Germany is one of the most candid and impenitent confessions of treason ever scripted by a subject and servant of the British Crown. Plotting a critical stage in Casement's path to the scaffold in Pentonville Prison, London, the first entry was penned shortly after his arrival in Berlin in November 1914. Despite significant silences and interruptions, the diary chronicles a defining moment in the destiny of both the movement for Irish independence and European diplomatic relations. The relevance of the account is further elevated by the fact that Casement quite clearly intended it for public scrutiny. In early April 1916, as he prepared for his departure for Ireland on board a German submarine, he left careful instructions for the safe-keeping of his papers and for the eventual publication of some of his writings, including this diary, which he considered to be a vital insight and full record into the logic behind his self-confessed 'treason'.

Most of the diary has survived in two identifiable manuscript sources; both are archived in the National Library of Ireland. The first section, written between November 1914 and February 1915, is contained in two blue notebooks: [MSS 1689-90]. There is then a gap of roughly a year, as described by Casement in a brief bridging entry and added at the start of 1916. A second document [MS 5244], with entries from 17 March to 8 April 1916, covers 134 numbered sides of script, with additional comments and marginalia added on 8 April 1916. The first page is titled *A Last Page*, and is inscribed on headed Irish Brigade paper. The pages were later bound in a black, hardback cover. Several photographed and typescript copies of this second document have survived. Supplementing these final entries are some fragmentary diary entries briefly describing events from 9–11 April 1916.[1]

In brief, the diary describes Casement's part in the move towards open rebellion in Ireland, and his negotiations with high-ranking military and political figures in the German General Staff. His reasons

---

[1] National Library of Ireland (henceforth NLI) MS 17587 (1) and (2) with four ink manuscript pages entitled *Rough notes of last days in Berlin*.

for going to Germany were pithily explained in an essay – *Why I went to Germany* – written in December 1915, and first published the week after his execution. This essay provides relevant background information, and is published as Appendix 1.

Early paragraphs of the diary provide some context, and sketch Casement's movements from late June 1914, when he departed Ireland for the US, and the early weeks of his time in the US, before the outbreak of war in Europe, in August 1914. The diary then comes to an abrupt halt. The outbreak of war changed everything. For several years, Casement had predicted that conflict was inevitable due to the trajectory of British foreign policy since the signing of the Entente Cordiale (1904) and the Triple Entente (1907). The war brought Casement into direct confrontation with his former

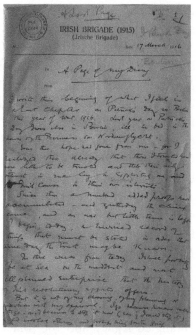

A Last Page – The opening page of Roger Casement's diary, dated St Patrick's Day 1916, and describing his last days in Germany before returning to Ireland aboard a submarine. [National Library of Ireland]

colleagues in the British Foreign Office. He remained in the US for the next two and a half months, working hard to try to keep Ireland out of the war. Conspiring with the Irish revolutionary underground in the US, he was eventually chosen to undertake a journey to Germany to serve as liaison officer and diplomat between Berlin and the U.S. It was an extremely perilous undertaking; he had been under close surveillance by the British secret services since the start of the year. By the time he set sail from New York, and travelling under a false identity, Casement was a marked man. The ship he sailed on, the *SS Oskar II* was intercepted as it crossed the Atlantic and ordered to dock on the Hebridean island of Lewis, whereupon it was rigorously searched. Casement was lucky to avoid capture.

A few days later, during a brief stop-over in Christiania (Oslo), agencies of the British secret state conspired to have their knighted consul general 'knocked on the head' before he reached Berlin. British embassy officials approached Casement's manservant, Adler Christensen, and a conspiracy was set in motion. This notorious incident became known as the 'Findlay Affair' or 'Christiania incident' – named after the British Minister (ambassador) in Christiania, Mansfeldt de Cardonnel Findlay. Over the following months, the confrontation mushroomed into a malicious and disagreeable embarrassment of misinformation, subterfuge, forgeries and false allegations. The British government eventually offered Christensen £5000 – with a relative value of over £400,000 in 2016 – to betray Casement. The plotting tormented Casement and it won him few allies, though he referred to it repeatedly in his diary, correspondence and published journalism. When this diary was first published in 1922, the incident was given central prominence even in the title: *Diaries of Sir Roger Casement: His Mission to Germany and the Findlay Affair* (Munich: Arche Publishing, 1922). Understanding this conspiracy between Casement and the British Government is fundamental to unlocking the deeper truths about the complications that emerged over Casement's own entangled legacy and the 'Black Diaries' controversy' that has come to dominate and determine his historical interpretation.

While Casement's diary contains various revealing entries about the conspiracy as it developed, Casement's narrative was most plainly outlined in his letter to Sir Edward Grey, dated 1 February 1915 (Appendix 2). This was distributed to various foreign embassies, and it maximised disclosures about the most nefarious action on the part of Findlay and exposed the British Foreign Office to a barrage of negative publicity. However, though the Findlay Affair is undoubtedly important to understanding Casement's bitter confrontation with his former paymasters, it obscures other dimensions of his mission to Germany that are no less important.

A few weeks after arriving in Berlin, and still travelling under another assumed identity (that of Mr Hammond, given to him by the German authorities), Casement made a forty-eight hour round-trip journey to the German General Staff on the Western Front. This is the first substantive event detailed in the diary. He described his route through war-torn Belgium, visiting several of the towns and cities that were exposed to the brute force of the German advance as the Schlieffen Plan was mobilised. This is an important account, by a seasoned investigator of atrocities, into the devastation resulting from the German presence in Belgium.

On his return to Berlin, Casement's real identity was revealed to the world's press, and his name was openly attached to the publication of a *Declaration of Goodwill* proclaiming Germany's peaceful intentions towards the Irish people. Over the following months, Casement met with several leading military and political figures including German chancellor, Theobald von Bethmann Hollweg. He commented on various matters, such as the news of the revival of British diplomatic relations with the Vatican, which he felt was another ploy to undermine Irish influence abroad. In December 1914 and January 1915 he travelled, for extended periods, to the camp at Limburg, in an effort to build an Irish Brigade from among captured POWs. Towards the end of 1914, he managed to sign a treaty with the German Government, setting down the organising principles of the Brigade. The ten articles of that treaty are frequently referenced in the diary. They too have been reproduced (Appendix 3).

By early 1915, as the war dragged on and his plans for the Irish Brigade failed to take off, he grew disillusioned with both the war and Prussian militarism. His diary shuts down for the next thirteen months. Much of what is known about Casement over the following year can be gleaned from his extensive correspondence and his propaganda writings. He travelled to several cities in Germany, including Hamburg, Dresden, Leipzig and Munich, although none of these journeys are covered in the diary. One revealing artefact surviving from this period is the fragment of film footage of Casement, shot by the US documentary film-maker, Albert K. Dawson. Both the film clip and the associated photographs, also by Dawson, reveal Casement's concern for how he would be remembered. They show him at work in his hotel room, and at his desk busily writing. The film would be exposed to an audience of millions in the US after Casement's execution in August 1916.

In an effort to provide some support for Casement and keep the revolutionary momentum going, the Supreme Council of the IRB in Ireland sent out Joseph Mary Plunkett to try to revitalise relations with the German General Staff. Over several weeks, Casement and Plunkett worked hard to stimulate German interest in the potential of the Irish cause. From Plunkett, Casement first learned of plans for a rebellion in Ireland, but he was largely disapproving of the idea and remained skeptical of what such a show of resistance would ultimately gain. Without the right military support from Germany, he felt that it would amount to little more than a sacrifice of precious blood, and that it could provide

Britain with a propaganda advantage. He nonetheless collaborated on the *Ireland Report*, setting out possible guidelines on how a German military intervention might contribute towards an Irish rebellion.[2]

Plunkett's mission was followed by the arrival, in the autumn, of Robert Monteith, who took over the day-to-day running of the Brigade. Fifty-three men were moved to a camp at Zossen, on the outskirts of Berlin, with the promise that they would be properly trained, but the Brigade never attained the proposed target of two hundred volunteers, and the German General Staff lost faith in the venture.

Casement spent much of the summer and autumn of 1915 living quite simply, in the small Bavarian village of Riederau on the banks of Lake Ammersee, south west of Munich. During these months he produced a significant body of propaganda writings. Much of his output was published under various pseudonyms in an English-language propaganda newspaper, *The Continental Times*. Some articles were then republished in the organ of the IRB, *The Gaelic American*. Casement adopted a position that belligerently and unreservedly attacked both the British press and the inner circle of the British Liberal Party, who, Casement believed, had been responsible for dragging the world into the war and betraying the cause of Irish Home Rule. What gives Casement's argument substance is that he had first-hand experience of working with the British foreign secretary, Sir Edward Grey, the minister who had given him considerable support in both his Congo and Amazon campaigns.

Over the winter of 1915, a combination of tropical fever and nervous exhaustion forced Casement to retire to a sanatorium near Munich, where he spent several weeks in early 1916; it was there he heard of the plans for a rising at Easter. Despite various ailments and low levels of energy, he made one last effort to exert his influence to stop the rebellion or, failing that, to return to Ireland to die for the cause. The second substantive period of his German diary – detailing the period from 17 March to 8 April 1916 – cover the last weeks of his mission to Germany. It depicts his high-level meetings with representatives from the German General Staff, the German Foreign Office and the Admiralty, before he embarked on board a submarine bound for the south-west coast of Ireland.

In the thirteen months separating these two sections of the diary, it is apparent how his attitude to Germany's political authorities had

---

[2] A version of the report is held in NLI MS 13085-5.

undergone a fundamental change. His initial belief in the sincerity of the support of the German General Staff for Irish independence had evaporated well in advance of his departure from Germany. Negotiations with some of the most senior officials in the German Foreign Office and German General Staff had turned acrimonious. Increasingly, his relations were undermined by suspicion and distrust. At times, Casement's inner reflections bordered on the paranoid. His sympathies lay with the German people, who were in thrall, as he saw it, to the curse of Prussian militarism. In November 1914, Casement had believed Germany would win the war; this was a view he no longer entertained when he boarded the submarine in April 1916.

As a whole, the diary is unusually revealing about the political mechanics of war. The narrative allows some insight into the working of German intelligence and the mentalité of senior figures within the German General Staff. Even today, a century on from the activities described, his account makes for profoundly harrowing reading, and demands awkward questions to be asked about the role of the secret services and covert propaganda activities during the First World War. The writing is infused with raw emotion: anger, frustration, determination, self-pity and guilt. Casement's deeply hostile comments against the British ruling establishment and the collective mindset of 'Englishness' should be understood in the context of the deep hostilities of the time, and his belief that the war was a great betrayal and the consequence of years of secret diplomacy and generations of political bungling by Westminster over Ireland. His disgust at the duplicity of British power is matched by his anger and exasperation, levelled at the German military officialdom.

Independent Ireland has found it complicated to incorporate the narrative of this decorated imperial official into its foundational history, an officer who played a pivotal role in both the intellectual and practical formation of the Irish Volunteers and then returned to Ireland to try and stop the Rising. The tendency in the troubled historiography of 1916 has been to downplay Irish relations with Germany. Equally, Britain has turned its back on the renegade traitor, and done its utmost to mask the logic of his treason. Both these positions are expediently simplified in and by the toxic dualism of his reputation as British 'traitor' or Irish 'martyr'.

The Politics of Diary Writing

On 1 February 1916, as Casement lay in a convalescent home near Munich, he wrote a personal letter to the Countess Blücher responding to her request asking if he would help her embellish her diary with a personal touch because, she confided, she lacked the gift of description. His response sets out some of his own thoughts on diary-keeping and hints at the reasons why he stopped writing his diary in early 1915:

> You know the charm of a diary is its simplicity. Its reality and the sense of daily life it conveys to the reader depends not on style, but on truth and sincerity. It should tell things but still more of the writer and his (or her) outlook on those things. Its personality is its chief claim to the interest of the reader – and no one can give the personal touch but the person who keeps the diary. I kept one for the first three months or so of my stay in this country, & then I gave it up because I became too personal! I found myself writing things best left unwritten – even unthought – & since I could not tell the truth, even to myself, I dropped the pen – a year ago.[3]

This remark recognised, too, the importance of his diary in ultimately justifying and clarifying his self-confessed treachery. By publishing his version of events explaining why he went to Germany, and why he had determined to further internationalise the issue of Irish independence and raise an Irish Brigade, the manifest honesty of his motives and the sincerity of his beliefs would add to the logic of his 'treason' an appealing, affective dimension. When his plans began to unravel, he gave up his routine of diary-writing because he realised how it might leave him vulnerable. When he restarted the diary in March 1916, he reflected on his reasons for the break in the narrative:

> I stopped that Diary when it became clear that I was being played with, fooled and used by a most selfish and unscrupulous government for its own petty interests. I did not wish to record the misery I felt or to say the things my heart prompted. But today it is my head compels me to this unwelcome task.

---

[3] Clare County Archives, Roger Casement to Countess Blücher, 1 February 1916. The letter was written in response to one from Evelyn Blücher of 30 January.

But the substantive record he kept of his last weeks in Berlin was undertaken with purpose. While recording his doubts about the rising and what it might achieve, he honestly admitted to the desperate and nigh impossible situation in which he found himself. He assiduously recorded his meetings with some of the most senior figures involved in the war and his deepening differences with the German spymaster, Rudolf Nadolny. But most of these encounters related mounting tensions and the frustrations he faced in his dealings with the German Government. A week before leaving he wrote: 'If my diary is ever published – as some day it may be – what a figure all these military minds or political minds of this great Empire will cut!' In his days before leaving he read excerpts from his diary to his closest friends and sympathetic officials in order to elicit feedback from them.

From these internal comments within the diary and from various comments made in correspondence, it is apparent that like many of his generation, he recognised the diary genre as a vital source in the recording and recovery of history. However, committing such private thoughts to paper had the potential to be over-revealing and potentially self-destructive. If his intention behind keeping a diary was to serve as an accurate record of his actions, he was acutely aware that there were 'special forces' at play determined to undermine his reputation and, by deliberate misinformation, to shape public opinion about his aims, purposes and competence.

Nothing, he realised, could be left to chance. The publication of his own version of events was therefore vital to his eventual exoneration from the calumnies that besieged him. Experience had taught him when undertaking official investigations into crimes against humanity in the Congo and the Amazon that governments would mount egregious campaigns of defamation to protect reputations. He had watched the power and authority of King Leopold II deny and undermine his campaign in the Congo and mount a counter offensive. He was conscious, too, that he was extremely vulnerable to black propaganda campaigns.

> For, with me in their hands, the 'archtraitor' and all the rest of it, the English government will try how [sic] most to <u>humiliate</u> & <u>degrade</u> me. They will not honour me with a high treason trial. I am convinced of that. Then I should become a martyr or a hero of revolutionary Ireland. They will rob Ireland of that & they will charge

me with something else – something baser than 'high treason' – God knows what – & what chance of a trial will I have on any charge they chose to get up against me?[4]

This prescient sense of how the British authorities would ultimately take control of his meaning and seek to deny his heroism prompted him to be particularly cautious about his legacy. His Berlin diary returns to a theme that runs through Casement's writing: the question of his archive. He recognised that papers, correspondence and journals or diaries were the very currency and legal tender of history. During his career as a consular official, he had generated a labyrinth of writings. Official correspondence was supplemented with an equally extensive body of letters to family, friends and political allies revealing his private thoughts and motivations. But Casement had learnt too that papers and narratives were vulnerable to manipulation and that writings could be used for strategic purposes that were highly questionable. There is one very telling episode from his Berlin diary that shows how he was prepared to deploy diaries in a malevolent strategy of misinformation. As his vicious engagement with Findlay and the Foreign Office deepened and was placed on a war-footing, Casement deployed faked pages from his diary in order to deliberately deceive and trick the British Government. On 24 November 1914, he recorded:

> On Sunday I saw Adler off at 11.18 to Sassnitz with two faked letters and two 'stolen' pages of 'my Diary' giving hints at impending invasion of Ireland by myself and friends here (50.000) 'by end of December'.

In adopting the diary as a weapon of misinformation, he provoked a stratagem that would ultimately prove personally devastating in the battle for his own legacy and place in history. In the prolonged and tiresome debate over the authenticity of the 'Black Diaries', it is astonishing that the implications of this incident have been ignored. Is the protracted campaign by British intelligence agencies to manage Casement's public meaning ultimately justified in the light of this episode?

While he recognised that papers could be purveyors of historical 'truth', he was equally conscious of how they could be highly incriminating.

---

[4] NLI 17026, 26 March 1916.

From various comments in other parts of his archive, it is known that he was quite prepared to destroy documentation if he believed it could end up in the wrong hands. On the voyage from New York to Germany in October 1914, Casement had thrown overboard 'the diary of his last voyage across the Atlantic, together with other papers and documents'.[5] The inference was that the document revealed information that was potentially incriminating to his revolutionary allies. On his way from Berlin to Sassnitz, on 1 February 1915, he diaried how he had 'burned some papers I found the enemy might seize if I were arrested'. For this reason the destiny and safety of his papers became a high priority as he prepared to leave Germany and return to Ireland.

It is also apparent that if Casement's trial had not been so deliberately restricted and managed by the prosecution, he might well have submitted his Berlin diary in his defence. His diary, he argued, revealed a more precise truth than the one that could be revealed under oath in court from witnesses. But his request to send the US attorney, Michael Francis Doyle to Germany to retrieve his papers was prohibited. In his trial notes, he made reference to the diary and why he had kept it. When speaking about the slightly unreliable memory of the soldiers used as witnesses to testify against him, he commented:

> But my memory is more precise than theirs – for I recorded most of what I said at the time or what was said to me in my diary – and that record is in existence – in another land – and some day can stand as evidence of the truth of what I now assert.[6]

The assertion of Casement's 'truth' has, however, not proved as straightforward as he had hoped and part of the reason is the troubled history concerning the diaries that have played such a critical role in the structuring of his narrative.

Dispersal of Papers

In the months before his departure from Berlin, he left detailed orders for the dispersal and eventual publication of his papers. Several of his closest

---

[5] Charles Curry (ed.), *Diaries of Sir Roger Casement: His Mission to Germany and the Findlay Affair* (Munich: Arche Publishing, 1922), 30.

[6] NLI MS 13,088 (5/v).

friends and collaborators became the appointed trustees of his documents. On 20 September 1915, he wrote a letter to Joe McGarrity giving details of documents that he was leaving in a strong box in the Dresden Bank mainly to do with the Findlay Affair.[7] 'The documents are important,' he wrote 'they are historic & I leave them to Ireland'. A letter pasted into his diary and dated Dresden, 3 January 1916 bequeathed 'all my letters, books, papers etc. in Germany or elsewhere' to Joseph McGarrity.

In the weeks before his departure, he deposited other papers with his inner circle of collaborators. Some papers were left with Gebhard von Blücher, a friend from his earliest consular posting to Lourenço Marques (Maputo), the capital of Portuguese East Africa (Mozambique). A significant tranche of his private correspondence with Blücher and supplementary documents are held

Joe McGarrity: Casement's ally in the US, who was bequeathed many papers from Casement's German archive along with other important personal papers [Digital Library@Villanova University]

in Clare County Archives. Further papers to do with the Irish Brigade were handed to the Limerick-born, Thomas St John Gaffney. 'He also entrusted to me a portmanteau containing his private papers with full instructions as to their disposition,' Gaffney recalled in his memoir.[8]

The most trusted executor of his orders was Dr Charles Curry, an American citizen, who Casement had befriended during his months residing in Bavaria. Little is known of Curry, but Casement appears to have invested great trust and faith in him. It proved to be a sagacious choice. His correspondence with Curry reveals his wish that his time in

---

[7] NLI MS 17017.

[8] Gaffney, Thomas St John, *Breaking the Silence: England, Ireland, Wilson and the War* (New York, 1930), 160.

Germany be carefully written up after the war.[9] In letters written to Curry before his departure, he sketched out a strategy for the gathering up and sorting out of his archive and the eventual editing of his papers. On 26 March 1916, on his final visit to Munich, he wrote two lengthy notes to Curry that included detailed information about his papers:

> I will send you a bundle of my 'Diary' (<u>very confidential</u>) and the papers of the poor little, forlorn 'Irish Brigade' those now in the possession of Lt. Monteith. All this 'raw material' should, with the letters & copies of my letters in the various trunks, allow a fairly complete history of my stay in Germany be put together ... The best person to edit all would be Professor Kuno Meyer, the Celtic Scholar.[10]

In a letter of 3 April 1916, written to Dr Charles Curry, Casement seemed to extend Curry's brief and asked him after the war to undertake a specific operation to gather up the papers and have them placed in safe hands. He ordered: 'You might open all the trunks – the two at Mrs Green's as well as the others – & go through the letters. Never mind books and newspapers get the letters sorted. All official ones & my drafts of replies & all letters referring to the "Brigade" together ... I will tell Mrs G. to let you have the trunks.'[11]

Since 1904, Casement had carried on a close correspondence with Alice Stopford Green on questions of Irish history, colonial affairs and their shared frustrations with the direction of Liberal Imperialist politics. Stopford Green knew Casement as well as any of his friends, but despite her tireless efforts to save him from the scaffold she was disapproving of his mission to Germany. Casement had suggested Kuno Meyer as the obvious editor of his German papers, but Meyer died in 1919. Another possible candidate was E. D. Morel, his collaborator in the Congo Reform Association campaign, but Morel was busy organising the anti-war pressure group, the Union of Democratic Control and was imprisoned not long after Casement's execution on some technical infringement of

---

[9] Principal correspondence with Curry is held in National Library of Ireland, there are copies of earlier correspondence held in the Public Record Office of Northern Ireland, T/3787/20-23.

[10] NLI MS 17026, 26 March 1916 – 'A Last Word for my True Friend'.

[11] NLI MS 17025, 3 April 1916.

the Defence of the Realm Act. Apart from suggesting possible allies who might edit his German papers, Casement set down some brief editorial guidelines. In a letter written to Dr Charles Curry, on April 9th, he commented:

> The Diaries are very poor stuff very poorly written and hastily put together – and would need much editing by a friend – for I often say things in them I should not like to stand for ever. It is so hard to see straight even when one is well and not troubled – and I am not well in body and have not been for long and then greatly troubled too in mind – so that my remarks are often unjust and hasty and ill considered.[12]

In a letter written on 6 June 1916, as he waited trial for treason in Brixton Prison, he confided to a relative:

> Some day a rather interesting account of my doings will see the light I hope – altho' I shall not be able to revise the proofs – but it will show a side to the picture that people now in this jaundiced time don't understand – or could not. I have left a pretty full record with a trustworthy executor, I hope.[13]

While the comment quite deliberately does not mention specific names, the 'interesting account of my doings' would appear to refer to the diary and other associated documentation that had been left with Curry, the trustworthy executor. Yet, despite the carefully stated intentions regarding his papers, it seems that a significant part of his archive did pass through the hands of British Military Intelligence. After the war, the authorities were keen to round up material on Casement's brigade and his German activities. A typed list compiled by Captain N.C. Harrington of G-2 Branch of the Department of Defence has survived.[14] However, there is no reference to the diaries on this list. Various papers in the possession of the Blüchers were handed over voluntarily to the British authorities and the English-born Countess Blücher, who had

---

[12] Curry, 197.

[13] Public Record Office of Northern Ireland T/3787/19/1, 6 June 1916.

[14] NLI 13085 1-i,

sought his advice on diary-writing, revised her view of Casement in the light of the German defeat, and wrote some highly critical comments about him in her popular volume of memoirs based upon her war-time diaries.

Publication of the Diaries

Notwithstanding his various instructions to Curry and others, making Casement's diary public proved difficult and controversial. Curry kept his word, and after the war he set about publishing the chronicle with the help of Joe McGarrity. Initially, the principal platform was the US journal, *The Nation*, founded in 1865 and the flagship publication of the political Left in the US. Between November 1921 and February 1922, as the negotiations for the Anglo-Irish Treaty were taking place in London, *The Nation* published weekly extracts from the war diaries along with associated correspondence.

Ater the founding of the Irish Free State, the diary was published in Munich.[15] Curry supplemented the daily narrative, from November 1914 to February 1915, with other documents. He included private letters between Casement and his sister Agnes; correspondence by Christensen on the conspiracy; and the foreword to an unpublished book entitled *The Findlay Affair*. A certain amount of strategic editing was employed. Several names were redacted, as many of the figures mentioned in the text were still alive. The most significant omission was the lengthy entry describing Casement's journey to the Western Front from 17–19 November 1914.[16] Casement wrote about this journey in some detail and it stands as a perceptive eyewitness account of one of the most controversial aspects of the war: German atrocities in Belgium. Although there was a brief acknowledgment to the diary in which he had detailed his last days in Germany in March and April 1916, none of it was included.[17] Curry's

---

[15] The original title was *Diaries of Sir Roger Casement: His Mission to Germany and the Findlay Affair* (Munich: Arche Publishing, 1922) a German translation appeared a few years later, *Sir Roger Casement: Meine Mission Deutschland während des Krieges und die Findlay-Affaire* (Altenburg/Thüringen, 1925).

[16] See *Field Day Review* 8, 'My Journey to the German Headquarters at Charleville' (Dublin, 2012), 23–44.

[17] See *Field Day Review* 8, 'A Last Page of my Diary' (Dublin, 2012), 45–83.

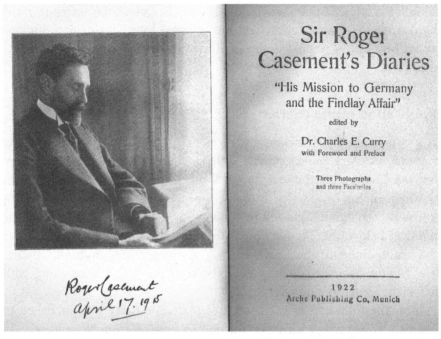

Sir Rogei
Casement's Diaries

"His Mission to Germany
and the Findlay Affair"

edited by

Dr. Charles E. Curry
with Foreword and Preface

Three Photographs
and three Facsimiles

1922
Arche Publishing Co. Munich

Roger Casement
april 17. 1915

The title page from Dr Charles Curry's edition of Roger Casement's German Diary, published in Munich in 1923 [Angus Mitchell]

edition was clearly intended to focus on the Findlay conspiracy and to publicise the antagonisms between Casement and his former paymasters.

Another significant difference between the published diary and the surviving manuscript version are the entries between 31 October and 2 November 1914, recounting Casement's journey on from Scandinavia to Germany. This included his highly explicit explanation of treason, written as he sat in the German Foreign Office, at 76 Wilhelmstrasse, awaiting his introductory meetings with Arthur Zimmermann and Georg von Wedel. What happened to the manuscript pages of these entries is unclear? One possble explanation is that the entries 'went missing' when the diary was rebound. Curry described the physical diaries that he received from Casement as contained in 'four quarto note-books of 180 pages each'.[18] Yet, the diaries that are held in the National Library of Ireland appear to

---

[18] Curry, 197.

have been rebound into two volumes. Both pagination and binding are somewhat puzzling and would indicate that rebinding work was carried out. But when or by whom is uncertain?

Publication of the diaries in the US unleashed another chapter in the war of words over Casement's reputation. Just as *The Nation* published its final instalment on 8 February 1922, Michael Collins was invited to the House of Lords by the Lord Chancellor, Lord Birkenhead, to inspect the so-called 'Black Diaries'. Alleged extracts from these documents had been strategically deployed against Casement, at the time of his trial, to destabilise his defence and turn influential supporters against him. Lord Birkenhead's determination to involve Collins in the authentication of the diaries would suggest that Casement was a sacrificial victim to secret diplomacy at the very foundation of the Irish Free State. On his return to Ireland after inspecting the diaries, Collins opened up a file in the Department of the Taoiseach entitled 'Alleged Casement Diaries' and thereby initiated one of the longest running historical controversies in Anglo-Irish relations.

Diplomacy apart, the Berlin diary is intrinsic to any deeper understanding of the on-going diaries' controversy and an informed interrogation of their authenticity. What the diary ultimately reveals about Casement is an extraordinary honesty about his 'one bold deed of open treason'. While his months in Germany might have ultimately ended in failure and his own personal isolation – a 'hopeless mission' – he never faltered from his belief that the logic behind his actions would be justified before the tribunal of history. In keeping this diary, he quite clearly intended to leave a record that would demonstrate that his intentions had been genuine, even if his situation had proved ultimately disastrous. By forcing the hand of the German government into accepting the cause of Irish independence, he ultimately repositioned the question of Irish sovereignty within an international framework. Even if Ireland still finds it hard to accept Casement, he has been acknowledged as the founder of an independent Irish foreign policy – a foreign policy centred on European integration and a compassionate concern for humanity, rather than the British Empire and the blind pursuit of commercial profit.

Notes on the Editing

In order to create a reader friendly text, certain passages have been edited out and the overall volume of words reduced by roughly 20,000 words. Whenever text has been omitted an ellipsis has been inserted. For those in search of more detail, two large sections of the diary, containing individual introductions, have been published in full in *Field Day Review* 8 (2012). These include Casement's journey to the Western Front and the entire text of *A Last Page*. Researchers requiring a complete version of these entries are referred there. The intention of this edition is to provide an accessible version of the diary for the general reader that is not encumbered with dense annotation, but can provide insight into one of the most extraordinary footnotes to the First World War.

The process of editing inevitably means making hard choices. The dates at the start of each entry have been standardised. On occasions it has been necessary to slightly rearrange the text, when entries belong naturally to a different day. Casement did not write up the diary regularly. Some entries are written several days after the events they describe. The narrative between Saturday 23 January 1915 and 11 February is in places quite confused in terms of chronology. A small amount of rearrangement has been done during this period in order to clarify. Occasionally there are two entries for the same day.

Casement included a significant amount of news about the war, and some quite dense paragraphs of statistics detailing British casualties weigh down the narrative and have been omitted.

PART 2
THE DIARIES

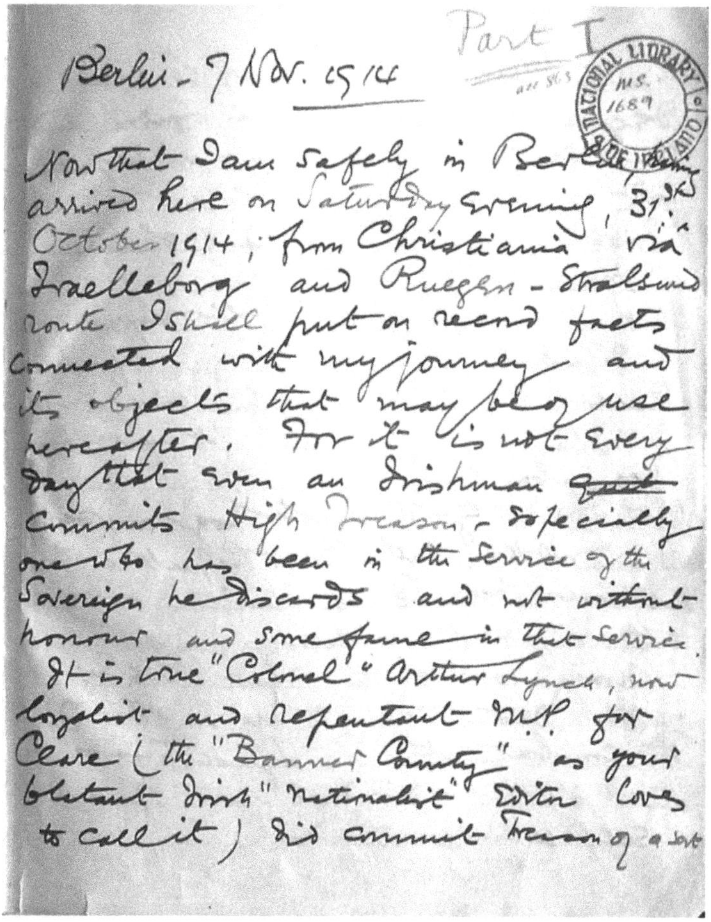

Part I

Berlin – 7 Nov. 1914

Now that I am safely in Berlin, (having) arrived here on Saturday evening, 31st October 1914, from Christiania via Trelleborg and Ruegen-Stralsund route I shall put on record facts connected with my journey and its objects that may be of use hereafter. For it is not every day that even an Irishman ~~quit~~ commits High Treason – especially one who has been in the service of the Sovereign he discards and not without honour and some fame in that service. It is true "Colonel" Arthur Lynch, now loyalist and repentant M.P. for Clare (the "Banner County" as your blatant Irish "Nationalist" Editor loves to call it) did commit Treason of a sort

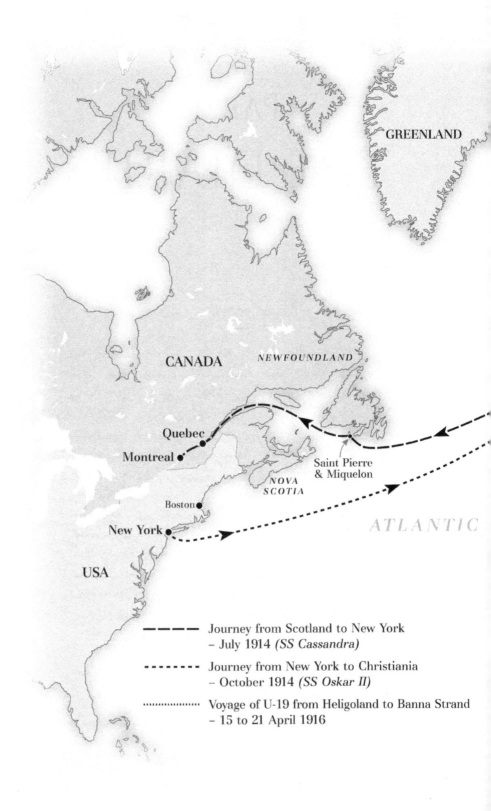

GREENLAND

CANADA   *NEWFOUNDLAND*

Quebec
Montreal

Saint Pierre
& Miquelon

*NOVA
SCOTIA*

Boston

New York

ATLANTIC

USA

— — — — Journey from Scotland to New York
– July 1914 *(SS Cassandra)*

- - - - - - Journey from New York to Christiania
– October 1914 *(SS Oskar II)*

·················· Voyage of U-19 from Heligoland to Banna Strand
– 15 to 21 April 1916

The Atlantic travels of
Roger Casement 1914-16

ICELAND

SWEDEN

NORWAY

Stornoway

Christiania
(Oslo)

Tory Island

Ängelholm

Glasgow

Malmö

UNITED
KINGDOM

IRELAND

Heligoland
Wilhelmshaven

Banna
Strand

London

Berlin

BELGIUM

GERMANY

Paris

FRANCE

ITALY

CEAN

SPAIN

ITALY

ALGERIA

MOROCCO

0   500   1000

Scale   Kilometres

A Brief Account of the Journey from Ireland to New York

Now that I am safely in Berlin, having arrived here on Saturday evening, 31 October 1914, from Christiania [Oslo] [...] I shall put on record facts connected with my journey and its objects that may be of use hereafter. For it is not every day that even an Irishman commits High Treason especially one who has been in the service of the Sovereign he discards and not without honour and some fame in that service.

[...]

When I left Ireland on 2 July last and Glasgow in the 'Cassandra' (name of ill omen!) on the 4th as a second class 'emigrant' to Montreal, how little did I think of what was before me!

I chose that route in order to avoid publicity and possible interviews at New York, and the quite probable attentions of the British spy bureau, whose agents in Ireland had been so maladroitly pursuing me since the beginning of the year.

I embarked on the 'Cassandra' on 4 July in the Clyde as 'Mr. R. D. Casement' my right name and initials, but without the prefix my knighthood conferred. No one suspected I was Sir Roger Casement, and one passenger once asked me if I was any relative to that 'well known Irish baronet'! I laughed and said I believed I was a near relation and that I knew him well.

[...]

On Sunday morning 5 July at 7 a.m. I looked from our port and saw far south the jagged precipices and towers of Tory Island. It was perhaps 12 miles off – and beyond it rose in blue lines Muckish, Errigal and the hills of my heart.[19]

---

[19] Tory is an island off the coast of County Donegal. Muckish and Errigal are prominent mountains in the northwest of County Donegal. In the following sentence, Cloghaneely is the village where Casement attended an Irish language summer school.

I could almost see Cloghaneely and the shining strand of Magheraroarty – whence two years before August 1912 – I had gone over to Tory with that famous party the fiddler, the piper and the rest.

[…]

The only objects of interest on the 'Cassandra' voyage to Canada were the icebergs we passed during two days when near Newfoundland.

These were the first I had ever seen and unlike most 'first sights' of much talked of things they more than realised all I had conceived of them in my mind. Great Arctic palaces, green and gold sometimes with a crystal sheen and a dazzling white as of concentrated snow they sailed past us bound to their doom in the Gulf Stream.

[…]

Newfoundland's coast line grew clear on our right a pleasant coast in a fine, transparent air.

I forget the towns we passed or dimly sighted – rather fishing settlements than towns – but I remember St. Pierre (and Miquelon), for there we saw the town well enough, where, in 1905, it had been suggested by some friends of Lord MacDonnell's I met at Mrs. Green's one night at dinner that I should go as consul. The post, I think he said, was then vacant and I was purposely idle at the time, having practically retired from the service over the Congo controversy. I had been so anxious to support Morel in his Congo fight – more <u>with</u> the Foreign Office almost than against Leopold – that I had asked to be seconded (without any pay) from Lisbon, whither the Foreign Office had sent me after the publication of my Congo Report in the beginning of 1904.

Lisbon had not agreed with me – still less the F.O. method of conducting the controversy with Leopold which consisted largely in running away from their own charges and offering apologies for my report.

So on December 1904 I seconded myself and so remained a freelance, devoting myself to Irish affairs, until in August 1906 Sir E[dward] Grey wrote to suggest my return to the Consular Service, when I went out first to Santos, then to Pará and finally to Rio de Janeiro <u>en route</u> to Putumayo.[20]

I thought of these things, as I looked at the little town of St Pierre, and wondered as we steamed past it, what might have been the difference had I accepted the advice that night at Mrs. Green's and 'applied' for St. Pierre. Happily I was then so well occupied in Ireland trying to keep Irishmen

---

[20] Casement's three consular postings in Brazil.

Alice Stopford Green: Irish historian and national activist, she collaborated closely with Casement on questions of colonial reform and wielded great influence in a variety of political, literary and artistic circles in both Dublin and London. She was one of only four women elected to the first Irish Senate in 1922. [National Library of Ireland]

out of the British Army and dreaming of an Ireland that might yet be free, that I gave no second thought to that after dinner suggestion any more than to a later one of Sir Eric Barrington that 'Stockholm was vacant and might be offered me.' I was immersed in Irish affairs all through 1905 and right up to the very day of my departure for Santos in August (or was it early in September?) 1906.

It was those 19 months in Ireland when 'seconded' from the Consular Service that moulded all my subsequent actions and carried me so far on the road to Mitchel's aspirations that everything I have since done seems but the natural up growth from the seed then sown.[21]

Some day I may try to write the story of the Congo and how I found Leopold, – of the Putumayo and that abominable London Company, and of the 'inordinate wild Irishman', who went out on both quests in the garb of a British official, but with the soul of the Irish felon. If the English had only known the thoughts in my heart and the impulses I had obeyed, when I did the things they took pride in, I wonder would their press have praised my 'heroism' and 'chivalry' as they did, or would that expatriated patriot, T. P. O'Connor, have referred to me at the Reading Election last November 'as one of the finest figures in <u>our</u> imperial history'? <u>What</u> will he and the *Westminster Gazette* and even my poor kind friend the *Daily News* say, when the Christiania catastrophe becomes public in England?

---

[21] John Mitchel (1815–1875) Journalist and revolutionary, his *Jail Journal* is considered to be one of the gospels of Irish nationalism and had a significant influence on Casement's political formation.

But I am anticipating and must return to the Newfoundland shores and the Bay of Anticosti and the Great Gulf of St. Lawrence.

We sighted the Marconi Station on the New Brunswick shore near Gaspé Bay and next morning were in the 'mouth of the St. Lawrence' and steaming close enough to the south shore to the point where the ill fated 'Empress of Ireland' went down.[22]

The banks of the river are extremely pretty and interesting and in some respects, at a distance, bien entendu, recalling the vistas of the mighty Amazon. But the Amazon is a river – a vast flowing sea of fresh water and this is a gulf of the sea right up to Quebec. Many towns and even cities were passed during the day and finally late at night we reached Quebec. I saw nothing of the city beyond the lights of the streets and those on the lately burnt Frontenac platform or promenade.

We left again early in the morning and then began the true St. Lawrence river, almost at once. Up to Quebec is a seaway – an estuary if you will from the Heights of Abraham it becomes a river – often vast in breadth, with many islands and distant far seen banks, sometimes narrowing to half a mile or a mile.

Again many towns and churches were passed and towards 6.30 p.m. the smoke of Montreal. I say smoke advisedly, for of all the filthy approaches to a beautiful site (but not city) Montreal, belching forth the blackest smoke in the world, surely takes first place. From the river little is seen but a noisome line of zinc and corrugated iron horrors – grain stores – of factories and warehouses and a shrieking railway, then the 'Docks' more corrugated iron – abominations and above the town the first glimpse of the rapids. We quickly docked and at 8.30 we had rooms at the Queen's Hotel. It was hot and I think the 15 or 16 July 1914.

The next day my Irish friend went on to his sister in Toronto, to enter a bank, poor boy! He had never been out of Ireland and hardly out of Cork County (save for a few weeks at a commercial school in Dublin). I saw him off at 7.30 on his long night journey to Toronto.

Next morning I took train for New York having written old John Devoy to say I hoped to see him at his office on Friday morning (18th or 19th).

The journey was long and hot and quite stifling owing to the American fear of fresh air. The windows of the carriages or 'cars' open only a little

---

[22] An ocean liner that sank 29 May 1914 with the loss of 1,012 lives.

Roger Casement and John Devoy seated together in a car during a procession through the streets of Philadelphia on 2 August 1914. [Digital Library@Villanova University]

way up from below and some of them will not remain open, but slide down again slowly and have to be constantly re-hoisted. Mine was one of these – so to breathe at all I had to put a hat box in below the lifted sash – to the scandal of the guards and some <u>very</u> uninteresting passengers. The dullest looking lot imaginable. The scenery compensated for the want of the picturesque in the human environment.

Lake Champlain we skirted for over 100 miles, I was told, often running along the edge of cliffs and precipices above its pellucid, aquamarine waters. I thought of the days when Mohicans and the Six Nations had here a hunters' paradise.

Poor Indians! you <u>had</u> life – your white destroyers only possess <u>things</u>. That is the vital distinction I take it between the 'savage' and the civilised man. The savage <u>is</u> – the whiteman <u>has</u>. The one lives and moves to <u>be</u>; the other toils and dies to <u>have</u>. From the purely human point of view the savage has the happier and purer life – doubtless the civilised toiler makes the greater world. It is 'Civilisation' versus the personal joy of life.

We got to New York about 8.30 I think – after a delightful journey from the point of view of scenery down the Hudson river to Manhattan Island. The shores of the Hudson and the Catskills were more lovely than I had expected.

I went to the Belmont Hotel at New York as it lay just opposite the Station, and from the first moment found Irish faces and Irish voices round me – the lift boys, the outdoor porters and the waiters in the bar and at cash counters were mostly either Irish born or Irish descended I thought. Some had even the brogue still lingering round the shores of that broad estuary of smiles that takes the place of a mouth in the true Milesian face.

Strolling down Broadway in the thought of perhaps locating old points of view, like Ponds' and the hotel he lived in 1890 a young Norwegian sailor spoke to me – and him I befriended – and told him to see me next morning. I mention him and this chance meeting, because he is destined to figure largely in the end of this story. His name was Eivind Adler Christensen, 24 years old, of Moss, Norway. He had run away from his father's house after getting a severe beating for playing truant at school, and had stowed away on an English collier; this when he was 12 years old. He was landed at Glasgow and left there, and some Norwegian sailors took him and so he became a fireman on a succession of Norwegian steamers.

When he met me he was out of work, starving almost and homeless.

He was grateful for my help and I saw him once or twice in New York, where, with the help I gave him, he got work.

It would take too long to record my early days in New York and at Philadelphia. After meeting old John Devoy on the morrow of my arrival at the *Gaelic American* office, who took me to luncheon at Moquin's, I met shortly afterwards John Quinn and Bourke Cockran – I then went to Philadelphia and saw Joe McGarrity and stayed with him a night, returning to New York to visit Bourke Cockran at Port Washington. The Ancient Order of Hibernians being in annual session at Norfolk, Virginia, McGarrity begged me to go to their Convention and address them in the name of the Irish Volunteers. I consented.

[...]

The journey to Norfolk was interesting during the latter stages across the wide bays, past old Point Comfort to Hampton Roads & the fair, very hot Virginian city of Norfolk. The town was all beflagged with green flags & stars and stripes. No flags anywhere shown save the Irish & American. The Hibernians were in session in a large Theatre – their President, ex-president and nominees for the presidency for the present Convention's Election met us in a deputation & in a few minutes Cockran & I were seated on the platform as guests of our countrymen, with Patrick Egan alongside us.

I was asked to speak first – & gave a short address, on the spur of the moment, on the situation in Ireland, particularly from the Volunteer standpoint – I avoided purely political references and to some extent I eulogised the Ulster men, to the evident content of the great majority. It was a shirt-sleeves and fan audience. Cockran followed with an oration and Egan spoke a few words too – and then we returned to our hotel and spent the rest of the day (Cockran and I) motoring out to Ocean View Beach until it was time to return by the evg. boat and train. I got off at Philadelphia and stayed with McGarrity.

With him some days were spent awaiting news of my pre-arranged coup for landing the guns at Howth. During the period of waiting for Sunday 26 July (the day I had arranged with [Bulmer] Hobson & E[rskine] Childers that the two yachts should arrive at Howth and the Dublin Volunteers should march out to meet them & get the rifles) I got a letter from Mrs. Green telling me all was well and that "our friends were on the sea." The threatening situation in Europe following the cowardly murder of the Austrian Arch Duke Ferdinand and his Consort and the ultimatum to Servia gave me cause for some anxiety.

At other times I should have been even more anxious – but the fears for the landing of the guns at Howth swallowed up all other fears for the time. I had told only John Devoy and Joe McGarrity of the scheme planned before I left Ireland. It was timed for the forenoon of Sunday 26 July. That Sunday I spent at McGarrity's in great anxiety and on tenterhooks. It was a very hot day. At 7 p.m. Joe and I walked down the fields in front of his house until full twilight fell and darkness came. We lay on the grass and talked of Ireland and often, watch in hand, said, 'now it is midnight in Dublin now 1 a.m. soon something must come over the cables.' About 9 p.m. one of the sub-editors of a Philadelphia paper I need not name rang up Joe over the 'phone and told him a news message had just come in that instant saying that a landing of rifles for the Irish Volunteers had been effected near Dublin that day, that the British troops had been called out to disarm the Volunteers and had fired on them killing several persons and securing the rifles. Joe flew down to the Hibernia Club. Later on a message came from him to his wife to tell me that the guns had not been captured by the troops but retained by the Volunteers.

We hardly slept that night. Joe returned about 2 a.m. (on the Monday morning) and told me he had <u>already</u> taken the steps necessary to have a great protest meeting for the following Sunday, 2nd August in one of the big Theatres of the City and had announced me as the chief speaker!

So whether I liked it or not I was now in for it up to the neck. I would have wished to keep quiet – but from every national point of view it was necessary this meeting should be held and if held that it

Howth Gun-running: Molly Osgood and Mary Spring-Rice aboard the *Asgard*, skippered by Erskine Childers. One of the boats that brought guns into Ireland in July 1914. The plan was first discussed in the house of Alice Stopford Green on the Thames Embankment in London, on 8 May 1914. [National Library of Ireland]

should lack no support I could give it, so I reluctantly agreed to a step already taken in my name.

The next day, Monday, 27 July, I was interviewed by some of the Philadelphia papers – and photographed – and the interview appeared in full in the evening papers, – particularly the *Bulletin*.[23] In this conversation I spoke very strongly of the lawless action of the British Authorities in Ireland,

---

[23] *Philadelphia Evening Bulletin.*

Beach until it was time
returns by the Sq boat and tra
I got off at Philadelphia and
stayed with McGarrity —
With him some days were
spent awaiting news of my
pre-arranged Coup for landing
the Guns at Howth. During the
period of waiting for Sunday 26
July (the day I had arranged w
[...] and E. Childers that the
two yachts should arrive at the
& the Dublin Volunteers should march out
to meet them & get the rifles) I got
a letter from Mrs. Green telling me
all was well and that "our frien
were on the sea".
The Threatening situation in
Europe, following the Cowardly murd
of the Austrian Arch Duke Ferdinand

12

and his Consort and the Ultimatum to
Servia gave me cause for some anxiety.
At other times I should have been far
more anxious – but the fears for the
landing of the guns at Howth swallowed
up all other fears for the time.
I had told only John Devoy and Joe
MacGarrity of the scheme planned
before I left Ireland. It was timed
for the forenoon of Sunday 26 July –
That Sunday I spent at McGarrity's
in great anxiety – and on tenterhooks.
It was a very hot day – at 7 p.m.
Joe and I walked down the fields in
front of his house until full
twilight fell and darkness came.
We lay on the grass and talked of
Ireland – and often, watch in hand,
said "Now it is midnight in
Dublin – now 1. a.m. – soon

culminating in the murder of women and children in the streets of Dublin – and I put the blame fair and square on the shoulders of Mr. Asquith.

The interview gave general satisfaction to the Irish in the city, while I learned it had greatly incensed the loyalists – some of whom wrote stupidly irate letters to my host.

From this on to Sunday 2nd August McGarrity was busy and more than busy in the arrangements for the Sunday meeting. I was a passive agent in his strong hands. He did everything. The Sunday came and with it a great deal of trepidation on my part.

[**Editor's note:** The following day Sir Edward Grey made his speech in the House of Commons that committed the British Empire to war against Imperial Germany. Casement remained in close and constant touch with the key figures in Clan na Gael including Joe McGarrity and John Devoy. On 24 August they met with a senior German diplomatic corps at the German Club in Manhattan. Beside the German Ambassador, Heinrich von Bernstorff, the German contingent included the leading German propaganda strategists in the U.S., Georg von Skal and Bernhard Dernburg; the Military Attaché, Franz von Papen, and his aide, Wolf von Igel.

In the immediate aftermath, Casement drafted a letter to His Imperial Majesty and avowed Irish support for Germany in a war that had been deliberately forced upon the German people. The signatories of this letter included the entire Clan na Gael Executive. Devoy's name was at the top of the list.]

To: His Imperial Majesty,
The German Emperor

New York, August 25, 1914

Sire,

The undersigned, representing many millions of the people of this country, either of Irish birth or Irish descent, desire very respectfully to place before Your Majesty what we believe to be the view of the vast majority of Irishmen not only in the United States but throughout the world.

In the first place we seek to give voice to the feeling of Irishmen in America. That feeling is chiefly one of sympathy and admiration for the heroic people of Germany, assailed at all points by an unnatural league of enmity, having only one thing in common, a hatred of German prosperity and efficiency. We feel that the German people are in truth fighting for European civilization at its best and certainly in its less selfish form. We recognize that Germany did not seek this war, but that it was forced upon her by those jealous of her military security, envious of her industrial and commercial capacity, and aiming at her integrity as a Great World Power that was capable, if peace were maintained, of outdistancing the competition of all her rivals.

Since peace was essential to the fullest German development, and since in the realm of peaceful rivalry Germany could not be overcome, those who were jealous of her growing peaceful means, determined to destroy by war what they could not meet by peace. This we believe to be the reason and the sole reason, for the present combination of armaments against Germany. For this reason we assert that Germany is fighting the battle of European civilization at its best against European civilization at its worst.

We wholeheartedly hope for the success of the German people in this unequal struggle forced upon them. Just as they have overcome by peaceful means the competition of their trading rivals, so we pray they may now overcome by armed manhood the unfair combination those rivals have substituted for lawful effort.

This said on behalf of our countrymen in America, we would bring before Your Majesty the condition of our countrymen in Ireland, and draw Your Majesty's attention to the part that Ireland necessarily, if not openly, must play in this conflict and in every conflict where sea-power is at stake.

The British claim to control the seas of the world, rests chiefly on an unnamed factor. That factor is Ireland. It is by the sole possession of Ireland that Great Breatin has been able for two centuries to maintain an unchallengeable mastery of the sea and by this agency to convert a small trading community into the wholly arbitrary judges of war and peace for all mankind.

If Europe would be free at home, she must be free at sea. If Europe would have peace within her borders she must deprive Great Britain of the means to provoke or precipitate war whenever, as in the present case, it may suit the interests of that power to substitute war for peace.

There cannot be peace in Europe until Great Britain's claim to the mastery of the seas, that great highway of the Nations, has been finally disposed of.

We are profoundly convinced that so long as Great Britain is allowed to control, exploit and misappropriate Ireland and all Irish resources – whether of men, material wealth or strategic position – she will dominate the seas. Thus the freedom of Ireland becomes of paramount, nay of vital importance to the larger question of the freeing of the seas.

Hoping as we do that Germany will win this war so unrighteously forced upon her by a combination of assailants, each lacking the courage to act alone, we earnestly commend to Your Majesty's attention this fundamental fact that to restore the equilibrium of sea power so grievously injured by Great Britain, to the detriment of the whole world since the Napoleonic wars, Ireland must be freed from British control.

While the fortune of war may not bring German troops to Ireland, the hearts of thousands of Irishmen go out to the German shores today. Thousands of Irishmen are prepared to do their part to aid the German cause, for they recognize that it is their own.

Should God grant victory to the German people in this struggle of brave men to keep the freedom they have so clearly won, we hope that Ireland may be permitted to contribute something to the triumph of that good cause. We beg Your Majesty to reflect that a defeated Great Britain, still retaining Ireland, is really a victorious Great Britain.

We beg Your Majesty to reflect that an Ireland freed by German victory over Britain becomes the sure gage of a free ocean for all who traverse the seas.

On these grounds alone, did not natural sympathy and admiration for a people fighting against such heavy odds leads us to address Your Majesty, we should hope for a German triumph over an enemy who is also our enemy. We pray for that triumph for Germany: and we pray with it Your Majesty may have power, wisdom and strength of purpose to impose a lasting peace upon the seas by effecting the independence of Ireland and securing its recognition as a fixed condition of the terms of final settlement between the great maritime Powers.

[**Editor's note:** Casement remained busy writing and publishing. His essays speaking out against the war and in support of Irish neutrality appeared in the *Gaelic American* and were published in pamphlet form. On 17 September 1914, he wrote to the *Irish Independent* encouraging Irishmen not to fight in the war; their responsibility lay in the fight for Irish self-determination and not in the defence of Britain's commercial and imperial interests. The letter was published on 5 October.

That same day, Casement, Devoy and McGarrity met at Judge Cohalan's house and agreed that Casement should travel to Berlin. The German ambassador Count von Bernstorff supplied a letter of recommendation for Casement addressed to the German Chancellor Theobald von Bethmann Hollweg and Casement left New York aboard the SS *Oscar II*

of the Scandinavian-American Line a few days later. He travelled under the false name of James E. Landy and was accompanied by his manservant Adler Christensen.

On 24 October, the steamship was intercepted and ordered by a British battleship to steer course for Stornaway, on the island of Lewis, off the northwest coast of Scotland, so that passengers and cargo could be inspected. Casement managed to avoid detection and the boat continued on to Christiania (Oslo). By then, the British secret services had worked out that Landy was their renegade official and efforts were

Scandinavian-American Line – Passenger List: [National Library of Ireland]

made to have Casement seized through the intervention of the British Minister in Christiania. Some explanation of the Christiania incident has already been made in the introduction. Readers who wish to understand Casement's version of the events should read his letter to British Foreign Secretary, Sir Edward Grey (Appendix 2).]

Eivind Adler Christensen: Casement's manservant and collaborator in the conspiratorial entanglement with the British Foreign Office. [Dr Charles Curry]

Imperial Germany with principal places mentioned in the text.

ON THE TRAIN

Saturday, 31 October 1914

I could not sleep well in the train. Adler was to watch and to make sure I was ready to change carriages at Engelholm at 5.45 a.m.. However, at 1.40 a.m., I wakened suddenly and opened the door of my carriage and found a guard who told me the time. I found, too, Adler asleep in the top bunk, but he wakened at once. From that time on to Engelholm I did not sleep. We reached it punctually – all the other carriages were closed, the inmates sleeping. The train stopped and we jumped out on the platform shifting the baggage more quickly then any porter. Meyer came from his Traelleborg coach to meet me on the platform; and in four or five minutes I saw with joy the Helsingborg car carried on with its sleeping passengers, while we got into the Traelleborg section that did not continue on its route for some time.

I found an empty sleeping carriage […] and at last lay down really tired out and slept to Malmö. Here we arrived about 7, and the glimpse of the beautifully clean streets, fine stone buildings and pleasant faced Swedes was a charming awakening. We had 20 minutes stop for breakfast […]

From Malmö to Traelleborg I did not sleep, but looked out on the flat, well-cultivated fields and pleasant homesteads of Swedish farmers.

At Traelleborg we embarked on the railway steamboat 'Queen Victoria' for Sassnitz – on the stormy white-capped Baltic. […] The steamer was very comfortable but the journey of five hours (or more) to Sassnitz was rough.

At Sassnitz we had delay in landing over the inspection of passports. Had Meyer not been with me, even with his telegram from Berlin, I should have had great difficulty. As it was they wanted to turn out my pockets and Adler's for letters &c. – and even did this with Meyer. These were stupid peasant reservists with '42' on their caps. The higher officials at last got us through, after a very close inspection of 'Mr James Landy's' passport, especially of the U.S.A. red seal and the lithographed signature 'W.J. Bryan'. At length we got away to the train – and Meyer and I into a comfortable first class carriage while Adler was put into a second class compartment in the corridor.

The landing wharf and all along the shore of the island of Ruegen where we landed was guarded by sentries; rough peasant soldiers of same reserve class. As we passed over the island of Ruegen we got here and there glimpses of fine houses, of farms in plenty and villages – the fields all bare, the shorn stubble of a most plentiful wheat crop, and truck loads of a large species of parsnip greeting our view. There were plenty of men about – and often fine looking men too, so it is clear Germany has still reserves of manhood left in civil occupations. Here and there a glimpse of the Baltic and some bay of the island was given us before we saw the church towers and semi-Byzantine minarets of Stralsund. Our train was run onto a ferry and we crossed the narrow breach of sea into Stralsund, where we had to stay a little time. From that on to Berlin the train filled up – and our carriage, which I think had been reserved for us at Sassnitz, got other occupants. Two of these were Junker landlords. One with an excessive Prussian beard, divided into two extraordinary waves that struck out almost at right angles from each other. Both were ugly. Meyer explained to me that these were typical 'small Prussian landowners'. Their talk was constant, was of war and their families and friends who had all got some one at the front.

Presently I notice them glaring at me. Meyer whispered that they were discussing the 'extraordinary insolence' of an Englishman being there, when one of them was about to call the guard to have me put out of the carriage – so Meyer said. Meyer intervened and explained that I was an American going to Berlin and that he knew all about me. The hatred against the English is so bitter in Germany, Meyer explained, that while there is only pity for Belgium, respect for France, frank enmity for Russia, there is for England, the 'Cousin', the 'good friend', who has betrayed Germany and tried to stab her in the back and to incite the whole world against her, nothing but an extraordinary hatred that exceeds anything felt ever in Germany before for any country with which the German were at war. [...]

We reached Berlin at 7.30 or 7.45 and saw some wounded soldiers and an ambulance waiting [...]

Richard Meyer: served as Casement's liaison officer with the German Foreign Office. Almost all communication to and from Casement during his time in Germany passed across Meyer's desk and the two co-operated closely on the formation of the Irish Brigade and the preparations for Casement's return to Ireland in April 1916. [Auswärtiges Amt]

Meyer had intended to take me to the Palast Hotel – near the Foreign Office – but on ordering the taxi driver to go there, the man looked at him amazed and said it had been closed since the beginning of the war – so we were driven instead to the Continental where Meyer got some rooms for me under the name of 'Mr Hammond'. I had decided to bury 'Mr James Landy' on the shores of the Baltic, after we had traversed the custom inspection there. The management were impressed by Meyer and were all bows and smiles – and so I was duly registered as 'Mr Hammond of New York', and they were told they would be responsible to the German Foreign Office if anything unpleasant occurred to me.

My room was 219 – with a bathroom – and Adler's 240 – close at hand. The prices are rather bewildering. Thus Adler's room, only two doors from mine, is only four marks – a smaller room and without bathroom, while my, by no means, magnificent room is 18 marks.

Meyer soon left me for the Foreign Office to report our arrival and to arrange for me to see some of them tomorrow. He begged me not to go out, or let Adler out, until the police had been advised – as English speaking men, without papers &c. and unknown to the police, would surely get into trouble. So we both stayed in the Hotel – and I had a quiet and lonely dinner in the restaurant – and then went to bed after a talk with Adler.

At last in Berlin! The journey done – the effort perhaps only begun! Shall I succeed? Will they see the great cause aright and understand all it may mean to them, no less than to Ireland? Tomorrow will show the beginning.

Berlin, Sunday, 1 November 1914

The Hotel is comfortable and quiet. Very few guests. [...]

I did not go out all day. Meyer called twice, to report progress. No one at Foreign Office at first. The Chancellor, von Bethmann Hollweg, and the Secretary of State, von Jagow, both with the Emperor at the French front – at Charleville I gathered later. At the Foreign Office only the Under-Secretary of State, Zimmermann, and the Staff. The second visit of Meyer, in the evening, was to tell me that I should be recived by the Under-Secretary on Monday morning at 11.30 – and that meantime they had discussed Christiania incident and he had shown them the document and the Kronen notes and explained the attempt on me – and that they would like to hear more of it also. Anyhow, he showed me plainly, I was a welcome guest – and I felt as easy in mind, as it is possible to be in so strange a position. Here I am in the heart of the enemy's country – a State guest and almost a State prisoner.

I wrote today to Major Lothes and the young Muller Beeck and also sent von Skal's letter to Maximilian Harden. I was sorry afterwards that I had written these letters so soon – but the inertia of a whole Sunday in this dreary Hotel was too much for me.[24]

The people are very civil in the Hotel. They regard me, Adler reports from the Servant's Hall, as an American millionaire – and he added to this belief by saying I had a fine steam yacht!

Berlin, Monday, 2 November, 1914

Meyer called for me at 11 – and took me on foot to Unter den Linden – close at hand – and down to the Wilhelmstrasse in which, at No. 76 is the Foreign Office. He pointed out to me the closed Russian Embassy in Unter den Linden and the equally closed British Embassy in Wilhelmstrasse – and further on in this street the 'Palace of the third son of the Kaiser' – a fine building with sentries outside. We met a Prince Fürstenberg in the Wilhelmstrasse whom Meyer knew – a cousin, he said of the prince whose splendid château at Donaueschingen I passed in May 1912 with Dick Morten and Heini.

The Foreign Office, No. 76, is an old fashioned, white, very plain house of the time of Frederick the Great or earlier. You have to ring at a wooden gateway door, and the door opens. We went upstairs and a servant man took our coats, hats and sticks! So different from the London Foreign Office where I have been so often chez moi! The waiting room we were shown into was a fine salon, well furnished and large, with fine oil paintings of King Frederick Wilhelm III and the old Emperor Wilhelm. Meyer told me I was to be received, first by the Under-Secretary of State, Herr Zimmermann, and then by Count Georg von Wedel, the 'head of the English Department'. Meyer left me alone a few minutes. Some officers came and went, cavalry men in grey.

---

[24] All these names were part of Casement's propaganda circle with whom he was conspiring in the US.

Strange thoughts were mine, as I sat on a big sofa in the centre of policy of the German Empire. No regrets, no fears – well – yes – some regrets, but no fears. I thought of Ireland, the land I should almost fatally never see again. Only a miracle of victory could ever bring me to her shores. That I did not expect – cannot in truth hope for. But, victory or defeat, it is all for Ireland. And she cannot suffer from what I do. I may, I must suffer – and even those near and dear to me – but my country can only gain from my treason. Whatever comes that must be so. If I win all it is national resurrection – a free Ireland, a world nation after centuries of slavery. A people lost in the Middle Ages refound and returned to Europe. If I fail – if Germany be defeated – still the blow struck today for Ireland must change the course of British policy towards that country. Things will never be again quite the same. The 'Irish Question' will have been lifted from the mire and mud and petty, false strife of British domestic politics into an international atmosphere. That, at least, I shall have achieved. England can never again play with the 'Irish Question'. She will have to face the issue once for all. With the clear issue thus raised by me she will have to deal. She must either face a discontented conspiring Ireland – or bind it closer by a grant of far fuller liberties. Coercion she cannot again resume. Laissez-faire must go for ever. 'Home Rule' must indeed become home rule – and even if all my hopes are doomed to rank failure abroad, at least I shall have given more to Ireland by one bold deed of open treason than Redmond and Co. after years of talk and spouting treason have gained from England. England does not mind the 'treason' of the orthodox Irish 'patriot'. She took the true measure of that long ago. She only fears the Irishman who acts; not him who talks. She recognises only action, and respects only deeds. Those men have killed England with their mouths time and time again – I am going to hit her with my clenched hand. It is a blow of sincere enmity, based on a wholly impersonal disregard of consequences to myself. Sure alone that it is in truth a blow for Ireland I should be a traitor did I not act as I am doing.

I have often said, and said it without the slightest concealment, that if ever the chance came to strike a blow for Ireland I'd do it. Well the chance has come. I am not responsible for it. The crime is not mine. It is England's own doing. Grey and Asquith are the real traitors. They have surely betrayed their country and her true interests to glut the greedy jealousy of the British commercial mind. Germany's sin has been her efficiency. They chose to build up a league of enmity against the people they feared to assail themselves, and having triumphed in their tortuous, ignoble secret diplomacy they joyfully hurried to the encounter when, at last, sure as they thought of their prey. For them, that so-called Liberal administration, I have nothing but unmeasured contempt. A scorn I cannot express. And for the 'governing classes' too of the pirate realm. For the people themselves and for many individual Englishmen, I have only deep sorrow, regret, pity and affection. But as Wilfrid Blunt said to me in Sussex at Newbuilding in May when I lunched with him and the lovely girl (the great granddaughter of Lord Edward Fitzgerald) – the time has come for the break up of the British Empire.

Even as he said he hoped now to live to see it, so I hope to be able to do something to bring it about. That Empire is a monstrosity. The world will be the better, the more sincere, the less hypocritical for a British defeat, for a German victory.

Many thoughts like these were with me as I waited. When I was shown into Herr Zimmermann's cabinet, I met a fair-haired very good natured face and a warm and close handshake. I like the man at once. He was warm-hearted as well as warm handed. He congratulated me warmly on my safe arrival and spoke of the Christiania episode in fitting terms. He asked me long about it – and I described the whole incident, and his comment was my own – 'Dastardly' he said – 'but it is what they do and have always done when their interests are at stake. They stick at nothing.'

I had written a hasty memorandum, in the morning in my bedroom – in my pyjamas – giving a fresh point of view and drawing in outline the form of declaration I thought the German Government might issue. [...] The memorandum briefly recited the cruel calumnies the British Government and their agents were spreading through Ireland, in order to defame Germany and to induce the Irish youth to enlist in their army of plunderers under the pretence that it was a war to protect Belgium and the 'small nationalities' – and went on to show that the German Government could quite legitimately defend itself from these atrocious charges of evil intent towards Ireland by making a formal declaration of its attitude towards my country. I read the declaration I suggested to Herr Zimmermann. He agreed with every paragraph and sentence, and when I had done took the whole paper from me and said 'I accept it entirely'. After an interview more cheering and full of spirit of good will than I had ever hoped for, I was taken by Meyer to Count v. Wedel.

Here I found a charming personality – a man of upright build; frank, straight brown eyes and a perfect English accent. Our talk was long and friendly. I told him I had left the memorandum and form of proposed declaration with the Under-Secretary of State – and we talked of the Irish soldiers in Germany and the line of action that I hoped to follow there. It is this step that appeals most to the Germans I can see. They perceive its full 'moral' value to their cause. Meyer said to me yesterday – 'If you do that it is worth ten army corps to us!' I made it plain beyond all misconception to Wedel that my efforts with the soldiers must be strictly defined as an effort to strike a blow for Ireland – not an attempt merely to hit England. I described the character of the Irishman

Arthur Zimmermann: Under-Secretary of State at the German Foreign Office (1911–16), he succeeded von Jagow as Secretary. He encouraged subversive activities among Irish, Indian and Russian revolutionaries. [Auswärtiges Amt]

and of the Irish soldier, and pointed out that any Irishman might commit treason against England for the sake of Ireland, but that he would not do anything mean or treacherous. He would put his neck in the noose, as I had done, for love of Ireland; he would not 'desert to any enemy' or forsake his own colours merely to assail England. In fact he must have an active cause, not a negative. If, thus, Germany made the declaration I sought as to the fortunes and future of Ireland in the event of German victory, I had little or no doubt scores, perhaps, hundreds of the Irish prisoners would follow me.

So said Wedel – 'It is clearly the declaration first of all.' He then discussed with Meyer and myself the steps for my safety in Berlin 'not alone from the British but from our own people.' He proposed going at once with Meyer to the Chief of the Secret Police and explaining things – and took me back in his taxi as far as the Continental where I got out. Later in the day Meyer returned with a card issued by the Chief of the Political Police, saying that Mr Hammond of New York was not to be molested […] This card I am to carry always and it will ensure me in case of any street trouble or enquiry. Adler is to have no paper, as being a

Norwegian he is not an 'offensive personage'. We both, however, are going to wear little American flags in our button holes – and this evening Adler bought them.

I went for a walk after dinner – Adler taking me to the Kaiser's palace and round it and then back down Unter den Linden again. We saw the fine buildings of that quarter – so many of them royal or imperial in origin and more than one pertaining actually to the Royal house.

Berlin is not imposing I think – from the glimpses had today – but it is fine. It is extraordinarily well kept and clean – and while the buildings are not lofty, they are massive and well built. Unter den Linden is, frankly, disappointing. It is not a fine thoroughfare and the shops do not impress one – neither do the Lindens. The latter are short and add little to the street so far as I can see – but then I saw them in the beginning of winter. There are too few people visible also. The street is wide – and rather empty of any human throng. The cross-street Frederickstrasse is, on the contrary, full of life, and I presume the true Berlin is rather this street than Unter den Linden. The Spree is a very insignificant river in the city – one crosses it before reaching the Kaiser's palace and again, a branch of it, on the other side. Now I am fairly launched on Berlin – and today sees me take up a definite position: 'Mr Hammond of New York' – not to be molested!

Mansfeldt de Cardonnel Findlay: the British Minister (ambassador) to Norway. With the authorisation of the British Foreign Office, he engaged in a conspiracy to have Casement 'bumped on the head' as he passed through Christiania on his way to Berlin in October 1914. The confrontation escalated into an on-going and bitter feud. [National Portrait Gallery, London]

My Journey to the German
Headquarters at Charleville

Berlin, Monday, 16 November 1914

I got a 'phone call from Baron von Berckheim of the General Staff, at 8 Moltke Str. about 1 o'clock asking me, 'Mr. Hammond', to go round there and see him between 3 and 4.

I went accordingly, in a taxi, to the address given. It is across the big Königsplatz in front of the Reichstag – I was shown up by a young orderly soldier who said he could speak 'Italianische' but not 'Amerikansche'! After wandering through many corridors, going to various rooms (all wrong) he waylaid a very pretty girl (possibly a typist I imagined) in a hat as if to go out who spoke good English and she directed us to von Berckheim's room, No. 182. He came at length, a young officer with sword and spurs in a grey cavalry uniform with riding boots and greeted me kindly & in good English. He said he had heard about me from Kurt von Lersner, and that he too, had been at the Washington Embassy and hoped to return there later on. We found the 'waiting room' occupied, so he cleared two servant maids out of a dining room – and there we talked. He explained that the 'Headquarters' (at the French front) wished me to go there at once. Von Lersner who knew me already had charge of the affair – was I ready to go? I said 'at once.' He said that arrangements would be made for my journey on the morrow, to leave Berlin by the night train for Cologne, where an automobile would meet me sent by Lersner to take me straight to Headquarters.

He explained that the journey was to be kept quite secret and that the Count who took charge of me would only know me as Mr. H. – and knew nothing of the objects. I would be simply Mr. H., an American, going to the front in his charge.

[…]

I spent the evening alone, as usual, taking a walk in the Thiergarten after a light 'dinner' at Hoffmann's restaurant, as usual, where I am now a recognised habitué.

Saw several detachments of recruits going off today – some in uniform, with flowers in belts and bosoms – some in plain clothes, with packages in hand of all sorts and mostly just wrapped in paper – women and friends walking alongside. The men – all young mainly – looked happy and smiling – and many were smoking. The passers by stopped to look with kind eyes on the sons of the Fatherland marching sedately to the trenches of death.

A quiet, patient, obedient and sure-hearted people this, if ever Europe had one. There is an entire absence of jingoism – and yet today, confirmation came of rumours of a great victory over the Russians. This is the first outcome of the battle Professor Schiemann told me of on Sunday.

[...]

Berlin to Cologne, Tuesday, 17 November 1914

Berlin is all beflagged today in honour of the Prussian victory. Von Hindenburg[25] the victor again! He is the hero of the Prussian heart – and rightly too – for this victory cannot fail to greatly aid the cause of Germany.

Today I sent Adler out to buy various things needed for my journey and arranged all details of his return to Moss on Saturday next (when his teeth are finished, poor boy!) With two faked letters and some pages of my 'Diary' he has 'stolen.'

[...]

Meyer called and told me that I should call on von Wedel at 5 or 5.15 & that he would call for me then to take me to F.O.

I went with him at 5 to 76 Wilhelmstrasse[26] & was shown into the Saloon to wait for v. Wedel who was just collared by an earlier caller. In this room I found Professor Schiemann – who was delighted with my story of the 'Christiania incident' (I had written out on Monday) which he had in his hand to get typed at F.O. and a copy of it sent with a covering letter to

---

[25] Field Marshal Paul von Hindenburg's military victories in 1914 at the Battle of Tannenberg and the Battle of the Masurian Lakes were being celebrated.

[26] Wilhelmstrasse is the street in central Berlin where the German Foreign Office was located along with other administrative organisations. The Reich Chancellery was located at No. 77.

the Emperor. Schiemann complimented me on the way I had written the 'story' – 'un vrai roman' – but one that he believed the Emperor would be greatly interested in. He told me that Fräulein Meyer had received a letter from her brother Kuno from Rotterdam saying his 'coffre' had not arrived and that he was sailing without it. Neither Schiemann nor the sister knows if this referred to the box of papers or to some ordinary trunk of clothes. Schiemann was alarmed and I shared his alarm, if it should prove to be Kuno Meyer's box of damaging papers. I pointed out that if, by ill luck, the English got hold of this they would certainly arrest Meyer anywhere at sea – even just outside New York. Schiemann left me in the waiting room to go and see Zimmermann; I waited on until 7 as Meyer came in twice to say that von Wedel was still kept by his urgent visitor. This waiting room of the German F.O. is interesting. It is furnished in crimson red, with claret coloured wall paper. There are two life sized portraits, one of the old Emperor William, the other of his father King Frederick William of Prussia. There are two busts (I don't know of whom) flanking the latter picture; and a photograph of the old royal castle of Goslar, Schiemann told me had been built by the Emperor Henry IV and is kept up and liked by the present Emperor.

[...]

At 7 Meyer came for me – and Wedel told he thought I should see von Jagow and perhaps the Chancellor at the front.

He told me to tell Baron von Stumm, the chief of the political department of the F.O. whom I should find there, 'everything.'

He then showed me the written copy of the <u>interview and declaration</u> – this the Declaration of Goodwill to Ireland – I had sent him on the 11th which had been sent to Headquarters and was now back amended and somewhat shortened.[27]

[...]

I got back the Christiania papers from von Wedel to show at the front, if necessary – and then I told him of the loss of Kuno Meyer's trunk and my fears that it might be his box of compromising papers. I pointed out

---

[27] The *Declaration of Goodwill* was a statement by the German Chancellor – drafted by Casement – intended to reassure Ireland of Germany's good intentions towards Ireland. Contrary to the official newspeak circulated in the British press and through war propaganda outlets ... 'that a German victory would inflict great loss upon the Irish people ... the Imperial Government formally declared that under no circumstances would Germany invade Ireland with a view to its conquest or the overthrow of any native institution of that country'.

that it might be as well to keep back the issue of the declaration until the truth was known, or even until we were sure that Kuno had reached New York safely. Von Wedel was anxious to issue the Declaration at once and told me he should like to give it out the next day. I agreed, provided they felt easy about the Professor's journey – admitting that I might be over anxious in this regard.

I left von Wedel about 7.30 with his final good wishes for my journey to the front, and his kindly face smiling after me as I turned down the stairs.

Meyer met me outside and told me it was settled that he should accompany me to the front, as there was room in the motor car. He would call for me at 9.30 at the Hotel.

At 9 p.m. von Berckheim came with my guide and guard the Graf von Lüttichau – a baldish headed young Prussian nobleman. He was in uniform, that of the 'Volunteer Automobile Corps.' All the necessary papers were with him.

Meyer came, and all three came to my room, where we arranged for Adler's passport to be visé, so that he could leave for Moss on Saturday without danger of the 'papers' I was giving him for Mr. Findlay's benefit being seized at the Sassnitz frontier on his way out of Germany.

Bidding poor old Adler (who nearly wept!) good-bye, 'Mr. Hammond', with his uniformed escort of the Baron and Count and his attaché Mr. Meyer, was bowed out of the hall by the manager and staff.

We walked round to the Friedrich Str Station and got our 'compartment' with some difficulty and delay. The train was crowded – and a great many soldiers and officers in it – and some wounded going back 'cured' – while stretchers were on the platform to have others carried off to the hospitals.

Finally we got off. The Count v. Lüttichau and I in one carriage, Meyer going into a sleeping car as far as Hanover where, he said, he would have to leave the sleeper and come and disturb us for a seat.

Cologne to Charleville, Wednesday, 18 November 1914

We reached Cologne about 7.30 a.m. getting a fine view of the splendid, old city from the bridge over the (always) hurrying Rhine.

[...]

The cathedral is magnificent. Altho' so new it looks old – and it soars up to heaven as if inspired with all the past of this glorious old city of the Rhine.

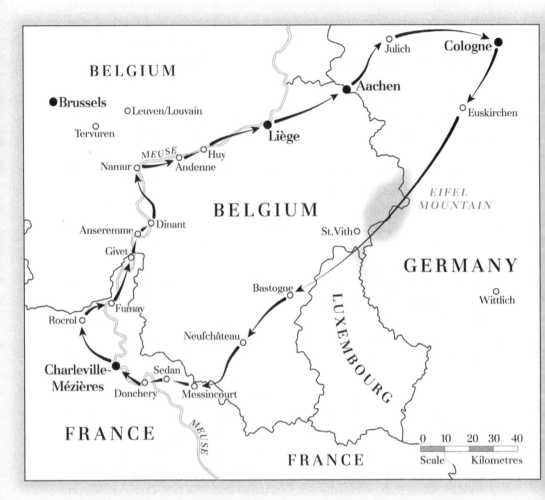

Roger Casement's journey from Cologne to the German
headquarters in Charleville-Mézières, 17-19 November 1914.

We went inside and found the nave filled with the devout crowds
of men and women kneeling and a priest I thought collecting – while
far up in the lighted chancel one could see and hear the distant chant
of the choristers. Cologne they tell me is probably 'four-fifths Roman
Catholic.'

After a very hurried dejeuner – coffee and bread & butter – at the Dom Hotel – for which I paid m1.50 – we left for Headquarters. [...]

The route taken was over the Eifel region[28] – going high over the tops of that arid region, where snow lay in places, and through northern Luxembourg into southern Belgium by Bastogne, through Neufchâteau and out into France near Sedan and so to Charleville-Mézières where the Emperor and the Headquarters of the German army and imperial government are. The distance traversed they told me was 270 kilometres and as we did it in 6 hours and stopped (only for short spells to find the road or look at the wheels &c.) many times our speed must have been fully 50 kilometres (if not more) per hour.

[...] The cold was intense and despite fur-lined gloves my fingers ached so much I had to take the gloves off & sit on my hands for nearly an hour to restore circulation.

[...]

We entered France by a road thro' Messincourt-Messimpre and were soon in Sedan of many memories.

Here again were very few traces of war or conquest – save that most of the fine houses had the shutters up – the families fled. The poor people, who could not fly, were there as usual, as along the countryside we had passed through. It was only on leaving Sedan to cross the Meuse we came across the first striking sign of the war. The fine bridge over the river, I remembered from 1912, was in the river – a few French labourers under a guard were repairing it – two tugboats lay also sunk deep on the opposite shore.

At Donchery a few miles out from Sedan, however, we saw the dread evidence of the recent combat. Donchery lay across the Meuse, on our right hand. There was scarcely a house uninjured. The whole town lay there roofless, empty, a mass of ruins. The church in the midst was a shapeless mass. The bridge destroyed – but as at Sedan, a temporary wooden bridge served.

At Charleville and Mézières, we found the town bridges all destroyed, but temporary structures had been run up alongside them.

Here, too, on the outskirts, were ruined and roofless houses – but in the two towns themselves – they are really one town divided by the

---

[28] Much of the Eifel region is now a national park in the south west of the federal state of North Rhine-Westfalia.

winding Meuse – were but few traces of destruction. Soldiers were here in plenty, and motor cars go leór. We drove to the former Prefecture now the residence of the Headquarters staff of the great German armies. Somewhere near, I knew, must be the Emperor himself.

We were shown in first to a room where a Lt. Nicolai (I think) received us where after Graf von Lüttichau and Herr Meckle had retired, Meyer explained who I was. This officer, however, spoke no English. I gathered that the Baron Kurt von Lersner (whom I had last seen in the Ritz–Carlton in Madison Avenue!) would soon arrive – so as we were all of us starving we went to the former dining saloon of the Prefect, where an excellently simple luncheon was served by soldier servants. Other officers entered while we four took of the plentiful dish of stewed beef, macaroni and boiled potatoes, with a plain white wine – and then we adjourned to the absent Prefect's drawing-room – furnished in a yellow satin, poor Madame La Préfet – & had our coffee. Here von Lersner found us and after a brief delay Meyer & I went to his room upstairs where we discussed the matter of the 'Irish Brigade' which is that nearest the heart of the General Staff I can clearly see.

Lersner told me of the steps being taken to collect the 'Irish Catholic soldiers,' who are prisoners of war, and to put them in one place where I could visit them. Nothing much has so far been done I gathered – their difficulty being largely that they don't know the difference between an Irishman and an Englishman! All are 'Englander' to them. However, after explaining things to von Lersner and discussing, too, the matter of the chaplain for the Irish prisoners, and even the possibility of

Kurt von Lersner: German diplomat and politician. Casement met with von Lersner in New York before journeying to Germany. [Auswärtiges Amt]

sending one or two of the men, released, back to Ireland to try and get a good priest to come here – as well as to tell the Provisional Committee of the Volunteers what I am doing here – I left Lersner with the understanding that, as soon as a few score even, or some hundreds of Irish prisoners – authentic Irish – are collected they will let me know and I shall go to the camp to interview the men.

Leaving Lersner we found von Lüttichau and Meckle and after a quest for 'quarters' we got a 'billet' for the night in the Hôtel de Commerce of Charleville. This we found with some difficulty and found there only one manservant in charge. He was a Luxemburger named Joseph left in charge when the personnel of the hotel had fled at the German approach.

Joseph showed us very cold rooms and said there was no food, or hot water, or electric light even in the hotel. All had gone. He got his daily 'ration' from somewhere. He had only a few bits of candles & these he doled out to us.

[…] At the Hotel Meyer met me and said he had been to the 'Foreign Office' – in a fine building in the Avenue Delafare – where he had arranged for Baron von Stumm the head of the political department to see me at 9.30 a.m. on the morrow. It was decided that after this interview I should return to Berlin – and Lüttichau begged me to try and get thro' my interview with von Stumm by 10.30 a.m. so that we might return by Dinant, Namur and Liège. This, a much longer route back to Cologne would be far more interesting as we should pass thro' some of the most famous spots of the opening stages of the war. Fearing the very damp sheets of a very cold, uninhabited inn, I wrapped my woollen comforter round my neck and my Irish rug round my body and then got into bed thus well protected by thick layers of wool from contact with the cold touch of the sheets.

I slept on & off till 8 a.m.

Charleville to Cologne, Thursday, 19 November 1914

[…]

Baron von Stumm spoke perfect English and told me of more than one talk he had had with Sir E. Grey. Of Grey's abilities he had a poor opinion – a mediocre intelligence, an inferior man, how is it that they think him so wonderful in England? I confessed I shared very largely his

Wilhelm von Stumm: Director of the Political Department at the German Foreign Office, he had tremendous influence at the highest level of German imperial power.
[Auswärtiges Amt]

opinion of Grey's abilities, altho' I did not doubt his honesty, to which estimate the Baron subscribed.

Most of the talk was mine. He asked about the Christiania incident and I described it fully and he agreed with me that it was well worth while to try and get Mr. Findlay 'caught in the act' through my man Adler – and then to make the whole story public and try and get him turned out of Norway.

We talked of the Volunteers in Ireland, of Redmond's recruiting dodges; of 'Home Rule' and of the prospects of keeping the Irish out of the army. I explained the Irish position to him clearly and closely. He admitted he knew nothing about it – that he had once been in Ireland (on a hunting trip I fancy) but that he knew nothing of the feeling of the people.

I told him of my larger hope – 'a dream if you will' – of an independent Ireland emerging from this war and he at once said it would be to Germany's interest to have an independent Ireland. I said 'Yes – to the interest of Europe at large'. As to the Volunteers and why we were not armed already I explained the situation in Ireland and how the British had 'closed the ports' as soon as the Irish Volunteers were started on 15th Nov. 1913 – 'just one year ago'. I said that Germany had herself very largely to blame for the position in which she found herself today – and he agreed. I said 'Why did you not make friends before the war with those who had reason to oppose England? – why did you not think of Ireland?'

He replied 'that is the best proof of our innocence, of our sincerity towards England – we believed she could be kept neutral – while she was plotting against us. Had we known – had we acted as she did – we should have had agents in Ireland, in Egypt, in India'. As regards my 'larger hope' he talked frankly. Germany had no objection, on the contrary only the desire to do it, <u>if possible</u>, but that while he fully expected Germany would win the war against France and Russia, and so conclude a general and, for her, successful peace, he did not know how far she could prosper in her fight with England towards the point of '<u>imposing</u> conditions of peace there.' That was all uncertain. There was no immediate or even probable prospect of the German fleet gaining a great victory, so as to clear the seas and render the transport of men and arms to Ireland possible. Were there, it would not be unlikely.

He believed the war <u>must</u> end soon – that none of the combatants, except England, could carry it on for a long period. France would go first – next Russia – perhaps both together.

And here a trenchant phrase was uttered. 'We will make peace with France – we pity them too – they and the Belgians will learn that England is responsible for their miseries – not Germany. <u>But what we hold we will keep</u>'!

It is this phrase rings in my ears. The Baron expressed himself deliberately, and the prospect it offers is, indeed for Belgium and France a dreadful one. 'What we hold we will keep'! He was quite emphatic in declaring that the German armies could <u>not</u> be driven back. Where they were they stayed – and it was only a question of months, possibly weeks, when the French & Russian endurance – and materiél – would give out.

We shall see. I do not think he was over confident as to the powers of resistance, or of maintenance of the present lines of the German armies – but I think it is highly probable that to secure a just and binding peace in Europe and so leave Germany free to tackle England – the Sea Serpent – the Baron's chiefs would agree to give up what they hold. Otherwise the war <u>will</u> go on for years – despite his estimate of French weakness – for neither France nor Belgium will agree, one, to a dreadful dismemberment – the other to extinction.

I told him England would go on for years. He agreed she might, but asked 'What can she do to us? She can't get near Germany. Her fleet is become a laughing stock. Her empire will and must break up – her diplomacy has been childish – for she has risked everything, more than we – and in future any little state like Norway or Holland, with a fleet of submarines can bottle all the British navy up in to ports. Thus while she may have been able to destroy our external trade she has not been able to use her fleet against ours or directly against our coasts. She cannot come near us. Her position has become ridiculous.'

I said that England counted on wearing Germany down 'as she did Napoleon' & that she would not care for the destruction of France – she would always counsel France to continue, even a hopeless resistance, as she did the Belgians at Antwerp – and rely on her ability to beget fresh forces for Germany and to redress the injured balance of power in Europe by calling in Asia, Africa, America. I pointed out that I was <u>sure</u> England counted on getting the United States in the field against Germany in the end – certainly if the war should go on against England. Her steps to this end had already been taken and I was convinced that if, by chance, the German fleet won a considerable victory (he shrugged his shoulders) there would go up a preconcerted and organised howl throughout the American press on behalf of 'the Motherland' – of a threatened 'common civilisation' and that England would spare no effort, no money, no means to compelling the Washington administration to take sides on her threatened behalf. Further there was Japan, and the grave possibility of the Japanese being brought to Europe in the end. The danger to Germany was a 'war of years' as England predicted. Von Stumm agreed that Germany could not go on for years as England might, but that there was any possibility of France or Russia holding on, even as long as Germany, he did not agree. Germany must win so far as her land frontiers lay and land forces went – but he was by no means confident of her ability to get at England 'this time'.

If she did, 'my dream' might come true! It would accord with her policy and interests. We discussed briefly, I more than he, the Declaration his Government had made at my instance and which I said I presumed would be issued that very day – I pointed out that while it went far on the road of our wishes it did not say all we wanted – and the fullest fruits could not be hoped from it alone – but that I was not 'impossible' and did not want them today to go further than they felt was wise.

We were agreed in aim – as to the means to attain it I knew these lay on the lap of the gods – and I was content to go on with the hope that the fortune of war wd. more and more bring about the possible realisation of my larger hope.

Von Stumm was clearly interested in our talk, and it was I who rose to leave and end the interview after fully an hour. He would have even kept me – but I pulled out my watch – it was 11.15 – and said I should not detain him longer. Meyer was waiting outside the door – and after a second farewell in the corridor to which he accompanied me I bade the

Baron & the travelling Foreign Office adieu and hurried downstairs and back in the motor car to the Hôtel de Commerce to get my things, to pay 'Joseph' a pourboire of 5 marks – instead of anything to the hotel for the night's lodging – & then to pick up Meckle and von Lüttichau at the rooms of the former.

When these were settled in the car and everything aboard it was nearly noon – and fully midday when altogether we steered out of Charleville on the road to Rocroi. The market place or grand place was showing a sprinkling of women & men with vegetables, carts and country produce – an attempt at a market. The women looked less downcast than the men. Small boys even begged from us smiling for 'einer pfennig!' – in bad German. An old woman with white hair came up to us while waiting outside Meckle's rooms and I heard her pleading voice and the words 'dans la misère.' I gave her 5 marks in spite of Meckle's protest that 'they all do this'. I said it might be so – but they were 'all in great trouble and misery' to which he & Lüttichau agreed. They remonstrated more at the amount than at the act – saying 50 pfennigs would have been enough.

(I had noticed during the hurried walks the previous evening to and from the officers' mess that townswomen were walking about with, or even waiting for, German soldiers! There was no doubt of it. I noticed more than one case – this to my mind gave convincing proof rather of 'misery' than of immorality. I did not tell my German friends of what I had noticed in this respect—for they would scarcely have understood my feeling I fancy.)

As we left Charleville – the ruined outskirts were often a new source of regret – the road to Rocroi lay northwards and upwards. The frost was strong and enduring, the fields and trees covered with it – and the air still and sharp. A few cabs came past – but as yesterday, the vast majority of vehicles met were either automobiles, like our own with men in uniform, or large wagon motors of red cross comforts or of provisions. Rarely with escorts, generally alone or in troops of cars – but once or twice we met horsemen – going through a strip of wood as we neared Rocroi we met a telegraph party out putting up a new wire through the forest – some trees were felled or being felled – and the second line being stretched along the existing single line.

Rocroi lies high, fully 1,400 feet above the sea. We did not enter the village or the fortress. We skirted the outer dry moat of the grass fortifications, diamond pointed Vauban-constructed may be – and went on through largely abandoned suburbs and damaged houses into the open hill country looking across the steep valley of the Meuse as it wound into the deep wooded hills of the Ardennes. The view here was splendid – despite mist and wintry gloom.

The steep cleft where the Meuse penetrates the Ardennes lay to our right the wooded hills on the far side being I judged close on 1000 feet above the gorge. Tufts of white mist clung to the sides of the hills & of the gorge itself. Every tree & shrub was like a fairy tree – each twig & branch a delicate branch of silver – and afar the frosted trees shone white on the darker ground.

Soon we came to the top of the ridge and the road stretched down before us, with great curves and sweeping angles into Fumay on the Meuse itself. We descended rapidly and ran thro' Fumay without pause. Here were many burnt houses – but the town was peopled again and shops open and people moving about their affairs. We were soon through this pretty little town and running along a fine smooth road that followed the left bank of the Meuse. The river about 100 yards broad, and deep brown. Every bridge was down. Some totally wrecked – others only partially injured. In some cases the piles alone had been blown up – & the iron superstructure had collapsed in the middle into the river, the two ends standing intact. In nearly all cases where a bridge had been thus destroyed by the retreating French, the invaders, (now the occupying tenants) had run up alongside, or in the near vicinity a wooden structure on piles that served all the immediate needs of road transport, but not of railway.

In several cases the wrecked bridges themselves had been already repaired – in one notable case, just before reaching Givet, the entire iron superstructure which had not been injured by the explosion that caused its collapse into the stream had been lifted again, well nigh intact, and as we passed it was being used in the ordinary way. Several of the (older) stone bridges of massive masonry had had only one or two arches blown up and in these cases the German engineers had already bridged the cavities with temporary ironwork and the bridges were again in use.

From Fumay we ran alongside the Meuse almost the whole way when the river made wide curves and the road took the short cut. Villages and little towns on both banks, nearly all showed traces of the havoc wrought no doubt so often by the retreating defenders as by the invading foe. What greatly struck me was that in several cases there were villages in close proximity, or little townships, one of which would be almost entirely

60

destroyed, the burnt and shattered frameworks of roofless and wall-less houses alone marking the site, while less than 400 yards away a similar village would present an entirely undamaged front and its inhabitants were going about their business seemingly unconcerned.

At Givet we came across the first evidence of a shattered <u>fortress</u>. Here on the cliff top more than 150 feet above the river I should say – perhaps 200 feet, the ridge was crowned with the stone wall and turreted bastions of a type of fortification no longer erected I imagine. Fine to look upon but of little use against modern guns. This battlement showed pregnant gaps where the German guns, from the hills across the river had battered it. At its foot, and between the roadway and the river, a long stone building of three stories – fully 250 yards long – which had been the caserne of a considerable French fort, was riddled with shell fire. Not a window remained – the walls had holes in them a coach and four could have gone through – the floors had often collapsed, and a great part of the roof was piled up in the mounds of debris that choked the basement. Givet itself had not suffered so greatly – although we could not see much of it as our car sped through. It was necessary to hasten, as by this much longer route it would take us all our time to reach Cologne in time for the night train to Berlin.

Soon after leaving Givet we crossed the frontier into Belgium – the former customs notice at the barrier 'À la Douane' still held out its arm across the road – but we had no customs search to pass, for today there is no Belgium!

Several of the road inspection posts here at which we halted an instant were in charge of Saxon troops, for the green and white standard of Saxony was often visible. The river cliffs as we drew near Dinant were perfectly charming. Great crags and peaks and pinnacles of grey limestone (I think) often garbed thick with dark green ivy, and crowned with a forest of birch and hazel and aspen trees rose some hundreds of feet sharp from the banks of the Meuse.

[...]

At Dinant we saw the great fortress (on the right bank) similar to that at Givet, but with no visible signs of wreckage at all. Even the notices 'Entrée à la forteresse' – 'Hôtel Lion d'Or' &c. &c. on the summit of the cliffs were quite undamaged. The cliff drops sheer, a wall of 250 or 300 feet from the centre of the fortress to the town, where at the foot a platform of land lies on which the old church or cathedral stood. It still

stands, but it showed many traces of the heavy fire – and the houses in
its immediate vicinity are only a shapeless mass of rubble – a pile of dead
bricks and mortar. The bridge that connects the two banks, right in front
of the Cathedral had been well blown up – but parties of Belgians – under
guard – were repairing it slowly, while a wooden improvised bridge 60 or
70 yards upstream connected the two banks and was full of traffic as we
passed. Meyer explained that all the gangs of French or Belgian workers
we had seen at work on bridges or roadways were paid for their labour.
In many cases I noticed houses that had been greatly damaged by shell
fire already well on their way to recovery – floors, windows, roofs &c. &c.
all being put in. The left bank of Dinant had suffered less than the right –
and as we passed slowly on out of the town we passed many people. Some
boys were playing see-saw – and we got courteous speech from any one
we made enquiry of.

Through similar scenes of destruction tempered by clearest evidence
of law and order erected on its base we passed always down the left bank
of the Meuse, through many charming resorts, with châteaux old and
new and pretty villas and well built villages and townlets to Namur. Here
we stopped to lunch (at 3.20 p.m.) in a restaurant

[…]

The City Hall and buildings near it were terribly shattered – and yet along side these piles of destruction shops were open, people moving about and no sign of war! Little boys were selling picture postcards – and I bought a batch of them from a nice little chap of ten or eleven with whom I talked in French outside the restaurant. Beggars too came – just as usual and besought alms or help from the enemy!

From Namur, we crossed the Meuse to the right bank, and with the priest explaining certain points of interest to the others we hurried on to Andenne. A good part of the destruction we saw was caused by Belgians themselves. Thus <u>all</u> the bridges for instance were their handiwork – and as artillery fire is mutual very much of the damage we saw was caused by the defenders. Thus the priest pointed out a ruined factory across the river which the Belgians themselves had destroyed. At Andenne, Meckle stopped the car to show me a gruesome sight and tell a horrible story.

First the story.

After the first passage of the German Army, when Andenne was already in German hands, a long column of German ammunition with a smallish escort was passing through Andenne on its way to the front. The town had already submitted and all the Belgian soldiers were scores of miles away.

At a signal, *given from the church*, the church bells ring out, and from all sides rifle fire was opened on the German column. Many men were killed – the punishment was not, as at Louvain, to destroy part of the town, but to seize a number of the men and shoot them then and there. Three hundred and fifty men were thus arrested, taken to the river front, lined up against a brick wall surrounding an empty yard and shot, and buried in two long graves between the wall of execution and the river. I was taken to this spot.

[…] Two workmen in corduroys were bending over the graves when we came up. They moved off – with averted faces. Some women and children, and a well dressed family were there too – but they slowly withdrew from the spot at the sight of the uniforms. How little these poor folk could have guessed that one man of that group was no German – but was the very 'British Consul' who had indicted their sovereign and his abominable Congolese system ten years before.

Sometimes, I must confess, when the present 'agony of Belgium' confronts me – and it cannot well be minimised it is in truth a national agony – I feel that there may be in this awful lesson to the Belgian people

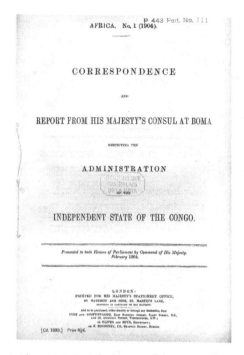

Africa No.1 (1904): Casement's report on the excesses of King Leopold II's administration in the Congo Free State ignited a furious war of representation over the European scramble for Africa. [Angus Mitchell]

a *repayment*. All that they now suffer and far more, they, or their king, his government and his officers wreaked on the well nigh defenceless people of the Congo basin. And with no such reason as the Germans. Germany offered Belgium fair terms – she asked only a 'right of way' to meet her foemen face to face on <u>French</u> soil. Belgium refused – at the instigation of England and preferred the arbitrament of arms. She relied on English promises and French support. Where are these today? Criminal as he was, Leopold II would never have landed his country in the awful plight this morally better King Albert has placed it in. Leopold before he opposed the German demand by force would have made England show her hand. He would have called her cards. He would have said – 'Yes, that's all very well to defend my neutrality! But can I do it? What help can <u>you</u> give? Where is your army – where your guns that are going to ensure the inviolability of Belgium if I resist the Germans?'

And if that question had been put, as it should have been put by the ruler of these betrayed people, what answer could England have made? She could not defend 'Belgian neutrality' and she knew it right well. She deliberately for her own selfish ends, in order to hinder, damage and weaken the German forces, put Belgium into the fire. However blameable Germany may be from the standpoint of international morality in forcing her way through Belgium, England is infinitely more blameworthy. For England <u>knew</u> she could not help the Belgians. She knew her promises of support were worthless. She knew that if Belgium resisted the weight of an irresistible invasion must crush the Belgian people to the earth and lay waste their thriving and prosperous country. All this she knew and yet

Sir E. Grey telegraphs to the Br. Minister in Brussels before war breaks out that he urgently begs the Belgian Govt. to 'defend its neutrality' at all costs! What a crime! Here, these two graves at Andenne, and the looks in the faces of the population as we pass away from it – dejected, scowling, uneasy and with all the evil of latent ill-will in many glances – should be laid at the feet of the British Minister and I thought too of von Stumm's firm statement – 'We keep what we hold'!

God in Heaven! What will it mean to these poor conquered people in the end if that be the irrevocable intention of the German Government!

That phrase has been ringing in my ears all the morning since I left Charleville and the 'Foreign Office.'

[...]

As our car topped the western heights beyond Rocroi and we began the descent towards the great cleft in the wooded hills where I knew the Meuse was clearing its way through the Ardennes I looked out on a scene that Caesar and his legions must once have eyed with something of awe. The vast spread of forested hills was the same probably today as then – the same white-frosted trees, the same tufted break of cloud half hiding half showing where the Meuse flowed into the northern hills. Only the men had changed – and these not much in mind. In place of Caesar you have the Kaiser! And Gaul is still the quarry. The Belgae that that first of the Kaisers was then advancing against perhaps by this very gap through Fumay and Givet have heard the tramp of many legions since those of Rome crossed the Meuse.

But what were the wars of Rome, the legions of Caesar compared to those of Berlin, to the army corps of the Kaiser!

[...]

In return for a partial promise to allow Ireland to erect a debating society on the banks of the Liffey at some wholly unspecified future date, Irishmen today are to give 300,000 men to the shambles in France & Flanders in order that the Englishmen, who is too valuable himself to be put in danger may 'capture the German trade.'

I rejoice mightily in my treason when I read these things – and think of those oleaginous scoundrels, like Haldane,[29] – quivering masses of

---

[29] Richard, Viscount Haldane (1856–1928) as both Secretary of State for War (1905–12) and Lord Chancellor (1912–15), he operated in the Liberal Party's inner circles of legal and political power. From as early as 1906, he was closely tied to Edward Grey and Britain's secret preparations for an eventual European war.

blubber – who are so busy killing the Kaiser with their mouth while trying to seduce my brave hearted countrymen to do the real killing – or be killed themselves.

If my treason does nothing else but save Ireland from this I shall have deserved well of my country. To keep our young men at home, for the future of our own country & for all her needs that is the counsel every true Irishman should give today. Thank God I came to Germany – and God be praised for the aid this people and their Government are giving Ireland today!

But this long digression leaves me between Andenne and Liège – in a hurrying motor car, with cold and darkness gathering in intensity.

We sped on through Huy past many factories, some silent, some at work until moments later we came to the outskirts of Liège – or Lüttich as my German friends call it.

We had some trouble in getting to the bridge, as the two that Meckle first steered for were down, and guarded – but we found a splendid bridge, with four columns of victory winged angels on top, two at each end—and over this we entered the busy part of Liège on the north bank of the Meuse. The river seems to be divided here into separate branches – so that more than one bridge is needed to cross it. The broad reach of the Meuse as we saw it from this big bridge was very fine, looking downstream, with a blaze of light from the city and a shining well lit riverside walk. We left the Bavarian priest at what had been the City Hall I presume – an imposing building on the Grand Place. It is now the headquarters of the German military governor – & orderlies, autos, motors, soldiers were coming and going. The streets were full of life – the shops well lit and the tram cars running filled with people. In fact, from inside no one could possibly say this city had recently been carried by assault and was now in the hands of a 'horde of barbarians' – *vide* the Anglo-Saxon press of England and England's dutiful daughter the United States of North America. Of all the lies England has distributed in recent years throughout the world, by her admirable system called 'free trade', I guess this lie of German barbarism and 'German atrocities' is the most wilful, the most perverse and the most evil intentioned.

As we hurried out of Liège, through crowded streets, past well lit windows and also by pleasant squares and esplanades I thought of the picture of Liège I had formed in New York and Philadelphia when the Anglo-Saxon lies were walking the streets of those cities. I suppose there

Ruined bridge at Liège. [Bundesarchiv]

is no people in the world so gullible as the Americans. That is doubtless why they invented poker. But the original poker face must have come from England – and I am convinced it came in the 'Mayflower', with an extraordinary pedigree behind it too and a family bible printed on the backs of the cards.

Leaving Liège, the suburbs, again on the south bank of the Meuse, which we recrossed by another bridge lower down stream, we stopped to ask the way from a crowd of workmen, A gendarme officer, a Belgian gendarme bien entendu, replied and *offered to guide us*.

He jumped on the footboard & we invited him into the car, and he took us up about 2 miles of our way on the road to Aachen – Charlemagne's city of Aix. This gendarme – he was an officer too – explained that the people were 'quite tranquil' now, and no trouble threatened. His talk was friendly enough and his manner too. The ordinary civil & criminal courts, Lüttichau and Meyer explained to me, were working as usual in Belgium and I noticed the ordinary gendarmes on duty in the streets – without arms or sidearms. The only armed men in Belgium today – east of Ypres and Dixmunde! – are German soldiers. After the treacheries of Louvain, Andenne, Termonde, Tirlemont &c. &c., it would indeed be madness for the army of the conqueror to leave arms in the hands of the population or their representatives. Meckle told me he had been shot at, in his car, at Tirlemont when going with despatches and that his earlier journeys thro' Belgium had been dangerous enough.

[…]

For the Belgian people I have nothing but pity—for their King and Government hearty contempt. These sacrificed the interests, the life itself of their country, to the interest of England. Léopold deux, with all his criminal career on the Congo, was a far better King for this unhappy people than this good King Albert.

[…]

These and thoughts like them were in my mind all the way from Charleville through ruined Givet, and occupied Namur and Liège until in piercing cold and mist we crossed the German frontier and sped towards Aachen, Jülich and Cologne.

The suburbs of Liège, so far as one could see from our car lamplights in the darkness, were almost all destroyed. We passed through village after village, or suburb after suburb of empty shattered and dismantled houses. Whether by German or Belgian shellfire no one can say now – then came fields – miles of them – and our lamps showed the barbed wire entanglements (like grape vines on low trellises) the Belgians had set up to impede the German advance against the ceinture of forts. None of these forts was visible – it was dark – all we could see was the barbed wire, acre after acre of the most worthless crop ever sowed by the hand of men. The wires were lit by the hoar frost – white and clear – laceworks of death. Meyer told me that the German troops had not crossed by the fields, but he came by the roads & so this wire had served little purpose – at any rate it was still there – intact and useless now. We went thro' Aachen without stopping, and thro' Jülich and reached Cologne at 8.50 p.m. The city seemed so peaceful, even gay and pleasant and clean and well lit –after the dark, barbed-wire fields around Liège.

From the hurried glimpse I have got of it I should think Cologne must be one of the pleasantest cities in Europe to live in. I liked it from the first – and on getting to the station at 9 p.m. my cold tired and hungry I liked it better still. The station was full of life – people of all classes and soldiers innumerable going and coming.

We got a hurried dinner in the Speisesaal[30] and then bidding Meckle adieu with a hearty handshake, Meyer, Von Lüttichau and I settled in sleeping cars for the night. As we crossed the Rhine bridge leaving the city, all the lights in our train went out. Von Lüttichau explained that this was a precaution 'leaving the fortress' against possible air-raids. Two searchlights were sweeping the heavens constantly. Our train remained in darkness until we had got well clear of the city defences, and then the lights were turned on and I went to sleep.

Von Lüttichau & Meckle, I am sure, were told sometime during the day by Meyer who I really was. They had taken me at first for 'Mr. Hammond of New York', but after the long interview at Charleville with the Headquarters staff and the F.O. this pretence was not sustainable. Their manner had grown more interested and when we parted, with Meckle at Cologne and with von Lüttichau at Berlin at 8 a.m. on Friday morning our adieux were warm and friendly and almost intimate.

---

[30] Dining room.

BERLIN

Tuesday, 24 November, 1914

On getting back to Berlin last Friday from our hurried visit to the Headquarters I found Adler still here, but prepared to go back to Norway on the morrow – with the sham letters I had written for Mr. de C. Findlay's benefit.

The declaration of the German Government on Ireland was not yet issued – and I wondered throughout the forenoon and after lunch at the cause of the delay, as von Wedel had told me on Tuesday last, before I left for Charleville, that it would be given to the press on Wednesday last. However, about 3 I happened to see the Midday Gazette – the *B.Z. am Mittag*[31] – & there it was.

> 'Deutsche Sympathie-Erklärung für Irland.
> Sir Roger Casement in Berlin.'

It was placed in big type & in the most prominent part of the paper – as a central 'inset' on the front page. Over columns was an article headed: '<u>Sir Roger's Aktion</u> – <u>Zu Seinem Berliner Besuche</u>', which was not only a sort of biography of me, but a eulogy as well.

[...]

All the evening papers as they came out had it in too – some with comment, others without.

[...]

At 5.30 von Wedel rang me up and asked if I could go to him at F.O. I went at 7 and he read me first a despatch from the German Ambassador at the Vatican saying that two good 'nationalist' Irish Priests had been

---

[31] Translates as '*Berliner Zeitung* at midday'.

got – thro' Mon. O'Riordan of the Irish College – one named Canice O'Gorman (a good enough name) the other Crotty. Both were ready to come for the work of the Irish soldiers.

[...]

The *Continental News* of Friday also has the Declaration in full – I give it here too. I have asked the Foreign Office to order 3.000 extra copies of the edition of the paper for the Irish soldiers later on –

[...]

The well known Irish Nationalist, Sir Roger Casement, who has arrived in Berlin from the United States, has been received at the Foreign Office.

Sir Roger Casement pointed out that statements were being published in Ireland, apparently with the authority of the British Government behind them, to the effect that a German victory would inflict great loss upon the Irish people, whose homes, churches, priests, and lands would be at the mercy of an invading army actuated only by motives of pillage and conquest. Recent utterances of Mr. Redmond on his recruiting tour in Ireland and many pronouncements of the British Press in Ireland to the above effect have been widely circulated, Sir Roger pointed out, and have caused natural apprehension among Irishmen as to the German attitude towards Ireland in the event of a German victory in the present war.

Sir Roger sought a convincing statement of German intentions towards Ireland that might reassure his country men all over the world, and particularly in Ireland and America, in view of these disquieting statements emanating from responsible British quarters.

In reply to this inquiry, the Acting Secretary of State at the Foreign Office, by order of the Imperial Chancellor, has made the following official declaration:

Official Statement

The German Government repudiates the evil intentions attributed to it in the statements referred to by Sir Roger Casement, and takes this opportunity to give a categoric assurance that the

71

The Continental Times, 20 Nov. 1914 [National Library of Ireland]

German Government desires only the welfare of the Irish people, their country, and their institutions.

The Imperial Government formally declares that under no circumstances would Germany invade Ireland with a view to its conquest or the overthrow of any native institutions in that country.

Should the fortune of this great war, that was not of Germany's seeking, ever bring in its course German troops to the shores of Ireland, they would land there, not as an army of invaders to pillage and destroy, but as the forces of a Government that is inspired by goodwill towards a country and a people for whom Germany desires only national prosperity and national freedom.

[...]

On Sunday I saw Adler off at 11.18 to Sassnitz with two faked letters and two 'stolen' pages of 'my Diary' giving hints at impending invasion of Ireland by myself and friends here (50.000) 'by end of December.' It should make Findlay's hair – such as remains of it – rise up and bless him and the day he got hold of Adler Christensen!

I spent the day quietly and met [Richard] Kiliani in the afternoon who told me he had found the Baroness von Nordenflycht in Berlin.

[...]

On Monday 23rd <u>Nov</u> I lunched with von Wedel's mother the Countess Groeben, at 3 Fürst Bismarck Str. A charming & beautiful old lady – perfectly delightful. She greeted with extreme warmth in the most clear English. There were also at lunch Georg, her son, Count and Countess Oppersdorff, he a Bavarian Catholic a member of 'the Centre' in the Reichstag and his wife née a Polish Lithuanian Princess. The Count spoke little or no English – but French (his mother was a Talleyrand-Périgord) but the Countess spoke excellent English. There was also present a tall, dark German I did not catch the name of – he a good English speaker. He met me on the stairs going up at 1.30 and

Gebhard von Blücher: the great-great grandson of the Prussian Field Marshal, he had known Casement since their time together in Portuguese East Africa. Casement sometimes stayed at the von Blücher household in Notting Hill in London. [*Memoirs of Prince Blücher*]

at once began to speak in English. He had been in India and knew the *Gaelic American* for when he saw my copy he said it had been excluded from India when he was there.

Count Oppersdorff full of sympathy for Ireland, largely on Catholic grounds, & very anxious to get the German Declaration in there thro' Church channels. (He was German Minister in Belgium before the war.)

I suggested Rome and he said naturally and that he would also try through Brittany!

The Countess (who <u>looks</u> 25) told me she had thirteen children! Two of her sons, 18 & 19 are going to the front in a few days as volunteers. I am to go and see them before they leave. I liked her greatly & we became fast friends & she talked much of Ireland – asking of the old Gaelic families & of the Irish language as did the others – Oppersdorff knew much about it.

At 5 the Nordenflychts called on me – the Baroness & Gussie – but just then came a wire from poor Adler detained at Sassnitz begging me to see von Wedel – so I had to hurry off to the F.O. & ask him to telegraph to Sassnitz. I also 'phoned & wrote to Meyer to same effect – & then walked a bit & dined, at Hoffman's Kellner.

On Tuesday, today, I was to go to the Baroness von N. – but got a 'phone to say she was in bed with cold – & just then a 'phone came from Blücher (Gebhard) at the Esplanade Hotel – to my great joy, & I hurried off to lunch with him there.

Berlin, Thursday, 26 November 1914

After my lunch with Blücher on Tuesday I talked with the Countess. She is in great distress for her young brother left with two broken legs in a captured trench.

He will try and arrange lunch with von Jagow & me – the Secretary of State whom he knows well. Von Jagow arrived in Berlin from the front a few days ago & the Chancellor comes too I hear for the Reichstag debates.

I worked a good deal in evening of Tuesday – it was very cold.

The papers from Countess Blücher are very interesting. I made out lists of some 300 Dublin Fusiliers 'missing' & see that hundreds of other Irish are captured. So much the better. The English fear of Ireland is clearly rising! Sir E. Grey's 'Ireland the one bright spot.' of 4 Augt. is a strange commentary on the terror and world wide activities they are displaying to keep Ireland 'quiet.' For every day fresh evidence comes to hand. I see by the English press of 11 Nov. – that the White Star 'mid week vessels now will go straight from Liverpool to New York with mails' &c. So a further nail in the Irish coffin!

[...]

But the best of all is the news that now appears in the Berlin press that England wishes to establish a diplomatic post at the Vatican! Shades of Persico and Leo XIII! Who will he be? Possibly the Earl of Kenmare – a loyal 'Irishman'! The report is qualified here by the press assertions that the Pope has refused the offer. The form it was said to have taken was that 'during the course of the war England would like to have a diplomatic channel with the Vatican established' – and that the Papal F.O. replied that it saw no good purpose to be served or reason for a <u>temporary</u> connection at this period.

The Pope probably wants to secure permanent diplomatic relations with England – and as 'the one bright spot' is clearly the object in view of British diplomacy, His Holiness will probably obtain, from English fears of the bright spot becoming brighter, the creation of <u>permanent</u> official relations between the Holy See and St. James's. It will be a triumph for the Vatican – and achieved moreover, over the spiritual and political heirs of the author of 'Vaticanism'! As to Ireland – the purpose to be served is clearly a harmful one. It is today as in the time of Parnell a fresh British intrigue against the spirit of Irish nationality. The Pope is to be enlisted on the side of British rule in Ireland – even as the Irish won't enlist to spread that rule abroad! But it is clear proof of the strength and reality of the national soul again uprising in Ireland. More even the British announcement of the Vatican <u>Entente</u> comes after the publication of the German Govt's Declaration of Goodwill towards Ireland.

Countess Blücher hopes sincerely I may succeed in raising a real good rebellion in Ireland – & so bring peace by terrifying the British Government.

I dined last night (Wed) with Professor Schiemann his wife & two daughters. He had got copies of New York papers for me *Gaelic American* several & the new issue of my brochure with the footnote about the Prince of Wales's 'going to the front' – to Brentwood Barracks (I see the poor boy has at length 'joined his regiment' in France!). Schiemann also had a letter from Freeman in New York with news – not very first hand I imagine – of Ireland – & a statement that of the 'recent lot of recruits taken from Ireland to the front, 3000 had gone over prepared to go over to Germany at first chance.' If only these people were less machine made they could get every Irish regiment in the British army to join my Brigade! But they will proceed only by machinery and not by individual intelligence.

[...]

I see in the *Daily Telegraph* of 16 Nov. 1914 a telegram from Washington saying that the Br. Ambassador had made representations about the spy Lody's[32] passport which was that of an American named Charles H. Inglis. In consequence enquiry is being instituted at Berlin & further 'new and strict rules regarding the obtaining of American passports for use abroad come into effect today (Nov 14) by an order signed by President Wilson having been issued, for the purpose of preventing foreign agents from securing passports for the purpose of espionage or for other reasons.' (Reuters)

I guess the 'Oscar II' & the passenger she brought to Christiania is one of the principal 'other reasons'!

Schiemann tells me that Kuno Meyer arrived safely in New York yesterday – 25 Nov. – so that now we may shortly expect the first blows in our double campaign. The Declaration of the German Govt. should have been with the press of U.S.A. at latest on Sunday last – probably Saturday 21st. I hope my two letters, sent by Meyer to be posted in R'dam arrive safely also.

I wrote to von Wedel y'day asking him to get some Irish flags and metal badges too for the troops – the *Continental Times* has my appeal to the Irish people on both Monday (23rd) and Wednesday (25) issues. Here it is as printed there. I have ordered 2.000 copies extra for the prisoners and I send some to Rome as well.

Meyer called at 12 & I discussed this latest effort at 'Vaticanism' on the part of Mr. Bull against Ireland. A minute after he left Count von Wedel rang me up to say the two priests had arrived from Rome and had been with him at the Foreign Office. They are in charge of a Dominican father, who will get them rooms in some quiet Hotel and then I am to see them. Wedel says they knew 'who I was' but did not know me personally No, they did not but I hope their views may become as mine before we part.

---

[32] The celebrated, German spy Carl Lody (1877–1914) was shot in the Tower of London in November 1914.

Gaelic American, 28 Nov. 2014: 'Germany pledges friendship to Ireland' based upon the 'Declaration of Goodwill' issued thanks to Casement's discussion with the German Foreign Office. [Digital Library@Villanova University]

<u>Nous verrons</u>. I told v. W. not to allow them to visit the Irish prisoners until I had seen them, and been there first.

[...]

I enjoyed my walk to and back from Schiemann's last night – especially the walk home from the Zoo and thus round by Potsdamer Str. Plenty of people in Berlin streets at night – not like London. I walked y'day afternoon (in rain) to Stettiner Str. and met lots of wounded soldiers with such kind-faced German nurses and 'guides' accompanying them. Part of the scheme of convalescence seems to be to have the men taken out and to theatres and shows, with such kind faced, smiling affectionate nurses acting as friends. Crowds of kind eyed people go with them often and press things on them and all are so full of courtesy, real affection and love for the soldiers that every day I feel more and more in love with German manhood and womanhood. A great people a good people.

No news yet from Adler. Meyer says he is certain he got away all safe and sound from Sassnitz on Tuesday (24th) after noon at 4.56. That means he should have been at Moss yesterday at 11 a.m. & perhaps today he may begin operations with '*ce cher ministre*.' Schiemann is anxious for me to publish the whole story to the world and quickly.

Coming out from lunch at 3 from 'Hoffmann's' Kellar the newsmen (not boys here, but <u>men</u>) were rushing thro' the streets with the *B.Z. am Mittag* with the (official) news from Headquarters that the Russians had been defeated near Lódz and 40.000 prisoners taken. The streets were full of pleased faces, hand shaking & smiles and flags were out in a trice from many shops and homes. The newsmen did a roaring trade, surrounded by crowds. But no jingoism or offensive hilarity!

They take their victories as they do their losses – with quiet repose of manner and expression. And yet this is a great victory and a big step on the road to final triumph, or a sound peace.

[...]

Baroness von Nordenflycht called at 5 & brought me the 1st edition of *B.Z. am Mittag* with report of Larkin's arrival in U.S.A. denouncing England and saying that there were no 'loyalists' in Ireland. Some *Daily Mails* and *Daily Telegraphs* of 20 Nov. to hand also. Furious and absurd statements about 'German gold' and 'German-American gold' spent on 'the Irish sedition mongers' who it is seen have stopped recruiting. Questions 'in the House' about an article in the *Irish Volunteer* of 7 Nov. – saying the only hope for Ireland was 'the downfall of the Br. Empire.' John

Redmond denounced the *Irish Volunteer* & disclaimed all connection with it. I like the 'German-American gold'! It used to be 'Irish-American gold!' – & when Redmond won the 1911 Election we remember the 'Dollar Dictator' campaign! But now – things are changed. Redmond is a jingo imperialist – quite 'one of us' – and it would be impolite to speak of 'Irish-American' anything now. Besides, there are no 'Irish Americans' now! They too are merged in the great loyal mass of friends of freedom fighting for the small nationalities – & there only remain such malignants as a handful of German-gold sustained Boers – like de Wet – and the German American offal in U.S.A. All the rest of humanity – including the Fijians, the Emirs of Nigeria, the Dyaks & headhunters of Borneo, the Esquimaux incidentals, and the Presidents of Liberia, Haiti, Nicaragua and Venezuela are burning to join the forces of the 'Allies' in defence of the public laws of Europe and the existence & liberty of the small nations.

These outbreaks of jaundice, produced clearly by German gold, were on Friday last 20th – the very day the German Official Declaration came out here in Berlin.

It will indeed be interesting (soon) to read the comments of the *Times*, *The Daily Mail*, the *Daily Telegraph* & the rest when that statement – the interview with 'Sir Roger Casement' are permitted by the British censor to appear. I wonder when that will be?

Or will they not be stopped? I fancy they will not allow the Br. Press to publish the Declaration – but they will instead begin an increasing volume of 'dénigrement' of me preparing for the day when the cat has to leap out of the bag. Anyhow, I have given them now some nice thrills that will certainly cause Sir E. Grey to revise his opinion that 'Ireland is the one bright spot.' Poor Ireland! If all I dream of comes to pass she will indeed be a bright spot on the map of Europe – in the chart of world peoples.

Berlin, Friday, 27 November 1914

I walked a good deal last evening – and wound up in the Thiergarten, Siegesallee and a seat in the pleasant garden. Not very cold yesterday – many were without greatcoats – a remarkable rise since Monday & Tuesday.

This morning, papers have more about Ireland – and quote a long article from the *Times* of 24th Nov. – attacking vigorously *Irish Freedom* and the *Irish Volunteer*. The latter enemy is the article of 7th Nov. I referred to y'day as having been denounced in 'the House.'

[...]

All of the servants & people here in the Hotel now know quite well who I am but I remain 'Mr. Hammond' still officially. All enquiries for Sir R. C. in Berlin have failed! No one knows where he is. I walk about with an American flag in my buttonhole and often go past the U.S. Embassy on my way to the Wilhelmstrasse. As soon as I have visited the Irish soldiers in their camp I shall return to Berlin to another Hotel and 'descend' there

Saoirse – Irish Freedom, November 1914 & *The Irish Volunteer*, 1 August 1914: Irish Nationalist newspapers that would be outlawed by the Defence of the Realm Act. [Angus Mitchell]

as Sir Roger Casement. Poor 'Mr. Hammond' will disappear, like Mr. Landy 'knocked on the head' in a more effective way than Mr. Findlay, H.B.M. Envoy Extraordinary achieved through Adler! I did succeed in knocking Mr. Landy on the head but the Holy Government failed in its Holy War on Sir R. C.

I see the real Holy War goes well – 'Territorials' have been sent to India! The Turks with 76.000 men and 10.000 Bedouins (and 5.000 camels) are reported as near the Suez Canal. General Maxwell, the British Commander in Egypt, is said to have 70.000 men all told – but some of them will be Indians and the majority Egyptians – and in the end the latter will surely follow the green flag. If Turkey breaks thro' the Canal as I think she may do, it may indeed bring about the downfall of the Fr. Empire – as Wilfrid Blunt prayed for it in May.

With the Canal gone Egypt goes – and with both gone I look for such an outbreak in India as must tax "the Empire" to its limit, and with Germany at the gates of Calais, and the Irish Declaration out I do not think Master John can spare many men, ships or guns for India. To hold down India he will have to appeal to Japan – and that spells his own sure and certain eviction from Asia later on. Once India falls the whole house collapses – for it is chiefly on India and her plunder the colonial scheme of robbery depends.

Meyer came at 12 & said the two Irish priests (from Rome) were out 'for a walk' and could not be found so I can't go till tomorrow. He tells me that in their interview with von Wedel yesterday they show that they had been given strict instructions to abstain from all politics! Good if they keep to that. Meyer said the German F.O. are now convinced that England is going to accredit an envoy to the Vatican! The name is even mentioned – possibly Sir Henry Howard.[33] I knew the instant I saw the telegram in the *Corriere della Sera* three days ago, that it would be done.

[...]

I said to Meyer that the fact that England was driven to this course was the clearest proof of the justice of my point of view. Ireland, instead of being as the English proclaim it "loyal" is the danger point – now that I am in Berlin and have got the German Govt to speak out. [...] We must

---

[33] Casement incorrectly refers to him as Charles Howard. The mistake has been rectified on subsequent occasions.

get the news into Ireland of the German Declaration – & at all costs get the Irish Brigade formed. I wired as follows to Cohalan to go by von Bernstorff in code:

> Have you sent special messenger to Ireland & if so wire me the date of arrival there – also have you sent priest here? Cable through Bernstorff. Casement.

How to meet the Papal danger is not yet clear. The best way is to make it clear that Germany will free Ireland if she wins the war and let England intrigue as much as she likes against that!

At the worst we can kill the recruiting – at the best we may get to Ireland with guns & officers & raise a first rate rebellion. The German Declaration is highly moral! – The British reply is prompt & highly moral too! Where Sir George Errington failed against Parnell – will Sir Henry Howard or another succeed against R.C. & the Irish Volunteers?

The *Continental Times* today has more about Ireland – & a further eulogy of me – & a notice about the 2 priests (O'Gorman and Crotty) from Rome. These two men may be a danger – I'll see tomorrow. If they are going to be agents of the British Govt. then they shall not get to the Irish soldiers at all.

Berlin, Saturday, 28 November 1914

I walked nearly all the way to the Baroness von N's last night in Hohenzollern Avenue – a long walk half way across Berlin – & I came back at 11 also nearly all way on foot. The streets are full of life long after midnight and I had a cup of coffee nearly at 1 am in Friedrichstr – the Regent's Street or Piccadilly of Berlin.

Today the papers give details of the destruction of the Br[itish] battleship 'Bulwark' at Sheerness, a fearful explosion and down she went, having sunk before the smoke cleared away. The houses in Chatham were shaken and windows smashed. The cause unknown, about 700 men lost some 22 (or 28) officers gone – God help them and their people. This, following the 'Audacious' and the possible sinking of the 'Canopus' by von Spee's squadron spells dreadful naval loss to England.

Then to Blücher and the Countess till nearly 2 p.m. I refused to see the princess yet. She is anxious to meet me, says she is Irish – (I believe her

Evelyn, Countess Blücher: born Evelyn Stapleton-Bretherton; her memoir *An English Wife in Berlin: A Private Memoir of Events, Politics and Daily Life in Germany Throughout the War and the Social Revolution of 1918* (New York, 1920) was based upon the diary she was encouraged to keep by Casement. [National Portrait Gallery, London]

mother was Irish but the Cornwallis West family are just what we know – English of the English.) The Countess B. is fine. She really would like to see England get not an overthrow, but a good birching from Germany.

I walked in the Thiergarten at 10.30 to 11.15 a.m. – lovely sun & soft air today & then I walked again back from Esplanade to my Hotel at 2. A message to go and see Father O'Gorman & Crotty at 4. They are in the Nord West Hotel in the Micaville – at Thurmstr 7.

The bar man told me that the evg paper *B.Z. am Mittag* had 'something about the big Irishman Sir Roger Casement' – & coming to my room I found it already on the table with a translation by my waiter.

Berlin, Monday, 30 November 1914

I went to the holy men at 4.30 & found Father O'Gorman a loyalist nationalist and Father Crotty, the Dominican (thank God!), a raging Fenian! <u>Both</u> promised me <u>not</u> to be 'agents of the British Government', as I asked them but to confine themselves strictly to their holy business. They are to be entirely 'non political.' The question is <u>will</u> they?

Will they not tell the men that their allegiance to King George V is a moral & religious obligation – if the men consult them? Fr. Crotty will not influence the men against my point of view – that I am sure – but

Father C.J. Crotty: In November 1914, Crotty was sent by the Vatican to Germany and began to work as a special envoy to Irish POWs, first in Limburg and then Zossen. He developed a strong bond with Casement and appears to have influenced Casement's own spiritual shift towards Catholicism. [Anthony O'Brien, Private Collection]

Fr. O'Gorman may. Both, however, are here (at my request too!) as spiritual guides only. If they stick to that all is well. I told them of the Vatican <u>démarche</u> & Fr. Crotty said '<u>That</u> will not help England in Ireland!'

I told them of Christiania & many other things – Fr. Crotty is a splendid big Irishman with the broad Milesian face – a relative of sorts of Leslie Crotty the singer – & I touched on him.

Fr. O'Gorman is chiefly influenced, I think, by the Belgian aspect of the case – the violation of Belgian neutrality & the alleged excesses there & destruction of life and churches. Had he seen Donchery with its ruined church in the midst of a desolation of ruined houses I wonder what he would have said. Donchery was quite the most obliterated town I passed.

Meyer called on me at 9 p.m. to say that the military authorities report that they have already found 2300 Catholic Irish soldiers among the prisoners! as I told them. They thought less than one thousand would be the limit. I told them all along England fights with Irishmen. Here is but proof of it. By the last official figures they had 15.400 privates of the British Army as prisoners of war. Since that return they have captured some 1500 – 2000 more at outside – so that of a possible 17.000 to 18.000 men they have already – with only a preliminary search too – got 2300 Catholic Irish soldiers! If we add those passed over, inevitably, in a search of this kind, conducted by foreigners, and the Protestant

Irish we should certainly find that well over 3000 (possibly 4000) of the 'British' prisoners of war are Irishmen – or about one fourth of the whole.

It points one way or the other – either there are many more Irish in the Army (as I have always said) than the Br. Govt admits – or else the Irish Regiments have been in the posts of danger from the first. Both explanations are true. The number of Irish soldiers is greatly swelled by enlisting in England and Scotland of Irish born boys or sons of Irish parents. Meyer, I think, told me that this preliminary search, however, was through Irish Regiments only! Already 300 or 400 have been collected into a special camp at Limburg near Frankfurt on the Maine – whither I am to go on Tuesday night to see the men.

I go before the priests go & will sow my seed first – & leave them papers & words of love.

On Sunday Blücher called & left me a *Daily Mail* with notice (21 November) of the pro-German demonstration of the Medical College of the National University of Ireland – the inaugural meeting. There were, it seems, wild cheers for the Kaiser and the German Army and hooting for Kitchener & the 'President of the Royal College of Surgeons and other gentlemen' had to withdraw! [...]

Blücher & I to Eden Hotel to see rooms there for Sir Roger Casement when he returns to Berlin. Then [...] to the Zoo a fine place, with good tigers and lions – & the Tea Room enormous. There must have been 1500 to 2000 people in the two big halls (at 4.30) & a good band playing – men, women & children & I could not believe it was the centre of a city beset by more than half the world in arms against the soldier boys of their people we saw so peacefully & happily at tea. Truly they are a great, calm, proud & <u>manly</u> race.

The evg papers announce that the Kaiser had gone to the Polish front! Is that good or bad? I fear bad news.

[...]

I had a delightful walk last evening in the Thiergarten – to the Konzertsaal by the Zelten & on to Moabit Bridge & back. Thousands of young soldiers out for the day – Unter den Linden swarming with them – handsome, strong, fine young fellows. All waiting only for the word.

[...]

Berlin, Tuesday, 1 December 1914

To Blücher at Esplanade at 6 & left a letter for Eoin MacN[eill] – enclosed in one to Mrs. G[reen]. – & this in one to Wambersin & Son, Rotterdam – this finally to go to Herr Ballin in Hamburg, who can get it through to England unopened – So B. says – this is the route Princess of Pless takes & it is on her advice.

[...]

B. says that the leading Germans still are not keen for war à outrance with England – at least the diplomatic world of Germany, of which von Jagow is the type. They wanted – and want! – English 'friendship.' The military machine, however (and happily), is under no such illusions and desires mightily to get at England – and, as B. truly says, the military mind in Germany dominates the civil power in every way and also has absorbed far the ablest minds of the land so that German intelligence is much better represented in Army and Navy circles than in the Foreign Office and governing administration.

This is evident! If the men who have controlled German 'diplomacy' & brought this country to its present state of colossal isolation in the world had had the war machine to run, I guess the French and Russian armies would now be near Potsdam.

[...]

The *Times* gives many particulars of the 'Sedition' in Ireland [...] They want *Irish Freedom*, the *Irish Volunteer*, *Sinn Fein*, & Larkin's paper all prosecuted for their active sedition and comfort to Germany

[...]

Albert Ballin: owner of the Hamburg-Amerika shipping line; in 1913, Casement negotiated with Ballin to bring his German liners to Queenstown Harbour (Cobh) on their transatlantic voyages to and from America, thereby breaking the British transport monopoly of routes in and out of Ireland. [Bundesarchiv]

The last *Times* to hand is <u>Wed. 25 Nov</u>. – & this still contains nothing about me. It is clear the Govt. tried to suppress the German Declaration, but must have failed – as Sir J Lonsdale question (from Amsterdam 28 Nov) shows that by Friday it was public property and had been raised in the Commons. It can have come out only through America.

LIMBURG

Frankfurt on Main, Thursday, 3 December 1914

I got here this morning at 7.10 in darkness. My train left the Anhalt Station at Berlin at 10.20 last night. The Crown Princess travelled too by the first part of the same train. I saw her arrive – very little ceremony, but all hats off.

There has been little to record the last few days. Tuesday I was unwell and stayed in my room all day. Professor Schiemann called late at night with disquieting statements about Adler that were unwarranted and malicious. Poor Adler! God knows he is bad enough without these professional inquests on him. I was annoyed beyond words – and disgusted.

[…]

Then last night, Wednesday 2 Dec the fall of Belgrade was announced after over four months' siege. The second capital captured in the war & both by the Germanic armies.

Things look <u>very</u> black for Servia – & there will be little pity for her fate. Her case is different from that of Belgium although the publication of the 'Anglo Belgian Military Conventions' of 1906 entirely upsets the Belgian <u>pose</u> of neutrality. She was no more neutral than France – or England. She deliberately allied herself with England 8 years ago – & England in 1912 dared to inform Belgium that she, England, would land troops in Belgium 'to defend Belgian Neutrality', whether Belgium consented or not! […]

I lunched yesterday at the Astoria Hotel with Baron & Baroness von Roeder. He is Court Chamberlain – Master of the Ceremonies. She was a daughter of Lord Rockingham. Of course her English was perfect; but her heart now entirely German and she shared all my views and hopes. Countess Blücher also there. She, poor lady very unhappy and <u>trying</u> to be German – but her heart still with her own land.

[…]

On getting to Frankfurt I came in the dark to the Hessischer Hof (formerly the 'Englischer Hof' I see) & took a room. About 9 the manager came to say that the Chief of the General Staff was in the Hotel & would see me at his office at 11 a.m.

This is General de Graaff.

I have a letter for him, from the Ministry of War, yesterday signed by the War Minister introducing me as 'Sir Roger Casement, an Irishman' & – stating that I am to visit the Irish camp at Limburg & have entire freedom with the Irish prisoners of war.

I also have, for general use, an Imperial Passport No. 2192 issued by the Emperor's 'Special Order' and signed for the Imperial Chancellor by one 'Dargitz', issued for 3 months from 2 Dec. 1914. The passport is for 'travelling in Germany' – and is issued to the 'Irishman Sir Roger Casement.' I showed it here at the Hotel on registering, and wrote my name, birth place, year & date of birth – & so now thirty four days after I reached Berlin I become myself! Here I am, I presume, the only (unmarried) or male 'British subject' at large in Germany, with a special Imperial passport and the full consent and goodwill of the Govt. – & to judge from the

manager's face, & the smiles of the waiters, the goodwill of the people themselves.

[…]

I have brought plenty of 'literature' for the soldiers – including a lot of copies of the new issue of my pamphlet 'Ireland, Germany and the Freedom of the Seas', which the Berlin F.O. has printed for me under the title 'The Crime against Ireland – and How the War may right it.' It is a reprint of the preface and then 6 articles & I have added as a 7th article 'The Elsewhere Empire' so that it makes a little book almost. The F.O. has had 2.000 printed

Casement's passport. [National Library of Ireland]

89

for me – and have done it very well indeed. The type, style, paper & general get up are excellent – I sent a copy to Schiemann – & will send out many to the press & to Americans here in Germany.

[...]

I found General de Graaff [...] at 11.30 a.m. in his office down by the Maine – a very charming man, knowing English well (a friend of the late King Edward VII, formerly, a native of Wiesbaden, I think) & in 5 minutes all was arranged.

[...]

I walked about Frankfurt a good deal, admiring the broad & beautiful streets and splendid buildings – & the general air of extreme well doing of people, houses & public buildings. The population is generally speaking, darker than the Berlin type – here the Hessian face is the predominant. On the whole the people are nice looking – good deal of Jew in some faces – & have the fine, strong, well shaped bodies I notice all thro' Germany – soldiers & sailors – very strong, well built young men are in evidence – & many young men & boys I met enough for a division in the streets!

No lack of fine, strong, handsome boys & young men. My old Hotel, the Frankfurter Hof (May 1912) is partly a Hospital – at back I find. The shops filled with Christmas things chiefly 'love gifts' for the soldiers and sailors at the front. Everything here in Germany today is simply a gift to the heroic forces defending the fatherland.

The crime and cowardice of England seem to me everyday to be magnified when I contrast her petty, mean, sordid spirit of commercial war & war of conquest over weaker peoples with this heroic spirit of all Germany, to face and overcome by courage, sacrifice and national discipline the hired hordes of Asia and Africa and trained millions of Russia and France too.

I agreed with General de Graaff, at night, after dinner, to leave on Friday at 8.30 for Limburg.

Limburg, Friday, 4 December 1914

This we did – in beautiful weather for Decr. The car a fine military motor with a huge War Ministry arms on the panels (the Prussian Eagles wings widespread long) that attracted attention & salutes from every soldier.

We were off at 8.30 and out to Wiesbaden, which we passed through, a perfectly charming town – the gardens well kept – but the smart Hotels shut up.

Prince Leiningen: born in Osborne house, Isle of Wight. His paternal grandfather was the half-brother of Queen Victoria. He accompanied Casement during his visits to Limburg and the surrounding region in late 1914. [Bundesarchiv]

A big garrison is there (3000 men) & about 4000 wounded, so that there is plenty of military life at present.

We got to Limburg, thro' a beautiful country with sunshine lighting the hills & woods at about 9.45 or 10 a.m. – having come quickly. There, at the Preussischer Hof were the General Exner in charge of the Irish camp & many other officers and among them Prince Leiningen who introduced himself as an 'old Harrovian'. He was born at Osborne.

We all went on to the Camp over the Lahn with a glorious view of the Cathedral on its rock right on the river. The camp not finished – a huge wooden encampment, very well put up indeed and with the greatest care being shown for the welfare of the men. About 400 French soldiers working at it & only some 300 'Irish' already collected. They looked a <u>very</u> wretched lot – half clad only in a miserable thin Khaki Stuff – they were pinched with cold, dirty & miserable & I felt ashamed of them beside the better clothed & <u>much</u> finer looking French prisoners.

The German officers (there were nearly 20 with us, following the two Generals) were all struck by the poor starving & generally poor figures of the Irish. I saw about 20 non-commissioned officers first in their room and spoke to them alone. O poor lot – one of them more English than the English themselves – he talked of 'getting back to England' – of 'squaring it with the Germans when we get them to England' and so forth. Others had the Irish face & eye – & (mostly young men) they had <u>horrid beards</u>.

The men outside looked even worse than the non-coms. & very unpromising material to work on I felt. The scum of Ireland – literally. Thank God for it, from one point of view – it shows so clearly that the blow we have dealt enlisting. Most of the men I saw were from the 18

Pope Benedict XV: on his appointment to the papacy in September 1914, he declared the neutrality of the Holy See and condemned the war as 'the suicide of civilized Europe'. He supported the mission of Catholic priests to attend to the needs of prisoners of war and similar humanitarian endeavours.
[Bibliotheca Apostolica Vaticana]

Royal Irish – with a few S. Lancashires! & Middlesex! & one I saw of the Leinsters. The General said that some 'English' soldiers had got themselves smuggled in as Irish and wd. have to be weeded out.

I talked to the non-coms for about 10 minutes – told them who I was & all about the 'Home Rule' fake & the Irish in America & that I was going to try to get arms & men into Ireland to join the Volunteers – but I said 'I don't think any of you are brave enough to do what I've done.' Some had themselves said they'd 'join the Volunteers' or 'go to America' when the war is over.

The worst was a young handsome lad only of the 18th – the one who spoke of 'England' & of 'us' all the time – & the 'lies of the Germans.' I saw <u>some</u> good Irish eyes – & one poor fellow outside among the privates, asked if I was Irish & when I said yes – he said 'God bless you, you look Irish too.'

I left them after only a few minutes talk promising to return tomorrow. I gave them the pictures of the Pope I brought from New York and lots of papers – including the *Continental Times* with the Declaration of the German Govt – & my 'Appeal to the Irish People' – & some English papers too with the usual lies. I left more for the 1800 others I heard were coming – and gave them to Major Grunert in charge of the camp under General Exner.

Then I visited with the Generals the kitchens. Excellent – clean & well built with huge boilers – in one kitchen half a dozen French soldiers were cooking. I tasted the food – a mixture of macaroni, potatoes & herbs, very good and <u>very</u> hot. One of the young French soldiers cooking was a splendid young fellow – about 6 feet, fair, strong – in blue puttee's showing splendid calves & with the figure of a young Hercules.

His face was fixed, no smile – blue eyes, civil & polite to the questions of his captors – but Oh! such a far off look! His heart in France – only his hatred here. I felt deep pity for the French. They were the men of a nation – a national army, citizens under arms – fighting for France. When I looked at them I understood the German pity and respect for the French.

For the Irish I could have no such feeling. They were not fighting for their country – they were indeed, as they are always called on the Continent, 'a mercenary army.' No spark of patriotism to fire the eye; The Crime Against Ireland stood there before me in these poor sodden sick faces. Demoralised into the ranks of the one anti-national army in all the world. God! what a crime it is.

I left the camp with a sense of despair. We all lunched together at the 'Prussischer Hof' in Limburg after General de Graaff (with Prince Leiningen) called on the Bishop to tell him the two Irish priests from Rome were coming as chaplains of the Irish soldiers. A 'phone to the General from Berlin asked if I had any objection to the two priests coming at once – and I said none at all – so de Graaff 'phoned back to say send them at once & they should be here on Sunday morning.

The Friday (4 Dec) afternoon, General de Graaff, his ADC & Prince Leiningen & I went on in the motor car to visit another prison camp being put up at Wetzlar – on the Lahn. The journey through a beautiful country – the heart of Hesse-Cassell up the valley of the Lahn. We saw afar off some splendid old towers on isolated hills – something like the Roman castles one sees outside of Rome – ruined messages from medieval Germany. At Braunfels a very fine schloss on the cliff over the Lahn. […]

Wetzlar, too, very picturesque with a fine old castle – & the river running through it.

The new camp being constructed, to hold at a pinch 20.000 men – is all of wood – not so solid as the camp at Limburg. Mostly French prisoners here – but 6 English soldiers – a poor looking lot – and six Russians.

[…]

We left the camp and on to Giessen – a fine town on the Lahn of 60.000 people and a University.

Full of life – schoolboys & students & some peasant girls in the charming country costume and some of the young men too in the <u>national</u> Hessian garb. The General and the two others got off at the station to wait for a train for Frankfurt and I stayed on in the motor which then set out to return to Limburg.

It was dark & the road uninteresting for that reason. We returned by Wetzlar and Braunfels & got to Limburg at 7 (or 6.40) where I had a quiet dinner & went to bed with a bad sore throat at the Preussischer Hof – it is a very comfortable clean, good Hotel – and extraordinarily cheap.

My excellent bedroom <u>with</u> ample breakfast – coffee, rolls, butter & honey (fruhstück) costs only 3 marks.

Bath free, and the bath is large, clean and airy.

A headwaiter who speaks good English and has young waiters, both boys, who speak only German. But all very civil, clean, smiling and pleasant faced.

The town of Limburg is quite charming – delightful old houses and streets round the Cathedral – and such a fine faced, strong, well shaped bodied population. Literally hundreds of young men and boys here still – and the more I see of Germany the clearer it becomes that she must win the war. One never hears a boast or a bragging word. There is simply quiet calm confidence in the power of the army (and the navy too!) & the patriotism of the whole nation. I gave away several copies of the *Crime against Ireland* to the German officers. The chief interpreter of the camp is a 'Professor' Brezien who speaks fairly good English – but will not leave me alone. He is constantly coming to see me on all manner of trifles and is, in fact, dreadfully officious.

[...]

A Major Grunert of the camp also speaks very good English – better than either General de Graaff or Professor B. He and the Professor have been in U.S.A. Brezien much at Philadelphia and Grunert at Washington.

Limburg, Saturday, 5 December 1914

On Saturday forenoon at 11 a.m. I went up to the prisoners with Major Grunert & the Professor – & spoke <u>alone</u> to some of the men & non-coms. They seemed already to guess the end in view and began saying they'd like to fight for Ireland. I told them of my plans & several of the non-coms said that 'very little persuasion would be needed.' that practically all would agree. One man came up & said 'How is Father O'Daly?' & then added 'I paraded in front of you, Sir Roger, at Six Mile Cross.'

I remember it well – the parade, not the man – that dreary Sunday evg in June last at the RC Church & the huge turn out – & Eoin MacNeill & I & Pat MacCartan standing on the wall & speaking to the men before the evening service. We left that for Dundalk that night in Pat McC's motor car – getting in at 11.30 p.m. to Dundalk – and now here is one of those Volunteers – a British soldier and a prisoner of war!

A good looking young man with a huge fair thick beard – & good blue eyes & a smiling brow. Some of the faces were good – those of soft hearted Irish boys – but many are not good and some are depraved & vicious. They look anaemic and

Eoin MacNeill: scholar-revolutionary and founder of the Gaelic League. A close friend of Alice Stopford Green, he was chosen as the first Chief-of-Staff of the Irish Volunteers in November 1913. MacNeill and Casement collaborated closely in Irish Volunteer recruitment rallies in the early months of the movement. [National Library of Ireland] sick mostly and say they were not well treated at Hameln and there they got 'English' fare – being 'English' prisoners of war! They said that the Irish Regts had been put in the front & sacrificed & that what the *Gaelic American* said was true in one of the copies I had left in the camp the previous day.

I asked if it was true that the Munsters had fired into the King's Own Scottish Borderers at the end and they said they had heard so, & they thought it was true.

Many said they had 'surrendered on purpose'! One young 78th man said 'We threw down our rifles at Lille – 400 of us'!

There is plenty of anti-English feeling – but no pro-German!

There is the trouble – they were well fed up with the lies of John Bull's press bureau before starting & then all the destruction they saw in France – especially of churches – they believe was wantonly inflicted by the Germans.

I left two exercise books with Sergeant MacMurrough of the Leinsters and with Timothy Quinlisk of the 18th to fill up with names of all men and regiments. These two are keen for the Brigade – so they say. Mac M. is a dark-eyed, black bearded Sergeant of the Leinsters from Belfast & once a postal clerk! He admitted his enlistment was due to 'financial trouble'!

Quinlisk is a boy, only 18 & 9 months, from Wexford – a corporal, I think. He writes well & is intelligent & says he will gladly join the Brigade.

Mac M. is 32. Both say they have read *The Crime against Ireland*, and like it much.

After a few words here & there & telling them I'd come up to Mass at 9 a.m. where as they said there was already an Irish priest to officiate! This I found rests on some opinion the men have that there is 'an old Tipperary man,' a clergyman here at Limburg.

In the afternoon I went in the car to Coblenz via Montabaur & other small towns. Prof Brezien came with me as *cicerone*. One of the two chauffeurs is a Doctor – studied at Jena for many years.

Both he & the other, a young Prussian type, steel-blue eyed young man, are volunteers like Lüttichau & Meckle. The car is the Staff car of the 18th. Army Corps Headquarters at Frankfurt & is left by the General with me for as long as I need it.

We crossed the Rhine from Ehrenbreits by the bridge of boats to Coblenz & went to the Coblenzer Hof where all four had coffee, wine, beer & cakes for 4.70 all told – very cheap indeed. The Hotel café fairly full of life.

The return journey was in darkness & I got to Limburg at 6 or so & to bed directly after dinner – the small waiter bringing me coffee and hot water at 9 p.m. His name is Rudolf Kuekelberg or some such – & walks with a military strut. All the small boys down to 4 and 5 play at soldiers & salute the car as we pass with a haughty Prussian pride. I bought some fine photos of Limburg today – showing the wonderfully placed Cathedral well poised on its rock.

Limburg to Frankfurt, Sunday, 6 December 1914

I went up to the camp at 8.15 (2 Doctors with me) & got from MacMurrough & Quinlisk 383 names of Irish prisoners. Some few, it

seems are really English Catholics, children of Irish-born parents, but themselves born in England. Several belong to the Middlesex and S[outh] Lancashire regiments. I got all gathered in one room – & told them of my idea of the Irish Brigade, and read out the conditions, roughly, that I should propose to the German Govt.

[...]

The following Irish prisoners of war, captured by the German army and now detained in the camp at Limburg, province of Hesse, Germany, voluntarily agree to enter the Irish Brigade on the following conditions.

The fine Cathedral at Limburg, visible from the prison camp. [Postcard]

1. That the purpose of the Irish Brigade now being formed in Germany shall be solely to achieve the independence of Ireland.

2. That the members of the Irish Brigade are enrolled in it solely to serve Ireland and to fight on behalf of the complete freedom of Ireland.

3. That no man entering the Irish Brigade does so for any pay, monetary reward or promise of such hereafter but solely as a volunteer in the service of Ireland with entire willingness to give his life and all he stands for freely and without reserve in his country's cause.

4. That the Irish Brigade, once constituted, while it shall be devoted solely to the purposes stated, with a view to securing the independence of Ireland by force of arms, shall during its stay in Germany be subject to the military discipline and control of the German War Office, and all members of the Irish Brigade shall be bound to obey all orders given to them by the competent German military authorities, whether officers of the Irish Brigade or not, and shall, in all respects, behave themselves with the same obedience and respect for German military authority as if they were German soldiers.

5. That the Irish Brigade shall be equipped by the German Govt. with a special <u>uniform</u>, having special Irish badge and that the Brigade colours shall be the Irish flag, the National Ensign as carried in 1798.

6. That as far as possible the officers of the Irish Brigade shall be Irish, or Irish Americans, but until such time as it may be possible to obtain the services of Irishmen with the necessary military training, the members of the Irish Brigade will obey whatever officers the German authorities may place over them, with the consent of Sir Roger Casement.

7. That Sir Roger Casement shall be in supreme command of the movements of the Irish Brigade – shall be responsible for its active employment in the field and shall accompany it in its active operations.

8. That a formal undertaking in writing, embodying these conditions in the name of the German government, and providing for the despatch of the Irish Brigade to Ireland with officers and military equipment to arm the Irish Volunteers, at the first opportunity, when it might be possible to despatch a body of men to Ireland, shall be drawn up and signed by the proper German Authority in the name

of the German government – and by Sir Roger Casement for the Irish Brigade and Irish Volunteers.

9. That in the event of it being possible to send the Irish Brigade to Ireland whether after a German naval victory or from other cause, the German Government will aid to the best of its ability to make that movement successful and will do all in its power to assist the Irish People, the Irish Volunteers and the Irish Brigade to establish a national government in Ireland.

10. That in the event of the Irish Brigade failing to reach Ireland, or in the event of peace being restored between Germany and Great Britain with Ireland still in its present relation to Great Britain then the German Govt. will send every member of the Irish Brigade to the United States of America at its own expense and enable him to land in that country.

[...]

I pointed out all the risks & dangers & said I wanted them to think it over & that I would come again in about a week to hear their answers. They said nothing. All kept quiet. I then returned to Limburg & picked up Fathers O'Gorman and Crotty at their Hotel & took them up to the camp.

They saw a good many of the men several of whom knew Fr Crotty or his brother, a priest it seems, once at Kilkenny.

I had both priests to lunch with me at my Hotel. We talked of the war & of Ireland & of the recent action taken there against the Irish national papers.

They are both well disposed more so than ever.

I decided to go to Frankfurt today & see General de Graaff to get further liberties for the men – & to allow the two Sergeants to come down & see me at my Hotel.

We left in the car at 2.45 or so – I alone in the car & the two chauffeurs. They chose a different road from that by which de Graaff & I had come. The route now taken was right up over the Taunus range leaving Wiesbaden well on the right. The towns and villages passed through were all of interest – particularly one with a fine ruined keep on a hill & a modern Schloss near – I think this was Cronberg – we passed one quite remarkable village down in the valley before going up the Taunus of quite medieval houses the external walls of the houses all joining & being erected on a rocky cliff. They gave the appearance of a vast fortified wall. In the middle ages these walls would have constituted a veritable defence. A ruined tower peered over the <u>straw</u> roofs – dark brown straw – of the high, fortified farm houses, all with their gables & beams & joists of dark wood.

Up in the Taunus pine woods there was snow & frost and these gave very striking character to the otherwise sombre woods.

From Cronberg we ran through a fine big village or town whence I saw a signpost pointing to 'Homburg, 3 Kms' – & we got into Frankfurt about 4.30. I found Prince Leiningen at ten, & he took me down to the General Staff headquarters where I had a long talk with de Graaff.

I told him the men were seemingly willing to join the Brigade, but that the matter would have to be worked very carefully & I should want fuller powers to do as I pleased with the men. I advised soap, shaving, tobacco to begin with. He agreed to all & wrote a letter to General Exner to this effect which I was to take back by the early train (7.57 a.m.) to Limburg.

De Graaff advised me to see either Bethmann Hollweg or von Jagow quickly & not to be content with von Wedel. He said that von W. was merely a "letter carrier" – & I should insist on the heads of the Govt. seeing me.

I wrote to von Wedel letter saying something of this.

I walked about Frankfurt a bit this Sunday after I left de Graaff and did not return to the Hotel until 9.15 to supper.

[…]

Frankfurt was crammed with life this Sunday evening – the Kaiserstrasse & the streets I remember from May 1912 were packed with people – men, women and children – & soldiers.

De Graaff & Prince L. were dining with 3 ladies – speaking English mostly. De Graaff's wife, one of these I find is an American – which accounts for something of his English.

De Graaff himself is quite the most charming of the German officers I have met. His manner is that of a Frenchman or a very polished Dutchman – lively, straight and gentle – his face is handsome, clean cut, grey hair and always a pleasant smile.

He tells me the General in command at Frankfurt, Freiherr von Gall, is interested in me – & I am getting a card from that old gentleman who is a pompous old soldier Leiningen tells me. The card came in due course. I had replied with a copy of my pamphlet *The Crime against*

Ireland – & am also sending a card with my name written on it. I had to explain to de Graaff that I had no cards yet as I had been under a false name at Berlin.

Leiningen presses me to go & see him at Heidelberg 'after the war.'

Mavrone – for me there is no after the war – or hereafter at all. All I am & have & shall be is here now.

It is all for Ireland – & I refuse to think of anything else or of any personal consequences.

My cold is very much worse and while de Graaff gave me Formamint – a harmless and useless medicament, Leiningen sent a vial of drops to my room with word to try 15 drops on sugar before going to bed. I did – the result was nil. I tried them again twice, during the night, but hardly slept and had a very bad night of it with a cough that rasped me to pieces.

I did not sleep at all – but lay awake wondering what would happen. I have decided, perhaps finally, on one thing. It is that I shall insist on seeing either von Jagow or the Chancellor. Both are in Berlin I believe. If I cannot get an interview with them, I shall take it as proof that the German Govt. is not sufficiently in earnest for me to go on further.

I will not accept the responsibility for putting a couple of thousand Irish soldiers into the high treason pot, unless I get very precise and sure promises both in their regard & for the political future of Ireland. If I learn that neither Bethmann Hollweg nor von Jagow can see me, & I care not what the reason assigned may be, I shall decline to continue our 'Conversations' & shall ask for a passport to enable me to go to Norway or Sweden.

These thoughts hardened during the night. I am not at all pleased with their attitude towards Christiania & from Blücher's (& Schiemann's) remarks it is clear they do <u>not</u> accept my view of the Findlay affair. I told Meyer so – & he got very red & shuffled, but from von Wedel's remarks about Adler – when I left the letter to be forwarded, it is clear they want me to drop the Christiania affair altogether & to drop Adler.

Now I am quite determined to do neither. I shall go on with the case against Findlay by every means in my power & I shall do all I can to help poor Adler to live a better life. From the point of view of the Irish Cause I am not sure that the case against Findlay is not more telling than would be even the formation of an Irish Brigade. Of course for the Germans, the Irish Brigade is most important. It <u>shames</u> John Bull's army & it knocks recruiting on the head in Ireland.

The Findlay business has no interest for them – & they do not appreciate its significance rightly or the vast effect it would have on public opinion in Ireland & U.S.A. But even if they did, it would be for me only – & not for them; & they are keen only on the things I can do that will help them. Quite naturally. But equally, quite naturally, I mean to convict John Bull's Govt. of being what I have always termed it a criminal conspiracy.

Then as regards the Irish Brigade the difficulties are appalling. De Graaff approves the Egyptian idea greatly – but thinks I could get the men off to Egypt without the German press knowing anything! He is afraid of a 'hell of a row' in the press any day about the 'special treatment' being shown the Irish prisoners of war. Even if the men all agree – the difficulties then only begin. How is discipline to be maintained – what are they going to do? Officers? By and by want of money? Both for them and me. I shall soon be penniless. The expenses have been far heavier than I anticipated – and one's hand is always in one's pocket. Travelling, changes of hotel and tips take up constant sums. The servants are <u>not</u> paid by the <u>big Hotels</u> at all! The waiter at the Continental in Berlin on my floor has to pay his sub-waiter 20 marks a month to help him. He told me none of the servants on my floor were paid, but that the others 'had no expenses!'

These are aspects of German method that are wholly repugnant to me. A callous disregard for the employed and a cynical disregard for the patrons too. For it is obvious if the servants are not <u>paid</u> by those engaging them they will not discharge their duties very brilliantly & if not well tipped by those entitled to proper service for nothing they will leave those who fail to tip them to whistle.

On the whole I find that with the exception of table waiting (which is a German science or philosophy of life in itself embracing a study of languages along with the art of laying plates & knives, always at the cost of the other party!) the service in German Hotels is greatly inferior to that in English. Bedrooms are not looked after nearly so well and valeting is a farce. The Hotels are clean – but the rooms neglected and there is no briskness of service as one sees in a big London Hotel upstairs – where the maids are bright intelligent and quick. Here they look listless, cross grained and ever expectant. By contrast the table service is always good – clean and fairly quick and the man or boy always polite and polished in manner, with a bow that no English gentleman could better and very few approach in grace or dignity.

With regard to the Christiania affair I am more and more determined to go on with it, just as I perceive the reluctance of the German authorities to my proceeding increases. I owe it to myself now. After Schiemann's disgraceful reference to Adler –and von Jagow's letter to Blücher that the latter told me held doubts as to the authenticity of the interview between Findlay & Adler I should be admitting the justice of these views were I now to withdraw. Besides there are the letters I wrote to J. McGarrity & 'Pat' & sent by Adler, which were handed by him to Findlay.

Those letters have long since been handed to the Foreign Office & constitute for Downing St. overwhelming proof of my guilt. To now retire from the affair, merely because Wilhelmstrasse does not like it, would be to make the Br. Government a present of my character indeed & enable them to poison the ears of everyone in Ireland and USA against me & to prove their charges from my own writings.

No, I must launch the charge against them – I must be first in the field with the accusation and part of the accusation itself must consist of those very letters on which they are now relying to base their charges of horrible treason against me. And no time should be lost either.

The Irish Brigade will have to wait. In any case the Germans can't complain of delay there. The proposition to separate Irish from British prisoners of war was made by me in August, early in August. It was accepted again & again & urged in the letter sent to John Kenny that he handed the German Ambassador in Rome on 3 or 4 September. Without exception all the German authorities jumped at the idea from the start – but altho' it had this highest backing no action was taken until long after I had landed in Berlin.

Instead of finding the Irish camp already long since formed on my arrival in Germany as I had expected and had even been led to expect before leaving New York, no single step had been taken of any kind.

On the contrary I am forced to take a long and exposed journey to the Headquarters to say again there what had already been said many times before, before an order is issued to collect the Irish prisoners – and then it is only on the thirty fourth day after I land in Berlin that I am permitted to set out to see the first batch of men so collected – and only the thirty-fifth day when I see a few of them for the first time. Today it is six weeks since I came to Germany – & I have seen a few of the men in a make shift way with no prior preparation of them.

Part of my plan had always been that they should have been got into a receptive frame of mind, by literature, special treatment &c. before I came in person on the scene. Then the men's minds would have been already enlightened before I came. Their hearts would have been heated and their imaginations awake. I would have been in their minds as the only Irishman at large in Germany, the open foe of England – & when they were told that 'Sir RC was coming to visit the camp' I would have been sure of a hearty welcome; & anything I had said of treason felony would have met with an instant response.

But these Germans cannot deal with the human understanding & they have mismanaged the thing as they do with all their 'Diplomacy'. I have had to introduce myself to a gang of poor devils; distribute the literature; point out my 'speeches' &c., &c. – & generally stand out from the first moment as an agent provocateur trying to stir up pro-German sympathies. It will take a great deal of careful work to undo the ill already done – & I don't see where the care is to come from.

The military authorities in charge of the prisoners know absolutely nothing of the purpose of the camp or the reasons for special treatment of Irish prisoners of war. & I am begged to <u>hide from them</u> all idea of any of my true purpose in visiting the camp! It cannot work like that. It is quite impossible. For me to get by stealth & in secret the adhesion of

Limburg: the POW camp where Irish prisoners were gathered and where Casement made largely unsuccessful efforts to recruit men into an Irish Brigade. [Anthony O'Brien, Private Collection]

2000 men to a propaganda of treason, conducted with <u>closed doors</u> in a military camp & with the officers in command ignorant of the game is a pretty fair sample of how these people (the Germans) mismanage their <u>human</u> problems!

Frankfurt to Limburg, Monday, 7 December 1914

I left Frankfurt at 7.57 in darkness.

I wrote von Wedel to say should require to see either the Chancellor or von Jagow before I committed the men – they will follow – but I don't go unless I get clear promises.

This morning's *Frankfurter Zeitung* has a telegram from London, 6 Dec – saying that (*Daily Telegraph* reports) the police have seized *Irish Worker* and the press & edition confiscated & there is also something about *Sinn Fein* I cannot translate. Fr Crotty said yesterday the *Leader* had been seized as well as *Irish Freedom*. The suppression of the *Leader* will put all the clergy 'agin the Govt.' Good! Last night de Graaff said there was a 'hell of a row' in Dublin – lots about me & the seizure of *Irish Freedom* and probably 'much more really than we saw in print.'[34]

The journey to Limburg is thro' a beautiful country – some of it near the country we passed yesterday up to the Taunus. A great <u>schloss</u> at Idstein, a huge place with an isolated ruined tower […] flies the red cross flag.

Further on we pass the extraordinarily picturesque village (with its ruined tower) I passed yesterday with the old house. It lies between Idstein & Cronberg & is in Nassau. There is no sign of snow on the hills today – but heavy rain in night and inky clouds. I shall go to bed at Limburg & send the letter to General Exner & ask to have MacMurrough & the young corporal brought down to my room where I'll fit them out & give them a good feed.

Father Crotty said yesterday 'The first thing is that England should be beaten!' I said almost the same to the poor Fürst zu Leiningen last night. He is most unhappy – he would really prefer to be in England! I can see that. He does <u>not</u> sympathise in his heart with Germany – or shall I say, his true feeling is with England & he wants only peace between them.

---

[34] This refers to various radical newspapers published in Ireland.

[…]

My defection is a serious blow to their pride – and if the Irish & Germans in U.S.A. are doing what I expect & hope I think we may put John Bull in the wrong box even in America!

At Eschhofen I see an old Church perched on a rock something like the beautiful Cathedral at Limburg. It is on the Lahn too, and we are now traversing its left bank going down to Limburg. This is the heart of Germany! – & as I write the spires & fortress like mass of Limburg cathedral rises close at hand.

Now to the hotel & bed to my treason felony!

I sent the letter to Gen Exner & then got the interpreter Professor Brezien to come & give him a letter for Exner – who had gone to the camp – asking for Sergeant MacMurrough & the young Sergeant to be sent down to me at the Hotel – I am in bed here – my cold much worse.

[…]

The Professor brought MacM and Quinlisk down to me about 12. I got him to bring them warm things, books & gave them a good dinner each. They talked long with me & it now seems there is much doubt whether any men will volunteer for the Brigade. They are very anti-German and think it is a German trick to get them to fight for Germany. So in one day they have changed their minds! MacMurrough & Q. say there is much diversity of opinion – but they would not commit themselves to say how many would agree to join the Brigade.

They 'wanted time.' I left them still with the list of names of 383 men & told them to try and find out & put a mark against each man – I was in bed all the time, with a throat with a band of red hot iron round it. General Exner came to see me at 2.30 with the Professor to interpret as he speaks neither French nor English – & he promised to do all I asked him to do for the men and to aid in any way possible.

I sent MacM and Q. back with the Professor at 3 – after many smokes & tea & cake. Neither impressed me very favourably. Both look rogues – especially MacMurrough. I may be wrong but I should think his enlistment was due to some serious defalcation – he says he had been a postal clerk. Quinlisk is only a boy – born in Wexford – but of a R.I.C. stock! Father & grandfather both sold to the British Govt.

The doubts I felt so strongly at the first glimpse of the prisoners here all revived. How could anything truly Irish really survive the free entry into the British army. No, these are not Irishmen but English soldiers – that is all.

[...]

Limburg to Berlin, Thursday, 10 December 1914

I am now in the train returning from Limburg to Berlin. We are going by Fulda, where artillery is being exercised as we pass. I left Limburg at 9 and got to Frankfurt at 11.07 & had to wait there till 12.58 to get this train, the direct express for Berlin.

[...]

Yesterday & the day before I spent ill in Limburg. I stayed in bed all day Tuesday & got an army Doctor to come to me & he gave me a good dose to stop the cough – some drops tasting of almonds, 6 times a day.

[...]

Last night the *Colnische Volkszeitung* had an account of a speech of Redmond at Tuam that puts the cap on his treason to Ireland. [...]

'130,000 Irishmen' according to this English scoundrel to take part in the most cowardly war even England ever waged for her selfish ends. Certainly if Ireland follows Redmond she deserves the doom of slavery, & degrading death so clearly the reward for helping England to assail Germany.

I went up to the Camp yesterday afternoon (Wed. 9 Dec) with the two fathers at 5 p.m. They were going to confess some of the men.

[...]

The more I see of these alleged Irishmen – the less I think of them as being Irish. They are the black blot on our claim to nationality – these same so-called 'Irish Soldiers' in the English army.

After supper I went round to see Frs. Crotty & O'Gorman to bid them good bye.

The former told me, when Father O'G had gone away for a moment – that Msgr O'Riordan was strongly against the recruiting of Redmond and co. – & that the sub-rector of the Irish College in Rome who is a better nationalist than Mgsr O'Riordan had got him, Fr Crotty, to come 'to be a check on Father O'Gorman.' He said – quickly – he was in full sympathy with my aims.

So far so good. Father O'Gorman has to return to Rome not later than 25 January – & then Father Crotty will have the men to himself.

But if I can't get 200 or 400 before that out of 2,400, I'm not much use – or rather the men are not much Irishmen. Several of them gathered round me with friendly eyes – mostly young men – & even a questioning look – was it Ireland, or tobacco? […]

Last night's telegrams also contained one from a Basel (Swiss) paper on the 'New Enemy' of England!

The Swiss paper commented on the outbreak of Irish sedition & the threatening aspect of this new attack on England. It said that 'what particularly attracted attention was that England, the home of free speech & of a free press, should now be violating both in Ireland.' […] Thus while Irishmen are to be armed out of Ireland, to do the work Englishmen themselves cannot or will not do, it is to be high treason to dare to bear arms in Ireland! What consummate tricksters and hypocrites the English are – and what eternal slaves and fools the Irish!

From Bebra we have turned and are now travelling up the course of a fine river with beautiful pine clad hills and innumerable picturesque villages with gable ended farm houses – lofty & old fashioned with a great many timbers showing. Many are straw thatched but others tiled.

On the whole I feel my week (or nearly so) at Limburg has been a failure. The chances of forming an Irish Brigade are poor enough – & if I cannot do that I may as well leave Germany – for there is nothing else to do here for Ireland but that.

We have just passed a wonderful old ruined castle on a hill across the river – a huge ruined wall with several battered towers the remains of some great stronghold of the Middle Ages.

(4.20 p.m.) We have just arrived at Eisenach – a fine town. The houses are well built, lofty and surrounding hills covered with towers, schlosses and other buildings – a really beautiful situation. The river, I see from the map, must be the upper Weser. Our line runs on to Erfurt, Halle & Berlin. It will soon be dark & I shall see no more.

[…] And here, in the heart of Germany, I pass through the best tilled lands I've seen in Europe – not a square yard wasted – the best fed people one can find in the world & this once quiet, university, medieval town, a large thriving, bustling city full of life, of industry & smoke! No one would dream this people was at war; the life of the country – as I saw it at Limburg – goes on the same and food is as plentiful & as cheap today as when on 2 August this war of devils was loosed against Germany.

When I look at this people, at their manliness of brow & bearing, their calm front and resolute strong chests turned to a world of Enemies, & then read the English columns of trash about Prussian barbarism & English heroism, I regret I am <u>not</u> a German. I used to be proud to be Irish. Since I saw the 'Irish' soldiers & read Redmond's speeches I feel ashamed to belong to so contemptible a race.

Bethmann Hollweg's speech at the opening of the Reichstag is given in bad English in the *Continental Times* of Dec 7. 1914, I got at Frankfurt. It is a fine speech – but too late. He recognises <u>now</u>, after the event, that England made the war!

And I, in Aug 1911, wrote on my way to the Putumayo that, if & when war came, it would be, it was already England's war. I was not only 3 years before the Chancellor, but I saw in peace what he has learned only through war.[35]

---

[35] This refers to Casement's essay *The Keeper of the Seas*. It is reproduced in Angus Mitchell (ed.), *Sir Roger Casement's Heart of Darkness: the 1911 Documents* (Irish Manuscripts Commission, 2003), 558-566.

BERLIN

Friday, 11 December 1914

I got to Berlin at 8.50 and drove to the Eden Hotel, where they were expecting me. Got a very showy and uncomfortable room.

Two beds but no chest of drawers, mirror or any receptacle at all for collars – hkfs and small things – simply two cupboards with coat rests in them – the two beds stretched across one entire side of the room – and the rest is a sitting room – a bathroom attached.

Price not stated. Very noisy tram line outside – so the windows shut – I walked a few minutes in Tauentzienstr.

[…]

I went to Foreign Office at 1.30 […] & saw von Wedel. We agreed 1st that I should proceed as I thought best about Christiania. […] We did not discuss my wish, expressed by letter from Frankfurt, to see either the Chancellor or von Jagow. I told him I would draw up in writing the conditions on which I proposed the Irish Brigade should be enrolled and he said all right.

Wedel read me a telegram that he had received from v. Bernstorff saying

1st that Cohalan – a trusty messenger had reached Ireland at end Novbr. –

2nd that the Declaration of the German Govt. had 'produced an excellent impression' –

3rd that Cohalan advised I should make no public statement about Christiania until I had clear proof.

This is all good news – so far as it goes. The bad news is in the public press. The German sea squadron of 5 ships – Gneisenau, Scharnhorst, Leipzig, Nürnberg and Dresden – has been overwhelmed by a huge allied squadron off the Falkland islands – the Gneisenau, Scharnhorst, Leipzig, (and Nürnberg

later) were sunk – the Dresden still in flight. All hands lost – including Admiral Spee and his two sons!

It is said the British had 38 ships gathered to meet this gallant little fleet of five! Another splendid triumph for British pluck! Asquith's 'We only ask for a <u>fair</u> fight' at the Guildhall is well illustrated in this encounter. The British were more than 7 to 1 and six of their vessels are said to have been battleships! What cowards!

[...]

Meyer called at 6.30 and told me the Irish badges were too dear! They would cost 1500 marks (say £60!) – and were not worth it. If this is the measure of their good intentions towards the <u>Irish</u> question the sooner I end with them <u>the</u> better. How can I trust any promises that rest on such a niggardly conception of their obligations as this shying at £60 for badging 2.000 men (say 6d per badge) represents.

[...]

At dinner 7.30 to 10 with von Roeder and the Baroness we discussed the war and nothing but the war with a Countess Oppersdorff – a sister of the Count I met at Countess Groeben's. The more I see of the 'governing classes' in Germany the less highly I estimate their intelligence. They are 'not in it' with the English – that is certain.

Eden Hotel; the hotel where Casement stayed for different spells of time when in Berlin. It was here that Karl Liebknecht and Rosa Luxemburg were interrogated after the Spartacist Rising of 1919. [Bundesarchiv]

Berlin, Saturday, 12 December 1914

[...]

When, today, at lunch here I said to Blücher that if neither the Chancellor nor von Jagow cared to receive me I thought my right course would be to leave Germany, he was already furious at my refusal to unfold <u>all</u> my plans to him and said that this was 'only vanity on my part.' I passed over the silly rudeness because I do not choose to quarrel with him – and said that I was entitled to the assurance of the highest quarter [...]

In my heart I am <u>very</u> sorry I came! I do not think the German Govt. has any soul for great enterprises – it lacks the divine spark of imagination that has ennobled British piracy.

The sea <u>may</u> be freed by these people – but I doubt it. They will do it in their sleep – and without intending to achieve anything so great.

England <u>enslaved</u> the seas of set design and far-seeing purpose and has held them in subjection with a resolute and unscrupulous will beyond all praise in themselves. These people, whose supreme interest it should be to have complete freedom and equality at sea, will not take the necessary steps in the direction needed beyond mere ship-building. That is an essential but other things, too, are needed to free the seas besides ships – just as other things are needed to hold them. England supplies all the necessaries – ships <u>and</u> brains – Germany thinks to do it by ships alone without brains and resolute, far-seeing purpose. A fixed, unchanging Irish policy is essential to freedom at sea of every power competing with England. That is the first rule to master.

[...]

At 6 I went with Blücher to call on Dr. Solf, the Minister of the German Colonies. Found him (after long wait) a fine type. Once Governor of Samoa. Knew Nigeria too. Very charming, great big, strong good man. I told him they would <u>have</u> to knock England out – there was nothing for it but that – and they must use all their brains and intelligence for that.

He agreed and confessed their brains diplomatically, were inferior to the English and that they were not trained to cope with English statesmen, 'pirates in evening dress.'

(I had called them 'very charming men, hereditary pirates of long descent' – and he had laughed approval and said 'Yes – I see, pirates in evening dress.')

I got a better impression of the German official world from Solf than from any of them. He confessed, too, that they had <u>all</u> been deceived by English 'nice manners' and 'hearty hospitality' and cited his own reception in Nigeria many years ago and the speeches of goodwill and '<u>cousinship</u>' exchanged – or professed rather by the Br[itish] officials. I assured him that was all part of the game – and said it would have paid Germany well to have engaged a few Irishmen as guides to the British character in international affairs! An Irish Imperial Chancellor would not have let John Bull wall up the German Michael as we now see him.[36]

Dr. Solf had read the manuscript of 'Ireland, Germany and Freedom of the Seas,' when it first came from Rome! He had it in his drawers he said – the mss – brought by Schiemann – and of course had read the translation the 'Achilles Heel of England.'

He was greatly interested in my explanation of the international value of Ireland to Europe and the freedom of the seas. He said he would speak to von Jagow and arrange a meeting. Jagow returns to Charleville on Tuesday he said.

I left him only at 8.30 p.m. – having previously met Frau Solf at his private house (in 66 Wilhelmstrasse). The Colonial Office is just like a private house – 62 Wilhelmstrasse – with nothing inside or outside that gave the least indication of its being the head of a great Department.

The Achilles Heel of England: Schiemann's translation of Casement's political writings circulated at the highest political levels in Berlin. [Angus Mitchell]

[36] Der deutscher Michel – The 'German Michael' is a popular national personification of Germany, similar to 'John Bull' or 'Uncle Sam'.

Solf said that the Declaration about Ireland was 'an entirely new departure in German foreign policy' – that until that statement was issued Germany had never said or done anything that implied a desire even to meddle in the 'internal affairs of another country.'

It is a new departure indeed. It was followed, as he admitted, by his own Declaration about South Africa – inspired, Blücher says, by my old friend Dr. Leyds, who is living at The Hague. Leyds had been so struck by the Irish Declaration, he got Solf to issue the statement that appeared recently in the press defining Germany's wishes and intentions towards the South African Union.

Dr. Solf said to me 'Why did Ireland never approach Germany before?' – and I laughed and said 'Why did you, in your own interests, never think of Ireland or seek first hand information as to the state of feeling in Ireland? You should have had an Irish policy, as part of your plan of defence against English aggression.'

He agreed entirely and we parted the very best of friends.

I went and dined with poor old Blücher at the Esplanade till 10.30 and then walked home by Potsdammerstr and the Spreebank to my Hotel – a delightful walk – the rain of the earlier day and afternoon now gone.

Berlin, Sunday, 13 December 1914

This morning Mrs. White of the *Continental Times* called on me – just back from Vienna at 11 a.m. She is a Viennese married to an Englishman. She was 'charming' and told me that in Vienna they were very anxious to meet me. At the F.O. where she had been, Berchtold and others of the F.O. staff were all hoping I would visit Vienna. So she said. They had read my 'Appeal to the Irish People' and were in full sympathy she said.

[...]

Berlin, Monday, 14 December 1914

Meyer came at 2.30 – after I had lunched with Mrs. Behrens the friend of Ballin. She wants me to go to Hamburg stay with her and meet Ballin – she says he can get any letter I want into Ireland.

[...]

At 4 I went to Mrs. Meyer's rooms in Nassauische Str. She has no word from Kuno yet. But she had an interesting card to him written by a young Irishman in Ruhleben camp begging to be released on the ground that he is Irish and the son of a Fenian! His name is Bryan A. Kelly of Dublin, an official of the University Gaelic Society who had come to Berlin to study & is now locked up as 'a British subject.' I will get him out, interview him, and if he is a loyal man send him first to Limburg to the soldiers and <u>then</u> to Ireland itself as my messenger.[37]

[…]

I shall draft today my proposals to the German govt. for the formation of the Irish Brigade. The idea is I formulate the conditions in writing, and they reply in writing agreeing and sign it by the Chancellor or von Jagow. Latter returns to the front on Tuesday.

A fresh success yesterday in Poland – the Russians again defeated with loss of 11.000 prisoners & 43 machine guns.

This morning's news too is interesting. The King George of England gave an interview to the new extraordinary envoy to the Vatican, Sir H. Howard – and the latter takes with him my friend J.D. Gregory as his secretary!

Ghosts of the Putumayo Indians! – how strange it all is!

Gregory, who collaborated with me in the F.O. to get the Franciscan Mission sent out by the Vatican and who was first in belauding me at Rome and in London – now goes to Rome to aid in belabouring me and in enslaving Ireland!

English rule is assuredly the masterpiece of dissimulation of the world.

I await with amusement the forthcoming comments of the English world on my 'treason' – but oh! <u>God save Ireland!</u>

The Pope has issued some rescript on 'Religion and the Fatherland' I gather. I wonder what it is?

Berlin, Wednesday, 16 December 1914

Adler returned last night at 7. I went to the Continental Hotel about my trunk and while there in he came. He had come in response to my wire

---

[37] For a report by Bryan Kelly on his meeting with Casement and associated documents see NLI MS 31,783.

of Friday last – but had not received my letter from Limburg sent through Wedel.

He reports Findlay in a state of abnormal excitement over my (reported!) doings. Adler spun a delightful web of lies! He talked vaguely, he says, of the 'Secret Society' in U.S.A., of its widespread organisation, of the wealthy accessions to its ranks of late, since the war, of the rich Irish American with his big steam yacht ready; of my commission to him, Adler, to charter <u>two</u> sailing yachts in Norway to meet me on the coast of Schleswig at an early date; of my complete system of intelligence, how I got 'word' from Ireland three hours after anything happened there; how I had agents 'in the Navy itself' – and how I was certainly going to get into Ireland with the American contingent in the yacht at an early date – probably, he said, I intended the Norwegian chartered boats for transhipment 'at sea.'

Findlay, he says, was pale, with beads of perspiration rolling off him and walked up and down the room in a state of wild excitement. He called him a <u>very</u> nasty name & said I was 'very clever – and a very dangerous son of a b.'!

He promised Adler <u>£10.000</u> for my capture! I am mounting up in value! He said it would be more than that – but that sure.

Adler implicated two great bankers he says – one in Norway & one in U.S.A. – and Findlay asked him if it was Armour's yacht[38] (the Kaiser's friend) I had got! So they think Armour is a Fenian too! It is quite delicious – I am to hear more today. I told Adler to stay at the Continental last night and I'd send for him today. He says that if I go to Norway, Findlay will 'go bug house' (an American euphemism, I believe, for 'going off his chump'). I may <u>have</u> to go to Norway before long – in any case – We shall see.

[...]

Berlin, Thursday, 17 December 1914

Yesterday afternoon Mr. Gaffney the U.S. Consul at Munich called with Aubrey Stanhope. Former has just returned from Ireland where he went to visit his brother, the Crown Solicitor of Limerick. He reports the country 'with Redmond' – but admits he was only some 48 hours in Ireland &

---

[38] A reference to J. Ogden Armour, the American meat-packing magnate.

T. St John Gaffney: born in Limerick, Gaffney was the U.S. consul general in Dresden (1905–12) and then Munich (1914-15). His pro-German and pro-Irish sympathies eventually led to his dismissal by US President Woodrow Wilson. Casement entrusted him with the care of the Irish Brigade in April 1916. [Des Ryan, private collection]

'saw no one' but his brother and a few friends at Limerick. His letters, addressed to him, had been opened by the Br. Censor – altho' sent in U.S. covering to Page.[39] Gaffney agrees that Redmond is betraying Ireland and is unworthy of support – but says the people hear nothing but lies and are 'fed up' with 'glorious British victories' and with equally atrocious German crimes.

I went today with Meyer to a Military tailors to order a 'sample' uniform for the Irish Brigade: a pale grey with a touch of green running thro' the warp – & then with emerald green facings, cuffs and collar & a harp on collar flaps & a harp with shamrock above on the cap on a green band.

I guess it will be a terror.

At luncheon […] I heard the church bells ring out suddenly – a peal of joyful news to all Berlin, I could not at first think what it might be – as I did not think these people rang the church bells for public festivity. In a few minutes I saw, from the restaurant window, the flags springing out from every parapet and window and streaming far and wide – I knew then. A great victory somewhere, but where? The waitress came with the 'tape' – It was brief, direct and positive. The Headquarters announced that the 'whole Russian front against Posen and Silesia, from north to south Poland had been completely broken and was in full flight with the German armies in close pursuit'! There it was! This is the 'news' I had been hearing rumours of for three days – from Schiemann and others. He told me several days ago that they 'hoped to corner eleven Russian army corps' – i.e. 440.000 men. It looks as if they have done this. There

---

[39] Walter Hines Page (1855–1918), the U.S. ambassador to Britain during the First World War.

was no doubt. Everywhere I found men sure, with a deep certainty in Hindenburg that he had done the trick and smashed completely the entire Russian offensive with overwhelming loss.

[...]

At 8 I went to Mrs. White's to dinner expecting to meet only Gaffney (the U.S. Consul of Munich) Aubrey Stanhope and Karl Wiegand – but met in addition Puttkamer and Mrs P. – and many more, all invited to meet me as the 'Guest of Germany.' The dinner was delightful, especially I liked one German officer, a Major Herwarth v Bittenfeld of the Headquarters General Staff. He had been at Washington as Military Attaché and spoke very good English and talked with great charm and good sense.

Puttkamer told me the victory in Russia was 'decisive.' It would 'end the war'! The Russians had been completely smashed and were in full flight and Hindenburg hoped to get the whole lot. They talk already of 200.000 prisoners – but all details are withheld still. Today the entire city is beflagged as I have not seen it yet. Everywhere streamers flying and a look of joy and content on every face.

The dinner revived me and the many sane views I met there. Mrs. White says I am sure of a hearty welcome in Vienna – the Austrians will be glad to help Ireland. A Colonel Emerson and his wife – American war correspondent – also there. He goes to U.S.A. on 9 January on a special mission of enlightenment. He told me he had read my pamphlet and liked it immensely – and hoped it had gone all thro' Ireland.

On getting back from Mrs. White's at midnight I found a letter from von Wedel asking me to go to the Imperial Chancellor at 12 (today) as Bethmann Hollweg wished to see me.

Jesco von Puttkamer: A long-serving German governor of Cameroon; Casement had dealings with von Puttkamer during his earliest official posting to the British consulate in Old Calabar. [Auswärtiges Amt]

Berlin, Friday, 18 December 1914

[…]

Jesco von Puttkamer, the old Governor of Cameroons, called on me this morning. I had not seen him since March or Feby 1895 – in Cameroon, when I was his guest and when I climbed the great peak with 'Gyp' my dear little fox terrier. He is old and white – but just married & full of life & hope still – and wished me all luck for Ireland.[40]

[…]

I went at 11.15 to von Wedel at F.O. who was more than friendly and told me they agreed to all my conditions as to the Irish Brigade.

The document I drew up on 15th last they had considered fully and with the exception of the following words dealing with German officers – they would sign it. The international law authorities at the F.O. had had it under consideration and found no flaw in it. It was not contrary to the rights of nations. There were precedents for it – apart from existing cases of the same thing in the present war. The precedents von Wedel cited were two – a Hanoverian legion formed in 1870 to aid the French in Paris, and a Hungarian legion that in 1866 fought for Prussia against Austria.

Von Wedel gave me a mass of London press references to myself – *Morning Post* and *Manchester Guardian* are very loquacious and latter speaks of my visit to Berlin as an 'act of monstrous baseness at first thought incredible.' Also as an 'act of treason to England and of double dyed treason to Ireland.' He also gave me a copy of the open letter to Lord Northcliffe sent out by my (former) friend Gardiner of the *Daily News* which Gaffney so volubly assured me (and I see assures the readers of the *Continental Times*) is written by Garvin.

Of Gaffney's wisdom I have not a high opinion and much too loquacious and not capable of thinking things out for himself.

Wedel took me round himself to the Chancellor's official residence next door to the Foreign Office. A fine palace. I was received and shown upstairs and sending in my card in a moment I was admitted to a large room where the Chancellor, in a grey uniform, was standing up. He advanced to meet me, shook me warmly by the hand, and led me

---

[40] This is the principal reference to Casement's ascent of Mount Cameroon in early 1895, Africa's fourth highest peak and the inspiration for a poem by Casement.

to a chair. We smoked cigarettes. He spoke in French, I in English, by agreement. I did most of the talking and discussed Ireland, the Irish in America and my hopes or 'dreams' of a free Ireland. Either now or later – but some day. He agreed that an independent Ireland, if possible of achievement, would be a good thing for Germany and for the freedoms of the seas – and a desirable thing to attempt. I said I was aware, fully aware that today, with the British Fleet barring the way and keeping all Ireland in jail, to think of an independent Ireland was 'fantastic' and he agreed to that. But I begged him to have an Irish policy for Germany in the future – for the next war would be a war for the seas, and then the cause of Ireland would indeed be the cause of Germany. He agreed. I spoke also of the Irish Brigade and of my hope that by its formation 'at least a hard blow could be struck at recruiting in Ireland' to which the Chancellor assented and said that that would be of great service.

We discussed at his request 'Christiania' and Mr. Findlay and the extraordinary later developments with Findlay's present offer of £10.000 for me 'anywhere in the North Sea or Skagerrak' and his entrusting the key of the back door of the British Legation at C. to my rascal Adler!

This latter act of Findlay's has, possibly, more amazed the German officials and more aided to convince them of the truth of the whole story than all the rest. Von Wedel (truly) said to me this morning 'It is incredible – a man in Findlay's position to so act with an unknown, with your servant!'

I said 'Yes – but that is the English character. You see I know them much better than you. To get me, to crush an Irish national movement they would commit any crime today, as in the past – they have no conscience when it comes to collective dealing – individually the Englishman is a gentleman often and frequently very charming – collectively they are a most dangerous compound and form a national type that has no parallel in humanity. Like certain chemicals – apart harmless, brought together you get an infernal explosive or a deadly poison.'

He laughed and agreed that my diagnosis applied to the disease.

I stayed with the Chancellor fully half an hour. He was interested and showed it and on my leaving he shook me warmly by the hand and wished me 'all success in your aims and projects.'

I returned to von Wedel at the F.O. next door and talked long with him over Ireland. [...] He said they would support me in every way and give me all the assurances I needed and that the Chancellor's reception of

Leonhard Fanto (1874–1958) produced a limited lithographic edition of his portrayal of Roger Casement during the latter's visit to Dresden in 1915.

[Above and Below] Albert K. Dawson's photographic portraits of Casement were widely syndicated. His accompanying sequence of film was seen by millions of U.S. citizens after Casement's execution on 3 August 1916.

A widely circulated press image of Casement from the latter weeks of his time in Germany. [Digital Library@Villanova University]

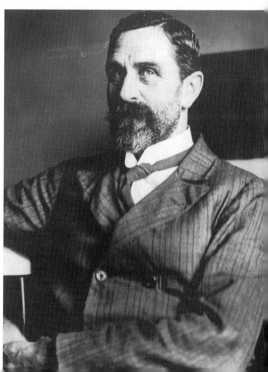

Casement's letter to the Kaiser, dated 25 August 1914, pledging support for Imperial Germany, was signed by the entire executive of the Clan na Gael. [Bundesarchiv]

Count Georg von Wedel directed the English Department at the German Foreign Office. Von Wedel worked closely with Casement during his months in Germany. [Auswärtiges Amt]

The German Chancellor, Theobald von Bethmann Hollweg, met privately with Casement in December 1914. [Auswärtiges Amt]

Hans Boehm was assigned by the German High Command to assist Roger Casement in his efforts to raise an Irish Brigade. [Auswärtiges Amt]

Eduard Meyer, brother of Kuno Meyer, a distinguished German historian of mainly ancient history. [Bundesarchiv]

Theodor Schiemann: historian, archivist and policy expert [Bundesarchiv]

Wilhelm Solf: scholar, statesman and diplomat; Solf served as secretary of the German Colonial Office until 1918. [German Federal Archives]

A picture of recruits to the 'Fighting' Irish Brigade. Casement's concerns about the potential military efficacy of the Brigade are perhaps evident in this photograph.

NCOs of the Irish Brigade Zossen. From left: Cpl Peter Golden; Sgt Major Keogh; Cpl O'Mahoney; Sgt Daniel Julian Bailey (aka Beverley); Captain Zerhussen (interpreter); Cpl Kavanagh; Cpl O'Callaghan; QMS H. Quinlisk. [National Museum of Ireland]

Father Crotty and Father O'Gorman: priests who attended to the spiritual needs of the Irish POWs. [Postcard, 1915]

r Henry Howard: British career diplomat and ousin of the Duke of Norfolk; in December 914 he became the first envoy to the Vatican r over 350 years.[Bain Collection]

Joseph Mary Plunkett was sent on behalf of the IRB to negotiate with the German Government. He collaborated with Casement on the 'Ireland Report' setting out how Germany might effectively intervene in an Irish rebellion. In this image, Plunkett is standing on the balcony of Casement's hotel in Germany. [Honor O Brolchain]

Robert Monteith: transferring skills learned as a soldier in the British Army, Monteith joined the Irish Volunteers. In October 1915, he arrived in Germany to take on the training of the Irish Brigade. He returned with Casement to Ireland on board the U-19 in April 1916. [F. Monteith Lynch, *The Mystery Man of Banna Strand*]

Sean Kavanagh joined South Irish Horse and was captured early on in the war He was an early recruit to the Irish Brigade. After the war, he wrote a memoir about his involvement with Casement. [Derek Kavanagh]

The figure dressed in a white suit in the lower right hand corner of this photograph has been identified as Roger Casement. While the physical similarities are striking the image cannot be definitively authenticated.

The camp at Zossen, a short distance south of Berlin, where recruits to the Irish Brigade were sent to prepare for the return to Ireland that never happened. Casement and Monteith visited the camp regularly to check up on the well-being of Brigade members. [Postcard images – Angus Mitchell]

En route for Ireland aboard a German submarine, the U-19.

Casement and comrades with captain and crew: from right going anti-clockwise Captain Raimund Weisbach, Roger Casement, Lieutenant Otto Walther, Daniel Julian Bailey (Beverley), Robert Monteith, unidentified.

me was to convince me of their friendship and regard and that I might trust them fully and to show that they trusted me.

I told von Wedel of the Hamburg-Amerika incident at Cork in January and of my conviction that the London F.O. had stopped it though the Emperor.[41] He said he thought it highly probable and would find out – that he was in very intimate touch with the Kaiser, frequently with him and could see him when he liked. In any case Wedel said in answer to me that whatever the immediate outcome of the war and fate of Ireland might be, I might rest assured they would pursue a policy of goodwill to Ireland commercially if they could not achieve a positive act of political assistance.

I then discussed with von Wedel the possibility of the Navy getting something out of Findlay's insane projects against myself, as reported by Adler. All is fair in war, and, if these fine gentlemen will stick at nothing to catch me, why not take advantage of their trap and use it for our common interest.

He agreed and said he would at once go to the Admiralty and discuss it and let me know and in any case I had better keep Adler longer than tomorrow.

At 6 I got a 'phone message from him to say the Admiralty were considering the matter – that at first they were naturally 'surprised at such a bombshell' but were now apprised of the particulars and he thought would take it up and so I was to keep Adler longer.

Otherwise Adler was returning to Moss tomorrow, with another sham letter and some further invented 'atrocities' of mine against England to keep poor Mr. Findlay at a white heat of 'criminal invention' against myself until such time as I might arrange for my own going to Norway to get him caught in flagrante delicto.

Now, the project is a twofold one to catch Findlay and catch some vessels of the British Navy at same time!

Findlay's hope is that I will embark off the coast of Schleswig in a sailing boat to join the phantom American yacht (Armour's or some one else's) at an assigned locality in the North Sea. Adler is to get copy of my plans and learn the exact spot, and let Findlay know the time to have British vessels there to waylay me. The scheme is simple. The answer is to

---

[41] At the end of 1913 and early 1914, Casement attempted to get the transatlantic passenger liners of the Hamburg-Amerika line to stop at Cork on their way to and from America, but the plan was blocked in Whitehall. Casement believed that Winston Churchill's hand was involved.

arrange a spot with the German Admiralty, when they too, shall be there – and instead of the British cruisers catching me they catch a submarine Tartar – a Diodon in fact! This is the thought today. How far it may go I can't say. Personally I don't like it. It is too British!

Also I am <u>not</u> sure of Adler! His air and manner have changed greatly since he came back or rather since he went away. He confesses that he now 'admires' Findlay! Findlay 'is a man' 'he sticks at nothing. He would roll these God d–d Germans up.' For the Germans now, since they held him up at Sassnitz, Adler has scorn and a sense of outraged pride. They treated him badly there stripped him, split his gloves open, took his gold coin and gave him paper money, extorted 7 Marks per meal, while he was detained 48 hours their prisoner pending the order from Berlin to release him, and read aloud to the crowd my letters to my American friends. This last extraordinary piece of stupidity it was that chiefly affects Adler. He says they 'are fools' and trying to fool me and get advantage of me and Ireland and give nothing in return but empty words.

There is also the recent German action Adler reports from Norway of the condemnation by the Kiel Prize Court of some Norwegian vessels with cargoes of timber that had been seized at the beginning of the war. These 'prizes of war' mean much to their Norwegian owners little to wealthy Germany, and Adler says public feeling in Norway is aroused at the decision of the German Prize Court and for his part he has become 'anti-German.'

Therefore with myself out of the issue his sympathies would be against Germany and on the side of 'the man' Findlay, 'who sticks at nothing.'

There is also the resentment he feels, the very deep resentment at the allegations against himself and his conduct while in Berlin, to which Schiemann referred and which Blücher told me had been conveyed in a police report to the F.O. I told Adler of this report last night – giving it as the reason why I found it impossible to take him on with me to Limburg and the Irish Brigade.

It makes him exceedingly bitter against the Germans and he is vowing vengeance. Knowing <u>now</u> all I do of his character, of its extraordinary complexity, I should feel gravely disposed to mistrust his fidelity in a matter, whence German ships were the issue as against British ships. I should even, now, be indisposed to trust myself to his schemes!

He is clearly beginning to feel that Findlay is a bolder, more uncompromising and reckless rascal than myself and Adler's deepest affection is won by extreme rascaldom. Utter unscrupulousness of action, so long as it succeeds, is his ideal he confesses. He was won to my side, he admits, only by my extreme trust in himself. Seeing how fully I trusted him on the voyage over, his honour (or what corresponds to it) came to the top and he determined to be true as steel to me.

Now that he sees me going off on my Irish 'journey' and he not to take part any more in my efforts, and this due to the evil (and indeed quite untruthful) reports of the Berlin police as to his conduct here, his rage against the Germans is almost swallowing up his affection for me. His face is changed. The old, boyish eyes and smile are gone and he does not look me openly in the face.

I think he is in <u>his</u> heart really regretting that – but no! I will not think that even. But I must see that he is ill disposed to the German cause and losing interest in mine, since he can no longer be associated with me in it and since he is aware that the Germans have 'scandalised' him so much. Therefore, I feel it would be far safer for all concerned to send Adler back to Norway and let him return to U.S.A. to work there. I told him much of this last night and said I would try to get him good work there, if he would promise to go straight and quite give up doing the things he confessed to me the last night before he returned to Moss he had done. And so there I left him this night.

[…]

I wish I could get word from Ireland. I sent a letter now 2 weeks ago via my friend here for Eoin MacNeill to go thro' Mrs. Green – but even if it reaches her hands safely I doubt now that she would dare (poor brave but frail lady) to send it on to Dublin. It would be too dangerous for herself and for the Professor. Besides they may have him locked up.

My only hope is that in their fury of rage and fear combined they (the British Government) will show their hand so openly against Irish nationality that Redmond and his gang of traitors will have to either repudiate England openly or repudiate the cause they have so grossly misrepresented for years and finally so cruelly betrayed.

In any case I hope all that is sincere and true in Irish nationality will he outraged by the attacks of the Government and that out of this accursed war of English greed against Germany shall be born once more in tribulation, in jail, in repression, the spirit of Irish revolt against English tyranny. May it be so!

Berlin, Saturday, 19 December 1914

Still no details of the Russian overthrow. It is clear that they are completely routed for the Austrian War Office accounts correspond with the German and say that along the whole front from Galicia to East Prussia the combined Austro-German pursuit of the enemy is taking place.

At the Esplanade Hotel last night a young German told me he had seen y'day morning already many trainloads of soldiers being brought <u>back</u> from the East front & going thro' to the West.

They were dirty and with beards he said & looked as if they 'hadn't washed', but were cheering & waving their hands & shouting 'Now for the English.'

The Emperor, too, I was told was leaving Berlin again for the front last night – I presume for Charleville. If, as <u>everyone</u> now is convinced, the Russian offensive has been completely broken, it should mean the return of a very large force of victorious troops & many guns & officers of ability for the renewed assault on Calais – Dover and Paris. I hope so.

Bethmann Hollweg said to me yesterday that 'Germany could not be beaten' – that not Russia, France & England would succeed in defeating her! I said I feared only the long continuance of the war possibly sapping German strength & allowing England's vast resources in the end to turn

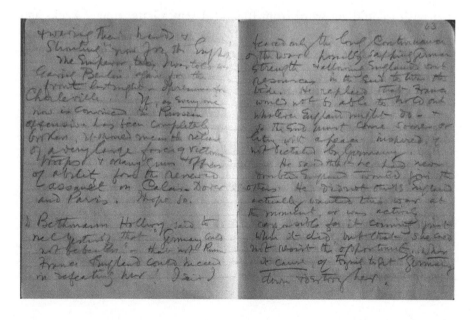

the tide. He replied that France would not be able to hold out, whatever England might do – & so the end must come sooner or later with a peace inspired, if not dictated, by Germany.

He said that <u>he</u> had never doubted England would join the others. He did not think England actually wanted this war at the moment, or was actively responsible for it coming just when it did, but that she could not resist the opportunity, <u>when it came</u>, of trying to get Germany down & destroy her.

He was convinced that England could have stopped the war but would not because she thought it gave her the chance of years of coming in with every prospect of success to destroy the German menace.

As to the pretext of Belgian neutrality that deceived no one now he thought, 'If it had not been Belgium, it would have been something else.' – I agreed and said: 'The detained British vessels in Hamburg perhaps' – 'Very likely indeed,' he replied!

[…]

Adler brought me the <u>key</u> of the back entrance to the Br. Legation in Christiania today – given to him by the Minister so that he might 'come in at any time'!

On Saturday evg I was the guest of a Colonel Emerson and his wife at the Hotel. He is here also. He is a war correspondent of the United Press and very pro-German and pro-Irish and has read my pamphlet 'with joy' he says and will 'use it to the best advantage.' The others were a Mrs. White and a Mr. Callan O'Laughlin, an American and once an Under Secretary of State under some previous administration. He was profoundly uninteresting. He has come to Europe as the U.S. 'Santa Claus' with gifts for the poor victims of the war and is returning very soon via England to U.S.A. He is impressed by German courage, calmness and greatness of soul & admitted so to me – but he gives the distinct impression none the less of being pro-British at heart & profoundly pro-Belgian. This is the pose of the average good American – Why did Germany 'violate Belgian neutrality!' They can get no further than this. That others and particularly England have again and again violated treaties and invaded neutrality they refuse to discuss or admit the bearing of. This war, to them, is simply a war undertaken by 'the Allies' to protect Belgium (and possibly Servia!) from Teutonic forceful aggression. While O'Laughlin did not assert this openly it was plain he <u>felt</u> it. He said, too, that 'many Germans' in U.S.A. were anti-German and pro-ally! Also that 'the Irish in America

were with England' – whereupon I contradicted him flatly and said I
believed the vast majority were strongly pro-German and assuredly anti-
English and cited in proof of my assertion the cancelling of Redmond's
announced visit to U.S.A., the dissolution of the Irish League of America,
the change of policy of the Irish World and the repudiation by Mr. M.J.
Ryan of Redmond's recruiting mission. He withdrew <u>instanter</u> and said
I probably know better than he did. I gave him before parting a copy of
my pamphlet *The Crime against Ireland* which he promised to read on his
way to England the next few days. That he should read it would be indeed
a miracle.

Berlin, Monday, 21 December 1914

Last evg (at 5.30) I went to Mrs. White's and met a number of people
chiefly from the press. The chief man of the <u>Lokalanzeiger</u> among them –
and one of the principal redacters of the *Vossische Zeitung*. Also a Swede,
the representative in Germany of the chief Swedish press – all were more
than friendly and the *Vossische Zeitung* man particularly. He said they
were only waiting for the naval fight to send an expedition, with me, to
Ireland.

[…]

I got a letter from Kuno Meyer today telling me (28 Nov) of his views
and of his having met Cohalan, McGarrity, Devoy and John Quinn. They
all disapprove the publication of the Christiania incident – and also of
my suggested expedition to Egypt. In the former case I <u>can</u> do nothing
at present – in the latter idea I am right and they are wrong – because as
Fr Crotty said The first thing is that England should be beaten. Since it
is highly improbable that the Irish Brigade (should it ever come to life)
could get into Ireland it would be a far more effective blow for Ireland
and against England to aid the Egyptian to expel John Bull than to remain
idle. These are the only alternatives I see – either to go to Egypt with the
returning Khedive and expel the English – or to sit down at Limburg an
der Lahn till the end of the war.

Of course a great naval victory by Germany would open the door to
Ireland – but this is not very likely. The *Lustige Blätter*[42] of tonight has a
good cartoon on this very subject – a German sailor and a big fleet bring

---

[42] A Berlin-based satirical magazine published from 1885–1944.

'Home Rule' to Ireland – while Pat says 'I've waited a very long time for that!'

I ordered 100 copies to be sent to the Irish prisoners and more for U.S.A.

I called on von Wedel again at 5.30, gave him K. Meyer's letter and told him of my interview with young Bryan A Kelly who had come to me twice today. Let out of Ruhleben (at my request) he will go to Limburg to convert the soldiers and later go back to Ireland with messages of good cheer to Eoin and others. He will be ostensibly 'interned' at Limburg without his own assent asked or given. Wedel agreed to all and will visit Frankfurt and Limburg and Kelly will go down on Tuesday as a 'prisoner of war.'

I also wrote Frau Nelly Zittel to come & see me – & she came y'day (Sunday) and she too will go to Limburg – ostensibly as a 'nurse' and will talk to the men in the right vein. She has been so long out of Ireland, however, (9 years) that her accent is now German & she forgets words and does not realise the great changes (for the worse) that the prolonged 'Home Rule' <u>fight</u> on the floor of the House and the 'trusting in the Liberals' has had on the heart and spirit of Irish nationality. I told her of these desperate evils and of how Redmond had gone over bag and baggage to the enemy and was now simply John Bull's recruiting sergeant in Ireland. She is a pretty woman, with blue Irish eyes and still a good deal of the gentle kindly Irish voice and brogue in her Germanised English.

The Chancellor left his card for me on Friday evg at the hotel.

Kuno Meyer: Celtic philologist and intellectual; Meyer founded the School of Irish Learning in Dublin and edited the journal *Ériu*. He was a close friend of both Casement and Stopford Green, who regarded him highly. Casement met with Meyer frequently in the days after his arrival in Berlin, before Meyer left for the US on a political mission. [National Portrait Gallery, London]

127

Berlin, Wednesday, 23 December 1914

On Monday evening I called again on Wedel at F.O. and arranged definitely about Kelly and Mrs. Zittel going to Limburg. She came in to see Wedel while I was there and we three discussed the matter fully – she will go after Christmas day – probably next Monday. I wrote General De Graaff about Kelly. Kelly is to go down today and at Limburg to report himself to the police and be 'interned' with the soldiers.

I also called to bid Major Lothes good bye. He goes out again to Chile to try and take 200 reservists to a certain place I will not put it down here even. I wish I were going too. I fancy the English may have already got hold of his idea for I see the U.S.A. authorities have held up a consignment of stores etc. for that place being shipped from San Francisco and yesterday I was told the English had seized the Chile mail to Germany on a neutral ship off Montevideo and thrown it overboard! A fine regard for the sanctity of treaties. These same English are shrieking to all the world against the bombardment of the Yorkshire towns and batteries. As I have always predicted they are now setting up a concerted yell in U.S.A. to try and get that country dragged in on their side. It will take <u>all</u> the strength of the Irish and Germans yet, in America, to keep Mr. Wilson 'neutral.' England will stick at nothing when the war she so selfishly aimed at Germany comes nearer and nearer her own shores.

Continental Times, 21 Dec. 1914. [National Library of Ireland]

Karl Vollmöeller: German playwright and screen writer; he is best known for writing *The Blue Angel*, the film that made Marlene Dietrich a star. [Bundesarchiv]

Yesterday, Tuesday, I went by appointment to see Dr Karl Vollmöeller at the Adlon Hotel. He had sent a telephone call to me on Saturday through Count Palby (a cousin of my former friend in London) begging me to call on him as he was sick in bed and wanted to meet me very much.

I found a fair haired, spectacled young German – or <u>almost a German American</u>. He is a journalist and a dramatic writer and I gathered had also helped in the Embassies of England and U.S.A. at times.

He wanted to help the Irish cause and write it up in the Berlin press and do all he could to advance 'my cause.'

I gave him my pamphlet – Puttkamer writes me that he has read the pamphlet and is so anxious to write an article on it in 'Der Tag' and to discuss this he comes to see me today.

[…]

I am to go at 3 today to call on Captain Isendahl at the Admiralty to discuss the ways and means of the Christiania incident and how to get Findlay. I don't think anything will come out of it. It can only be carried to success by my going into it personally and that would conflict with the Irish Brigade.

Last night I went to Professor Edward Meyer at Gross Lichterfelde West Weg and met a party of professors there – among them the Director of the Berlin Museum – an officer in uniform covered with medal ribbons – Major [Theodor] Weigand. He knew Mrs. Green – 18 years ago! Had gone on horseback with her to Troy! He had found her charming and said she spoke 'excellent German.'

Berlin, Thursday, 24 December 1914

I went at 3 to the Reichsmarineamt [German Imperial Naval Office] General Staff and found Captain Isendahl and another officer waiting. We discussed Findlay at length – and it was settled that 'Mr. Hammond' will embark at Gothenburg for Christiania direct (avoiding Kragerö) on 8 January. After that Adler will know nothing of his intentions. Adler will inform Mr. Findlay of this – and then two sketch outline maps of Ireland and Great Britain with hypothetical 'mine fields' were given me (at my request). Two of the mine fields will close the Irish Sea North and South – from Port Patrick to Galloway and from Carnsore over to Wales. These to be laid 'about the 15 January.' Mr. Findlay's only chance of catching 'Mr. Hammond' will be when he travels by this small Danish S/S 'Mjölnir' from Gothenburg to Christiania. I asked no questions.

I took the maps to Adler and he traced them on paper and did it well too and brought them to me at 7.30 this morning. Then I arranged the tale he is to spin Findlay in addition to the two maps. Part of the tale is that I left for Vienna today and so allowed Adler home for Christmas. Also that I met the Khedive and 'stood beside him' at the salute on Tuesday. That a special messenger arrived from New York last night with good news. This is true for a Dr. Ewald arrived by the Norwegian S/S 'Kristianiafjord' (to Bergen) and got to the Eden Hotel last night and at once asked for me and I met him at 11 p.m. on going up to my room. He is vice president of the American Truth Society under Jeremiah O'Leary and told me that all was going splendidly in U.S.A. – the Irish-German alliance there a firm and stern reality for Wilson and all the rest of the Anglo-Saxons. No possibility of getting the U.S.A. 'roped in' against Germany now he says – 'there would be a revolution.' The German-American press had come out with great headlines over the Declaration of 20 Nov. and the *Staats-Zeitung*, said the next German <u>Dreadnought</u> should be named '<u>Sir Roger Casement</u>.'

I called on Wedel at 6.30 (after seeing Meyer at F.O. and telling him of the 'plot') and he brought in Graf Montgelas who is taking his place while he goes off for Xmas. I told him of what Fräulein Meyer had told me of Professor Macran of Dublin University (Trinity) who is here in Charlottenburg and he agreed that if Macran will speak the truth for Germany they will release him and send him home to Dublin. He said it 'all lay with me'– that if I said so they would do it – that anything that I asked for of that kind they would at once assent to. So I shall see Prof Macran soon & if he is a decent Irishman he shall go back to Dublin.

Meyer brought the sample uniform today for 'an officer' of the Irish Brigade. It fits me well and I shall wear it!

At 11 as I was going to bed Dr. Ewald came to speak to me having just arrived from New York which he left on 12 Dec. He says all is going well – the Irish and Germans a solid mass and Redmond entirely repudiated and my coming here a subject of great rejoicing to all the Irish and Germans. He wants me to return to U.S.A. 'if I can' and take up the direction of the Irish movement there – but that is out of the question. He had not seen Kuno Meyer and only knows J. O'Leary and is not in the 'inner circle' – but he can tell of things within public knowledge. The pro-German feeling is growing according to him.

Today at lunch with Countess Hahn, the Princess Hohenlohe who is here in the Hotel brought her sailor boy (about 15) a fine handsome lad – Ctess Bernstorff the wife of the U.S.A. Ambassador, my friend, was also there with her son, a young officer of the Imperial Guard of Cuirassiers – like his father the Ambassador.

[...]

In the West, the Germans have stormed many French-British trenches in the last three days and killed large numbers (700 'English dead' at one point) & taken some 2000 to 3000 prisoners. Once the battle in Poland-Galicia is definitely decided in favour of Germany & Austria I expect they will leave the further handling of the Russian hordes to Austria & turn 500.000 victorious men into France & Flanders and break thro' towards Paris & towards the channel at sometime.

Meantime the British 'Protectorate' over Egypt is announced with a 'Sultan' of Egypt. The proclamation is signed by Milne Cheetham (my old friend from Rio de Janeiro!) and is a delightful specimen of British hypocrisy and double dealing combined with the arrogance of the successful burglar who has got his victim robbed and bound. John Bull is doing it all 'for the welfare of the dear Egyptians!' Equally he has 'no quarrel with the Caliphate' – only with the 'usurpers' of power at Constantinople! Everybody who acts for his own interests, except John Bull, is an 'usurper', a 'traitor', a 'lunatic' or a 'barbarian.'

If Turkey gets into Egypt it will be the beginning of the end!

Berlin, Sunday, 27 December 1914

Christmas & Stephen's Days have come and gone. Adler left for Moss on Christmas Day only – having been detained at last moment on Thursday by Meyer for fear of possible trouble at Sassnitz again. I saw him off.

[…]

The war news the last few days is disappointing. No real gain in Poland – the Russians have got large reinforcements and are holding the Bzura line 30 miles west of Warsaw.

In Flanders several English attacks repulsed and yesterday's bulletin shows heavy English losses near Nieuport and at Hubert – 'over 3000 dead' – 819 soldiers and 19 officers prisoners and 14 guns and some others. During the last week the English losses have been well over 6000 killed and prisoners – the German officers say the new English army is not so good as the first – the regular army. That must be pretty well used up and disposed of now.

[…]

LIMBURG REVISITED

Friday, 8 January 1915

It is nearly 2 weeks since I wrote in my diary. I have been ill and greatly upset at failure of my hopes.

Adler left for Moss and Christiania on Xmas Day only, which I spent so quietly in Berlin with Countess Hahn in the evening.

From that on I had several interviews with Professor Macran of Dublin University. He promised to be a true and faithful witness to the 'truth about Germany' if released – so I obtained that and he and his wife actually left Berlin for Ireland last 6 January. They should now be in Holland, en route via Rotterdam or the Hook of Holland.

[…]

On Tuesday 29 Dec. I went to the Irish prisoners at Ruhleben,[43] near Spandau. There are 163 nominal 'Irish' there – Catholics – I saw a few, young sailors from Rush and elsewhere and one charming youth of 17, Paul O'Brien, son of a Cork man and an apprentice on an English steamer. Only 17. I think all should be released as an act of goodwill to Ireland by Germany.

It would make the English and their Govt. furiously angry – and would do great good elsewhere – in Ireland and U.S.A. The fact that the German Government had released nearly 200 civil prisoners merely on the ground that Germany wished well to Ireland would make England foam at the mouth – and would make <u>everyone else</u> pleased throughout the world. I have advised this.

I discussed it with Professor Macran who said it would be a 'very nasty blow to the Br. Govt.' He has become entirely 'rebellious' at heart since

---

[43] An internment camp of mainly civilian prisoners of war, located about 10km to the west of Berlin

our first meeting – & is really sorry not to be in to the neck with me! He told me so – all red in the face. Strange product of Trinity – but the Irish blood will out – even in a Trinity professor. He is to call on Gertrude [Bannister] at Caversham, on Mrs. Green, on Eoin MacNeill, (through Sarah Purser), on F.J.B. possibly – and of course, too, on Nina – but that is to be arranged thro' Gertrude. I sent £15 (part £5 gold and rest German money) by him for Nina – to hand to Gertrude.[44]

I got the terms of the agreement between the Imperial German Government and myself on the Irish Brigade by a special messenger from F.O. on Monday evening 28 Dec.[45] I drew up the conditions and by letter on 23 Dec. forwarded them – and they now reply, in due form, accepting them fully in a letter covering my conditions – in English and German – dated 28 December and signed by the Under Secretary of State for Foreign Affairs Zimmermann with the official seal of the F.O.

I left Berlin, after having got this document, which contains a clear acceptance of an independent Ireland and its recognition by Germany, on Wednesday 30 Dec. by the 10.36 a.m. train getting to Frankfurt at 7.30. I had got a bad cold on me due largely to the sharp thaw after Christmas and the cold at Ruhleben and on getting to Frankfurt I had to go to bed and stayed there in bed till Saturday the 2nd January 1915.

I saw Prince Leiningen once – & then General de Graaff on Saturday evening, to arrange for the release of Bryan Kelly as soon as I wanted it. Kelly had come to Limburg, to be imprisoned on Wednesday 23 Decr – and he is to give me a real view of what the men truly think. That was the plan. On Sunday 3 January I came on to Limburg by the early morning train – still with this bad cold on me. I found the two Irish priests Fathers Crotty and O'Gorman both very well and delighted to see me. The latter confirmed publicly to me that he had 'entirely changed his views' and was now fully pro-German & in full sympathy with me and my plans for an independent Ireland through German help. He has repeated this several times and says my brochure did very much to change his views and that he agrees with every word of it.

---

[44] This list includes the artist, Sarah Purser, Casement's sister, Nina, and his cousin Gertrude Bannister.

[45] Casement is referring here to the document that came to be known as the 'Treaty' or the 'Irish Verses'. See Appendix 3.

In the afternoon of Sunday 3 January we went, all three, to Balduinstein to call on Pfarrer Berkessel who spent years at Cashel in the old days of Dr. Croke in the early '80s. We found him quite a delightful man, with a charming mind and person and a warm regard for the Irish. His conversation was altogether delightful, full of reminiscences of Irish (and English) personalities and he entertained us with the greatest good will till the evening train brought us back to Limburg.

On Monday 4 January I changed my hotel – the Nassauer Hof where I found two rooms, one an excellent sitting room – for 4.50 per day.

On Tuesday, 5 January, I got a letter from Adler from Grand Hotel, Christiania, telling me he had seen Mr. Findlay on Sunday 27 December, and that all was going very well and Mr. Findlay was very keen to catch me on my projected 'raid' to Ireland. [...] In the afternoon I went up to the camp, along with the two priests – I very soon saw from the manner of the men that all hope of an Irish Brigade from such a contemptible crew as are there must be entirely abandoned. Some of them insulted me – but all showed clearly the utter slothful indifference of that type of debauched Irishman to any appeal but to his greed. They complained of 'ill treatment' of 'want of food' and were anxious for tobacco – but were full of ill will to Germany and in many cases 'more English than the English themselves.' I did not see Kelly and made no inquiry for him – but wrote and telephoned to Frankfurt for his immediate release.

I came down from the camp at 6.16 p.m. in dark and mud – in a very despondent mood after the revelation of Irish depravity I had witnessed among these 2,200 so called 'Irishmen.'

At 6.20 I got a telephone from the F.O. as follows. Time 2h 10mts.

'Following telegram for Hammond just received from Frederikshald. Meet me train arrives 7.24 Berlin, must see you, good news. Christensen.'

Very soon after I got 'phone calls from Mr. Meyer asking me what I should do and saying he would go to the train to meet Adler. I said I did not want to go to Berlin unless absolutely necessary and to keep me informed by wire. At 7.20 a.m. on 6 January I got a telegram sent off in the night saying – 'your coming not necessary. Christensen returns tomorrow morning.'

I wrote to Meyer telling him that I thought there was no hope of getting the soldiers to do anything and asking to be kept informed of the new 'plot' against me arranged now – I wonder what Christensen's 'good news' is?

I hope it means that these scoundrels have fallen into their despicable plot to kidnap me. The daily papers speak of 'English mines laid off the coast of Norway' – and give some details & the names of steamers Norwegian – detained by them. This seems clearly part of the British 'action' to prevent my contemplated Wolfe Tone descent on the coast of Ireland.[46]

I must possess myself in patience and wait for developments. I hope it may mean several of their pirate craft caught in their own net laid for the one Irishman today they are really afraid of! Good! They are afraid of me. My price has gone up to £10,000 and poor Adler is anxious to get their money 'to give me' (poor soul) so that I may fight them with their own 'purse.' I have laughed at this and told him we must never touch a penny of this money 'given' to him.

On Thursday 7 January Bryan Kelly presented himself at the Nassauer Hof and after breakfast I went with him to Frankfurt at the request of the General de Graaff by telegram and got him a pass for Berlin where he is asked by phone from the F.O. to call on Friday morning (today) at 11 a.m. and report himself to Mr. Meyer.

I wrote by Kelly to Meyer asking for him to be allowed off at once to Ireland.

I had a long talk with Kelly. He reports the men as 'quite contemptible' – that they steal from each other, are despised by the German guards and the French prisoners alike. The latter will not associate with them in any way. Kelly says that the young men, or boys might be got together into a Brigade if one could get them away from the older men. There are many 'Englishmen' he says among them – born in England and no more Irish than any ordinary Anglo-Saxon. He says they are in no case to be trusted and that to think of doing anything for Ireland with such creatures is hopeless. He regards them as 'hired assassins and cut throats' and says that they boast of the 'blood money' they will get on their emancipation and return 'to England.'

---

[46] A reference to the leader of the United Irish, Wolfe Tone, the father of Irish Republicanism, who negotiated French support and the invasion of Ireland during the 1798 rebellion.

Kelly was to go to Berlin by the night train. I returned to Limburg, after seeing General de Graaff by the 8.30 train that got me in cold and wet at 10.45 p.m.

Today Friday 8 January, the interpreter (at my request) brought young Sergeant Quinlisk down to me at 9.30 a.m. I kept him till 11 when he was taken again to camp – with some papers. He reported that he was assailed by the men – but he would 'fight it out.' They threaten to inform on him and have him hanged as a traitor on 'return to England.' He showed no fear – and said he did not care – that he had done his duty to Ireland and was not afraid of them.

He confirmed – only more so – Bryan Kelly's statements and said they were a contemptible cowardly lot of brutes. Both Kelly and I decided yesterday that it would be a great mistake to allow these ruffians out on Sunday to Mass at the Cathedral and I told the General so. He agreed that it would be very unwise. This will greatly disappoint the two priests – especially poor Fr. Crotty. Father O'Gorman returns to Rome in eight days or so and Father Crotty will be alone. However I think it may be best to break up the 'Irish camp' at Limburg altogether. There is no reason for it now. All hope of getting these men to strike a blow for Ireland is at an end – and so far as I can see, my mission to Germany too. It will be impossible to expect the German Govt. to make any further declaration about Ireland when the only Irishmen in Germany boast that they are English and repudiate with scorn the idea that they should fight for Ireland! How can anything ever be done for such a people? Here are 2200 Irishmen as Quinlisk said this morning, and said himself 'not one to fight or work or lift a hand for Ireland.'

I said that Quinlisk could not be left to his fate at the hands of these men. He admitted that while he despised them and was quite prepared 'to face the music' that he thought it exceedingly likely the men, and the 'co-conspirator' MacMorrough especially, would try to have him tried for treason in England. The English government would be delighted to have a victim.

So I said to Quinlisk that I should apply for his release and send him to America and he jumped at the idea. It is the only way to save him. Even so, there are dangers for him – grave dangers, poor boy! He is a fine type – brave and fearless. A Wexford boy from the Christian Brothers school. Only 19. His younger brother, only 17, was shot through the heart he tells me near La Bassie – '10 miles below

La Bassie.' He saw him killed. Quinlisk's contempt for his comrades is wholehearted.

He asked nothing from me – made no complaint and was quite prepared to be put on trial for high treason.

[...]

Most of my thoughts are very sad – I am very despondent. How to lift up & vivify a land that has such cowards as these to represent it! On the other hand both Fr. Crotty and Fr. O'Gorman are splendid – and both give me good news from Ireland. The Rector of the Irish College in Rome, Monsignor O'Riordan returned from Ireland on Xmas eve and reported that the recruiting was 'dead.' Redmond had failed. He had tried to get up a meeting at Limerick, and no priest would attend. Fr. O'Hagan, the Vice Rector, wrote to Fr. Crotty in similar strains. Also they said that the Irish ecclesiastics in Rome are all against the new British Envoy to the Vatican. Cardinal Gasquet, one of the four Cardinals who live in Rome for international work and who is called 'the English Cardinal', gives a grand reception for Sir Henry Howard and the two Fathers tell me the great bulk of the Irish party in Rome will not go near it. They especially say that educated opinion in Ireland is beginning to change.

Limburg, Wednesday, 13 January 1915

I am still at Limburg – there is nothing here to record save continuous rain. I have not been again to the camp – but have had long talks with General Exner about the men and the 'Brigade.'

[...]

In the House of Lords of London I see Lord Curzon asked about 'Sir Roger Casement' and what would be done to him and the *B. Z. am Mittag* of Berlin of Sunday last, received last night by post, gives a long article on me. Lord Crewe seems to have said that 'very sensible punishment was due to Sir Roger Casement'! Yes.

Meantime I have been delayed in writing a letter to Sir E Grey which I have long contemplated I have drafted some of it. It recounts my own attitude towards Ireland since I left the F.O. service on 30 June 1913 & the acts of the previous Br. Govt. against Ireland & then it brings the whole charge of the attempted crime of Christiania straight to Grey & the Br. Govt.

I propose writing this letter while here at Limburg & sending the original from Berlin, through the American Ambassador, to London, &

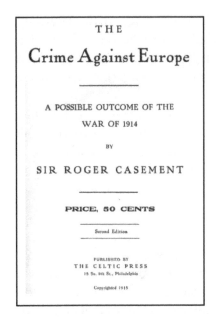

The Crime against Europe: Casement's volume of historically-based propaganda essays, written between 1911 and August 1914, was published in different editions in both the US and Europe and translated into both German and French. [Angus Mitchell]

handing copies formally to the Ambassador himself for transmission to his Govt. – as well as complimentary copies to the Norwegian Govt. the German & the Austro-Hungarian – & also getting one to the Pope.

[…]

Here in Limburg almost daily men proceed for the front. On Monday a number went off with flowers in their rifles. A fine body of young men – 19-21 – 250 strong, in grey uniform paraded on Saturday – splendid types of tall young Germans.

The land is full of men – & full of courage, certitude of victory & absolute faith in the great destiny of Germany.

No one who sees these people close can doubt for a moment in the national greatness of Germany or in the certainty that these people cannot be overthrown.

When the announced 'two millions of men' of Lord Kitchener come, as they say, in the spring, Germany will have a new army of 700.000 men in the field and with the help of God she should do more than hold her own against all comers.

A debate on recruiting in Ireland also took place in the House of Lords and it is admitted that all Redmond's efforts have failed and that the 'Nationalist districts remain untouched.' So far we have won. Lord Mayo attributes the failure to 'the seditious literature' that flooded the country. Me! – and friends of Ireland!

Meantime I am urging the release of all Irish prisoners at Ruhleben on the grounds of German goodwill to Ireland. This will please the Irish people and greatly irritate John Bull. If the Germans are wise they will do it as a gracious act to Ireland. Fr. O'Gorman takes many copies of my pamphlet to Rome on Monday.

[...]

Limburg, Thursday, 14 January 1915

No news from Berlin at all & so none from Christiania or the Skaggerak. I presume either the 'Mjölnir' was not molested by Br. cruisers on her journey from Gothenburg to Christiansand and so the coup manquéd; or that Findlay has – at last! – found out how Adler has been fooling him, or else that Adler's hurried return to Berlin & abrupt departure again for Norway meant a complete change of plan, of which I know nothing yet – & probably now shall know nothing. It is on the other hand, highly probable Findlay and the Foreign Office have found out that I am fooling them and that all Adler's fairy tales are only designed to get fuller proof against the British Legation in Norway of criminal conspiracy.

The last *Gaelic American* to hand has some very foolish utterances on the subject of my journey across the Atlantic showing clearly that the editor knew of an attempt against me. To thus let the cat out of the bag is to give the show away to Washington Embassy and I think it is highly probable Mr. Findlay has decided now to drop his dealings with Adler. But I must wait the latter's return to Berlin and full report on all.

Neither von Wedel nor Meyer have sent me a line.
[...]

Limburg, Friday, 15 January 1915

It still rains. I am daily nearly at the dentists' who is fixing up my teeth well. Father O'Gorman returns to Rome on Monday next, via Würzburg and Lake Constance. This leaves Father Crotty alone with the soldiers. I have secured permission for Father Berkessel of Balduinstein near this to go and come freely in the camp and to hire a harmonium to play Irish songs &c. to the men. He and Father Crotty will collaborate.

I have not been to the camp since the afternoon I went up with the two priests last Tuesday week – and it has rained daily.

I have been waiting here chiefly in the hope that Father Nicholson of Philadelphia would come. He was to have sailed on 18 December for Naples. Last night, however, I got a letter from Mr. Meyer saying they had received a cable from von Bernstorff saying Father Nicholson had not sailed on 18th but would probably go on 30th but they had not heard since if he had actually sailed.

Meyer said nothing of Christiania, so I am as much in the dark as ever as to the meaning for Adler's sudden return and telegram to me and equally sudden return next day. What was the plot? The German F.O. are very peculiar people – and one never knows where one is with them.

Meantime Limburg is full of life. Soldiers and recruits come and go daily. This morning a new batch of the New Year's men came by an early train, in the dark, and were singing through the town. They were fine, tall young fellows – mostly fair haired boys of 20 or so – big strapping young men – and all looking as simple and happy as if they were going to a fair instead of to a shambles in cold, mud, rain and slush.

The war news is comparatively nil – save for frequent captures of French at Soissons, and along the line and in the Argonne.

On 12th and 13th the Germans took prisoners 3200 French and many guns, and for several days previously it had been pretty much the same. Since the 1st January the French have lost some 6000 to 7000 prisoners and possibly many more killed and wounded, and a great number of guns.

The German advance on Warsaw is held up by the bad weather – but they are within 30 to 35 miles of it. On the seas there is little to record – German submarines off Dover in this morning's *Frankfurter Zeitung*.

The Note of the U.S.A. Government to England is printed in full in the *Continental Times* of a few days ago. It is a slap on both cheeks to the power that has posed so long as the guardian of the freedom of the seas. Meantime England has replied and apparently sticks to her 'rights' which consist in, practically, holding up the trade of the whole world lest, perchance, some of the goods crossing the oceans might possibly find their way to Germany. It is the clearest illustration of the fundamental truths enunciated in my pamphlet 'Ireland, Germany and the Freedom of the Seas.' I see, by recent *Gaelic American* that this is going strong in U.S.A. and it seems to furnish the text for many resolutions at the meetings now being held in U.S.A. to protest against the British attitude towards Neutral States. Dr. Dernburg is reported to have spoken lately in New York and to judge from the speech as given in *Continental Times* it was largely based on my argument.

My own course is not at all clear. Now that I have practically abandoned the idea of the Irish Brigade, there seems little object in remaining in Germany. The Government will not want me, I am sure. Once the hope of the Irish Brigade is gone, they will feel little interest in the other aspects of the Irish Question. Those remain for later settlement – when, after this war is over, the great question facing all maritime nations will present itself more acutely than ever. The control of the seas by one power, and that power the least tied to European obligations, is a standing threat to the welfare of all the peoples of Europe. This war will demonstrate that. It has done so already.

I believe Germany will achieve a successful peace as against France and Russia, unless Italy takes the field for the 'Allies' (with Roumania possibly too). With Italy remaining neutral and Roumania neutral I agree with von Hindenburg 'the nation with the better nerves will win.' That nation is Germany. Her greatest resource is that her people are one and united and march, fight and die as one man – prince, Herr and peasant. I believe with the Chancellor that 'Germany is unconquerable.' With France exhausted and Russia having had enough of it, these two powers must find their interest is in peace – and they will make peace what ever England may say or do when that day comes.

If Germany can only win France to her side she would then be able to settle the question of the seas, too, as well as of her land frontiers. But France will not forgive quickly or forget easily. She has a bad Government, and no great man or men. The French soldiers at the camp here say openly, I hear, that France has been 'put in the fire' by England and for English interests alone. The truth comes slowly to a nation – but quickly to its defeated citizens.

There are now close on 250.000 French prisoners of war in Germany and close on 350.000 Russians. The figures are mounting by thousands each week.

The German navy I am told is ready for the attack on England 'by end of January.' Part of the programme is said to be the formal notification of a blockade of all the east coast of England. The first time in her history the 'Mistress of the Seas' will have had this indignity put upon her! It is von Tirpitz's aim – and he may well be able to carry it out.

Limburg, Saturday, 16 January 1915

A fine morning that turned into a cloudy rainy day. Still at the dentist.

The last three days have seen a veritable battle at Soissons, where the French attacked the German position north of the Aisne, and after a first success were finally driven south of the river with heavy loss. They left 5200 prisoners between 4 & 5000 killed on the field (and how many wounded is not given) as well as 14 guns, 7 machine guns & a lot of other things. Poor France! She is paying dear indeed for the Entente Cordiale of the defunct King Edward VII.

How long her tenacity will stand the strain is hard to say, but to judge from the French soldiers, prisoners here, there must come a great awakening with defeat. These men will not speak with or associate with the Irish prisoners. They call them, and rightly, 'English' and despise them as frankly as their German guards do. On all hands I hear the most unfavourable comparisons between these 'alleged Irishmen' and the French prisoners of war. The latter work cheerfully and are civil and well behaved. The 'Irish' are lazy, dirty, & have a most forbidding aspect – slouching, hands in pocket, loafing and cheering 'dear old England' all the time.

They expect that this Motherland of theirs will arrive with 2.000.000 of men in the spring & smash Germany – when they will be freed in triumph and get 'home' to England and get their accumulated 'blood money'. They have said these things to me and to the two priests, and both Bryan Kelly and young Quinlisk told me this.

The attitude of these men is one of the things that must make an Irishman despair of Irish nationality and almost despise his country. Kelly called them 'contemptible'. I endorse the opinion to the full. Even Father O'Gorman, who is to some extent 'pro-English' thinks them 'miserable specimens of Irishmen'.

I have just had a long distance call from Berlin from Mr. Meyer saying Kelly has not gone yet but will leave very soon now, & that he, Mr. M, has written me 'tonight' a letter 'with some things of interest'.

[...]

I got from an unknown correspondent today a cutting from some unnamed German paper giving a long article on Ireland by Professor

Open-air mass at Limburg [Postcard, 1916]

Pokorny of Vienna with many quotations from my old *Dublin Review* article of July 1913 on 'Ireland, Germany and the Next War'. He did not know the writer – but quotes it – and then later on refers to my visit to Berlin.

I heard today that the Kaiser had been in Limburg lately at the Irish camp incognito.

[…]

Limburg, Monday, 18 January 1915

[…]

Cold weather came last night – and it is now freezing and snow. The change from the continuous rain since I arrived on 3 January (my dear brother Tom's birthday) is a very pleasant one.

I have two rooms at the Nassauer Hof looking out on the big square of Limburg, where well nigh every morning troops parade, and detachments of Landsturm[47] or Landwehr or Volunteers in grey, march off either to entrain for the front or on some route march in the neighbourhood. A fine company of 250 young volunteers marched through a few days ago.

The recruits (for 1914) I am told are the most interesting.

---

[47] The Landstürme was the German equivalent of the Home Guard.

144

They are young men of 20 & so strong, fair and healthy & all with fine limbs. They march off with songs in the early morning to the station while the streets are dark. There are no tearful adieux, or sad faces. They go as if to a great duty, proudly, smiling – and smoking cigars – their friends pressing their hands and smiling too.

Some of the Landsturm have gone with flowers in their rifles.

[...]

Of my own affairs there is nothing of much interest. I have seen General Exner thrice about the camp and he has promised to do all in his power to help the cause. But I have no faith in these poor types of 'Irishmen' – demoralised and Anglicised.

Even Fr. Crotty, who tried to think well of them, gives them up. They have discovered that he is an out and out nationalist and wants to see Ireland free – and they pass him by rudely now – many of them – or in silence or even make remarks to the effect that 'they' are 'good Redmondites'. He says they are the scum of Ireland, and richly deserve the sound hiding the Germans gave them.

The German non-commissioned officers and the men despise them openly – and draw very invidious comparisons between them, their bearing, and the French prisoners beside them. The latter are men of a country – men knowing the cause they fight for, and citizens of a citizen army just as the German soldiers are. All one great armed community. The 'Irish' are sold hirelings – hired men, who have no native land, no cause and no object in the war save to win 'blood money.'

[…]

Father O'Gorman left for Rome this morning, and declares himself a quite convinced pro-German now. He has been won over completely and says he will be a faithful witness in Rome, and will see the Holy Father in private audience.

Limburg en route for Frankfurt, Thursday, 21 January 1915

I left Limburg an Lahn on Thursday 12.10 having bidden General Exner good bye the previous day. I left a copy of the agreement [treaty] with Fr. Crotty to keep safe and sound always. I propose having a certified copy of it too. At Frankfurt on Thursday afternoon I called on General de Graaff and told him of the situation in the camp and he promised to do all he could to help.

BERLIN

Saturday, 23 January 1915

I got to Berlin [...] at 8.20, having travelled all night from Frankfurt, and came to the Esplanade Hotel to be near Blücher and also Lay, the U.S. Consul General, whom I wish to consult on my proposed letter to Sir E. Grey, denouncing the criminal efforts of H.B.M. Minister at Christiania. I also want to apply for American citizenship and find out what steps I can take in advance to procure it.

[...]

I wrote Meyer on getting here & sent it by messenger to his house, 3 Sommerstrasse, & got telephone reply to say he would call on me at noon. He came & at once told me that Adler's sudden return, notified to me by the telegram to Limburg, was due to the fact that he had extracted from Findlay a written promise, 'in the name of the British Govt.' to pay him, Adler Christensen, the sum of £5000 sterling on my being secured & handed over to the British!

This precious document, signed by Findlay on official Legation paper, Meyer assured me they had at the Foreign Office and would 'show me' (!) when I called. I said I should call on Wedel at 5.30. Meyer suggested a plan for catching Findlay's vessels and suggested my seeing Isendahl tomorrow, Sunday. I agreed, pointing out that now that I had got the convincing proof I should have to use it very quickly to forestall the inevitable action the British Government would, I felt sure, announce when Parliament assembles in February.

I went to Wedel at 5.30 & after some delay Meyer brought several bound volumes of official papers (dealing I perceived with my visit to Berlin & having letters of my own filed among them) and in one of these three volumes reposed in a special docket Findlay's pledge to Adler. It had already been numbered and sealed with a paper seal of the Auswärtiges Amt! It promised Adler not only the £5000 for my body 'with or without companions' but guaranteed him 'immunity for his action' and to send him to U.S.A., if he desired it.

British Legation,
Christiania,
Norway.

On behalf of the British
Government I promised that if,
through information given by
Adler Christensen, Sir Roger
Casement be captured either with
or without his companions, the
said Adler Christensen is to receive
from the British Government
the sum of £5000 to be paid
as he may desire.

Adler Christensen is also to
enjoy personal immunity & to
be given a passage to the
United States should he desire it.

M. de C. Findlay
H. B. M. Minister

The highly incriminating authorisation signed by Findlay on British Legation headed paper pledging diplomatic immunity for Christensen, if he provided information leading to the capture of Casement. Casement circulated the note widely. [Charles Curry]

The letter is the most damning piece of evidence, I suppose, ever voluntarily given by a Government against itself!

I told Wedel that the document was mine, my property and that I should use it quickly and outlined my intention of formally charging Grey with responsibility for a dastardly criminal conspiracy – & also of my intention to inform the Norwegian Government & to go personally to Norway to do so. He agreed, in a perfunctory sort of a way; he suggested that they should 'pay' all Adler's expenses while engaged in getting this paper from Findlay – to which I declined to assent. I pointed out that the matter was one between me and the British Government & that Adler was my servant and I could not allow him to accept money from the German Government. He has already been given 400 marks to cover his expenses in returning to Christiania to carry out the 'Mjölnir' incident – & they say produced 'no results' & they don't know why.

I left the F.O. at 7 after a talk with Meyer who gave me a long letter from John Devoy of 1 January in New York and also one from Adler, in pencil, written in the train when he was going back to Christiania from this after bringing the Findlay guarantee. They kept it for nearly three weeks!

I then went on to Adler and found him just writing a long letter to myself to explain things. This he gave me unfinished and I add it to the 'dossier.'

His account of how he got Findlay to give him the written pledge is the most amusing one. He could have got plenty of money instead – £500 as an 'advance' – but he swore & said he would not go a step further in the matter unless Findlay gave him a written pledge. This Adler said:

'I did for you; you told me not to get money from him, but to do all I could to get him to commit himself in writing – so I held out. I swore at him, cursed him, & told him to … himself (a fearful sailor's sarcasm) & left him. He stormed & protested & said his word was that of the Br. Government and he had pledged it to me.

'I left the Legation & he sent after me & brought me back & remonstrated again. I stuck to my guns, and was more and more insolent and rude and stalked off. As I got to the gate down the avenue, the footman ran after me & said the minister wished to see me. I told him to tell Mr. Findlay to … himself & went on. Then a man came to the Grand Hotel & asked me to go to the Legation again – and so I went. Mr. Findlay said he would give me the written promise and I said "All right, but here now, I want to see you write it with your own hand," whereupon he sat down and did it, I standing by.'

On getting this proof Adler tore back to Berlin, sending me the wire to meet him and informing me of the 'good news'. I was then at Limburg. […] Meyer met him at the station & to him Adler gave the Findlay pledge 'to be given to Sir Roger Casement.'

Meyer promised to give it to me & took it from him on this condition.

That was on 5ᵗʰ January – and although I wrote repeatedly asking to be informed of the state of affairs I got no reply from Meyer or Wedel. They had determined to stick to the Findlay proof, for their own ends, & to bluff me out of it by offering to pay all Adler's 'expenses'!!!

As to the 'Mjölnir' voyage it failed because Findlay said that Adler must travel with me, so as to get a hold of my 'box of papers' and incriminating documents when the moment came. Findlay said 'If Sir Roger is alone, and he sees a man of war coming he will throw the box overboard – so you must be with him to get a hold of it and keep it for us.' A wise precaution!

Adler went to Christiansand to meet the 'Mjölnir' there on 9 January as I had directed him in the 'new instructions'. Findlay sent a special man with him to telegraph my movements, etc. after arrival. When, however, I did not appear on the 'Mjölnir' at Christiansand, Adler had to explain the reason to Findlay by letter only that, owing to his refusal to give him (Adler) the guarantee he had warned me that I might not be safe on the 'Mjölnir', so I had not travelled by her. This he had done from 'revenge.' Findlay accepted the explanation and the position is where it was practically when I sent Adler back to Findlay on Christmas day with the 'Mjölnir' plot. With this great change – that I now hold the warrant of shame and ignominy His Majesty's Government signed by their own Minister in their name!

Adler says a good plan can still be devised to catch Findlay's ships. *Nous verrons*. I have caught more than that. I have caught the British Govt. in flagrante delicto – & with all the difficulties put in my way, too, by this stupid, pig-headed German Govt. And now these men actually have the audacity, the bare faced audacity, to seize my proof and regard it as a 'State paper' of their wretchedly run Foreign Office! Truly they merit all the opprobriums Billy Tyrrell heaped on them in the London Foreign

Office that November day in 1912 when he was discharging his soul into my ears – and Lichnowsky outside the door and announced as he spoke! It is almost impossible to have true dealings with them. You never know their mind save that if there is a wrong way to tackle a <u>human</u> problem they are likely to choose it.

This Zeppelin raid over the East coast is a proof. They rejoice at a silly exploit – that can only damage the German cause in the eyes of the world – for the English will represent it, through all their myriad channels of public perversion, as a 'deliberate murder of women and children.' I told Wedel so – & after first demurring, he agreed & said that I had expressed his opinion.

In the evg, after leaving Adler, I dined with Blücher and Baron von Roeder (the Emperor's Master of Ceremonies). Von Roeder agreed entirely with my judgment on the Zeppelin raid over East England and said he had that very day been saying this very thing to Count Oppersdorff, the Catholic chief of 'the Centre.' Oppersdorff had asserted that the raid was a great thing and just what was wanted.

As regards the Irish civil prisoners in Ruhleben, von W. says they cannot release the whole 163 as I had urged, as an 'act of good will to Ireland' but would let out some 20 or so if I selected them – as was done with Kelly and Professor Macran. The former got off safely two weeks and more ago & Kelly followed a few days ago.

I got [...] handed me at the Continental Hotel, a letter from New York, from Padraic Colum of 16 Decr. last, forwarding me a letter from Bulmer Hobson of 22 October last, from Dublin. Three months & two days to reach me! Colum said in his very brief covering letter that 'the correspondence in the *Tribune*' which he sent me would amuse me. It did not come. The outer letter was opened – but Bulmer's letter closed. This letter of B's gave me only the Volunteer news of Ireland & showed the quite disgraceful part Redmond and his nominees on the Provisional Committee had been playing since the gun-running at Howth on 26 July.

Dear old John Devoy's letter was a very welcome one – along with some bad news it had much good. Among other things that a special messenger who had been sent to Ireland (following my request by cable early in Nov) had brought back a satisfactory report and also that my sister had been kept advised and supplied. So my anxiety on her head, poor desolate, lonely old girl, surrounded by sneers, jibes and hatred, is somewhat diminished.

[...]

I told von Wedel [...] that were I sure of getting over I should return to U.S.A. but the risks are too great. And yet I know not what to do. To stay in Berlin or in Germany, idle, inactive and with the huge disappointment of the Irish Brigade failure staring me in the face, & with no hope of further action by the German Govt. [...] Besides I have not the means to live here. Life is very expensive and I must stay at expensive hotels and incur constant outlays. It would be better to retire to Norway – convict Findlay up to the hilt – get H.M. Gov't exposed & <u>if necessary</u>, return to Germany, should Father Nicholson succeed with the soldiers.

[...]

Count Blücher gave me some copies of the *Times* up to 7 January – full of German 'atrocities' and plausible accounts of the 'Allies' progress in the

Bulmer Hobson: The friendship between Casement and Hobson was critical to the preparations for the 1916 Risi Hobson was a tireless grassroots campaigner and instigated various republican / nationalist initiatives including Dungannon Clubs, Na Fianna Éireann and edited newspapers such as *The Irish Peasant* and *The Republic*. [Bulm Hobson, *Ireland Yesterday and Tomorrow*]. This photograph of Hobson and McGarrity would suggest that Casem was in touch with IRB networks a full decade before his mission to Germany. [Digital Library@Villanova Universi field. Soissons with its loss of fully 20.000 French and 35 guns had not then come to hand.

Blücher is, (as usual) full of ridiculous stories.

[...]

Berlin, Sunday, 24 January 1915

[...]

Meyer came to lunch with me (and tried to pay for it although my guest!). We went (with Adler) to the General Staff of the Admiralty, where I saw first Admiral Behncke – & then Captain Isendahl & the other Captain Heydell [...] Adler told them the whole Findlay story to their intense amusement. They asked to see the guarantee and Meyer said 'impossible to take it out of the F.O. as it is a State Document' – this in my hearing, but in German; Adler told me of it and looked at me as it was being said! Nothing decided there as to my return to Norway. They will let me know.

I told Wedel y'day that the Findlay letter was mine & I should use it quickly against the British Government not against Findlay, their poor agent. He hummed & hawed & deprecated haste but could offer no real objection and had to say 'of course, Sir Roger, the letter is yours when you need it.'

Fr. Nicholson came to see me in the morning and had long talk about Philadelphia &c. &c. I showed him the agreement about the Irish cause of 23 Dec. which greatly interested him. A historic document he truly called it. I spent the afternoon also with Fr. N[icholson] and Adler at the Excelsior Hotel & spent the evening with them – Adler removed there from the Continental Hotel & Fr. Nicholson very kind to him.

I was more and more uncertain how to act about Findlay with the Germans silently stealing the letter & practically saying to me "you can use this only as we choose" my hands tied. However I decided to write my letter to Grey. This I had begun in Limburg on 12 January, but had been forced to keep over until I was aware of the end of the 'Mjölnir' incident.

I met Lay, the U.S. Consul General today (Sunday). I left my card on him yesterday after arriving and by appointment to talk with him on Monday at 2 in the 'Rotunde' of the hotel.

Berlin, Monday, 25 January 1915

Professor Schiemann called, but I got him away quickly as Fr. N. was coming. Latter to lunch with me – and asked him to come at 5 to go to F.O. with me. I intended he should see the Findlay letter without telling them in advance. They are having it photographed for me.

[...]

At 5 I went with Fr. N to F.O. & saw Wedel at 6.30 only after long wait.   He got the Findlay letter from Meyer who brought it in a portfolio (like a baby being nursed & with a look of grave dislike on his Jew face) – & Fr N. read it, while I copied it in pencil on my knees. Wedel turning his face aside but seeing me doing it of course.

I said I wanted to make quite clear the exact terms of it & particularly of the 'immunity' granted Adler.

Berlin, Tuesday, 26 January 2015

Still in doubt how to act – my wish is to write Grey, renouncing all honours, recounting his crime & go to Norway to send the letter thence & challenge investigation on spot.

Began writing the final form of my letter to Grey, but only a draft of what I <u>think</u> of saying.

Fr. Nicholson in morning – & told him all about the Findlay letter and the F.O. here bagging it & keeping me for 3 weeks entirely ignorant of its existence and how I only learned thro' the fact that Adler had returned unexpectedly & I found him here.

I saw the Baroness von Nordenflycht & Gussie in the afternoon and told them all – not about F.O. here or my doubts of them but only of the Findlay incident & letter.

I dined on return with Fr Nicholson at the Excelsior, giving him last words. He goes Limburg in morning by 8 a.m. train. I back at 1.20 a.m. in deep snow to Esplanade.

Berlin, Wednesday, 27 January 1915

Today the Emperor's birthday. I wrote two letters to von Wedel – one on the day – and one about the Irish civil prisoners at Ruhleben, and sent them by special messenger.

Britain's Foreign Secretary, Sir Edward Grey, was a strong supporter of Casement's consular work in sub-Saharan Africa and the Amazon and supported his knighthood in 1911. However, Casement grew increasingly critical of Grey's ministry and wrote an excoriating letter to Grey in February 1915. [National Portrait Gallery, London]

[…]

Busy most of day on my letter to Grey writing steadily – discarding much. The difficulty is how much to leave out of it – to put in all the details a huge mistake.

[…]

I saw Mr. Lay, the U.S.A. Consul General, at 2.30 & asked if he perform certain notarial duties for me. I want an established record of the Christiania affair – and certified copies of a Declaration (my own) and to deposit copy of the Findlay guarantee. I did not tell him what it was I wanted, beyond to take an affidavit and obtain a certified copy of a document – for purposes of record.

He said he would let me know if his functions as acting British Consul permitted him to do this.

Father Nicholson left for Limburg this morning.

Berlin, Thursday, 28 January 1915

Writing my letter to Grey all day nearly & discussing things with Blücher – who is very angry at the Foreign Office business here over the letter & says he will tell von Jagow.

I went to F.O. at 6.30 & saw von Wedel & told him I had made up my mind to write Grey fully & to go to Christiania – he agreed. I said I should send the letter ahead by Adler probably and follow as soon as I could and fight the matter out in Christiania. Essential, I pointed out to act quickly as when the London Parliament assembles on 2 February there will be questions about me and then, if the Foreign Office there know they have failed to catch me, they will make a fine show of 'moral indignation' against my 'treason' & take some overt step. I want to be first in the field & expose them – before they get the ear of the world.

Wedel agreed and said I must act as I thought right. He is a gentleman & a friend.

Berlin, Friday, 29 January 1915

Got the Esplanade typist to type three copies of my letter to Grey finished. Got photos from Meyer of the Findlay letter to inclose.

All hurry & haste now to get ready for the flight to Norway. Decided to go myself on Sunday with Adler. I told Meyer and von Wedel. Former said would get 3 good private detectives to go with me – and so protect me and do all they could to help. Von Roeder and Blücher very much against my going to Norway. Meyer has a silly scheme for me to go there and try and get Findlay to kidnap me and through my three detectives to catch him and his and hand them over to the police. I rejected this on von Roeder's and Blücher's advice – and decided only to go to Norway openly, as myself, to challenge Findlay and invite the Norwegian Government to investigate the whole affair.

Berlin, Saturday, 30 January 1915

Busy writing all morning. Gave typed copies of my letter to Grey to Meyer to get typed for me. I want 20 or 25 copies – to send out to various Legations and public quarters, as soon as I have posted to Grey – and I am begging Meyer to see that copies are sent to the Berlin press too. He says they will publish it textually with the photo in 'N-D All Zeitung' – & cable it to U.S.A. &c. &c.

I took letter to F.O. at 5 p.m. & gave to Meyer for typing. I went on to tea at Astoria with von Roeder & Baroness von R. to meet a Fräulein de Bunsen, a cousin (but a German) of the Sir M[aurice] de Bunsen once at Lisbon or Madrid. A pleasant woman. I did not tell von R. I had decided to go to Christiania in morning as he would object I knew. Blücher was there also. I did not tell him either that I was off to Norway.

To Excelsior & told Adler come early & get my baggage & go to the Stettin Bahnhof with [it] for 10.33 train to Sassnitz.

Berlin, Sunday, 31 January 1915

I left the Esplanade early & walked to Stettin Bahnhof alone in snow & cold over Thiergarten at 9.30 a.m. At Station Adler found that the 10.33 train to Sassnitz misses the boat! A fine change of plan. The train only gets in at 2.59 to Sassnitz town, 20 minutes by train from the wharf, & the boat goes at 2 p.m., a change of hour due to the presence in the Baltic of some (supposed) English submarines. One of these attacked the gunboat 'Gazelle' a few days ago off Rügen itself & torpedoed her. So the mail boat to Traelleborg now crosses only by daylight – & owing to this change of plan one has to leave Berlin the night before, sleep at Stralsund, & go on to Sassnitz thence by an early train to catch the boat at 2. Accordingly when Meyer came at 11 with the three detectives the thing had to be all changed.

I returned but to the Continental Hotel where I spent the day in grave doubt.

Meyer brought me the 20 copies of the letter to Grey typed last night at F.O. but so full of errors I had to send them all back. He came at 6.45 p.m. again for me & hurried me off to the Station with the three detectives & Adler. Everything in confusion. He tells me the German Admiralty sent to warn me that the English submarine might stop the mailboat in the Baltic & demand my surrender! The Staff think it possible.

If a spy is at Sassnitz they wd. surely do it. What did I propose?

I said I should go on & if this happened I'd resist & not be taken alive. Wd. the detectives fight too? Meyer said 'Surely – they will fight to the death.' Adler agreed also. We left at 7.18 – the three detectives in a 2nd class car – & Adler with me. At Stralsund at 11.50 & to the Bahnhof Hotel – & to bed in my clothes greatly upset and wondering how best to proceed. Not afraid of the submarine but of the action of the Br. Govt. in Norway, their influence there, their power and gold and my own penniless and defenceless position. To go out, single handed, to thus challenge the mightiest Govt. in the world and to charge them publicly with infamous criminal conspiracy through their accredited representative is a desperate act. I have no money; no friends; no support; no Govt., save that of the one bent on destroying me, to appeal to. They are all-potent and will not sacrifice Findlay without a fight and in that fight they must win. Such were my reflections through the night.

Berlin to Sassnitz, Monday, 1 February 1915.

After a hardly spent night – I got up at 5.30 & was got off at 6.50 (I think) for Sassnitz.

Arrived there about 9 & to the Monopol Hotel to wait for the boat. There I went over the pros and cons with Adler, burned some papers I found the enemy might seize if I were arrested and finally decided to return to Berlin tomorrow instead of going on. I told the three detectives this & sent wires to Montgelas (Wedel being away at Frankfurt I knew). Spent a miserable day.

The Baltic partly frozen. The Sound between Stralsund & Rügen quite frozen over hard & passages cut for the boats and train ferry. Sledges with bells in Stralsund. Swedish faces & blue eyes on many. A charming old city. The three detectives cannot help me really. It is not kidnapping now I fear – but the direct, open assault of the British Government & some demand for my surrender or else a law case in which with all their wealth & power, poor Adler & I would cut a sorry figure.

Sassnitz to Berlin, Tuesday, 2 February 1915

Left Sassnitz at 9 a.m. & arr. Berlin at 4 p.m. about. To F.O. & saw Wedel & told him why I had returned. He said he thought Findlay would never <u>dare</u> to fight or protest – that the 'guarantee' was too damning. I said all the same the risk was far too great of defeat & that I purposed sending my letter to Holland to be posted there & then when that was done & sure of to send out copies to the Govts. here represented. He agreed.

Decided to send Adler back to Moss at once to get his things, see his people & tell them & then return to Germany so as not to be there when the letter comes out or into Grey's hands as they might try to arrest him so as to bluff a poor penniless wretch & <u>compel</u> me to surrender to defend Adler.

Meyer came at 6 or 7 to the Continental Hotel where I took room (again) on 4th floor this time – I as Sir R.C. – no longer 'Mr. Hammond.' Meyer agreed to all. He came twice, at 6 & then again at 8.30.

A cruiser was to have gone over with my boat he said from Sassnitz – to Traelleborg to safeguard me against the lawless submarine.

He told me a pro-Irish Society[48] had been formed in Berlin <u>that very afternoon</u> and had put up 50.000 Marks as a first contribution to the Irish Cause which wd be placed at my disposal to spend as I thought best in the interests of Ireland. Generous indeed – but I cannot accept – at any rate it must be left to my friends in U.S.A. to decide.

Berlin, Wednesday, 3 February 1915

At Continental Hotel. Made a few slight changes in the letter to Grey & sent it to the Esplanade Hotel (typist) to copy for me. 3 copies to be ready by 5 p.m. Meyer undertook to get it off to Holland by special

---

[48] The name of this society in German was Die Deutsch-Irische Gesellschaft.

messenger tonight at 8.49 p.m. to be posted in Hague tomorrow. Adler left for Moss at 8.40 this morning via Warnemünde & Copenhagen. He should get there Thursday forenoon & leave at 8 p.m. again to return via Copenhagen & see his sister there.

I took the letter – final typed copy – for Grey to F.O. at 5.30 p.m. & gave it to Meyer & a copy to him for translation to German. He promised send it faithfully.

Then to the Hotel Astoria where I dined with the von Roeders & Blücher (whom I had already taken into my confidence) & to whom I told (the Baron & B.) all the change of plan & the new way of procedure against the Hereditary Enemy.

Very wretched & miserable all night.

Berlin, Thursday, 4 February 1915

At Continental Hotel most of day – gave a second copy of my Grey letter to Meyer for the German F.O. to have officially. Got 25 copies in all typed by the typist at Esplanade. She is splendid. Got all the letters ready to go out to the Legations & Embassies here with a covering note to each Minister.

Then to the Nordenflychts at 6 & stayed to supper with them. Told them I wanted to stay with them & they offered me a room there.

Meyer thinks the letter will by 'out' here by Saturday and I want to escape reporters.

Berlin, Friday, 5 February 1915

Two telegrams from Adler. One y'day saying arr[ive]d well & one to say he was leaving & wd. be here Saturday or Sunday.

Got all my letters ready for the Legations &c. &c. sent three copies to Rome – one to Mon. O'Riordan, one to Dr. O'Hagan & one to Fr. O'Gorman – begging them to use publicly & show Holy Father.

Stayed in hotel all day – busy & very anxious. Meyer told me they would not publish here first. Only after Rome or some country had got it out first. I agreed, as wise.

The letter should have been with Grey today. In the evening paper there is a telegram from Amsterdam, 5 Feb, saying that Grey in the H[ouse] of C[ommons]s had said in reply to questions – that 'Sir R's pension would be suspended pending investigation into his action against Gt Britain' & in reply to another question he said – the public liar! – that 'he did not know whether Sir RC was in <u>Germany or not</u>' !!!

Within a few hours of making that statement he should have rec'd my letter from Berlin.

Berlin, Saturday, 6 February 1915

Sent a long letter to John Devoy with Grey letter – also posted one – registered to Bryan & State Dept. – & then sent out all the following by head porter in a taxi:

1. To the Norwegian Minister
2. U.S.A. Embassy
3. Italian Embassy
4. Austro-Hungarian Embassy
5. Spanish Embassy
6. Swedish Legation
7. Danish Embassy
8. Dutch Embassy
9. Portuguese Embassy
10. Swiss Embassy
11. Greek Embassy
12. Roumanian Embassy

They were out by 10.30 a.m. to 1 p.m.

I wrote to Graf Larisch at the Austro-H. Embassy privately, asking his help to get the letter public in Vienna.

Dinner Blücher came too & said Larisch wanted a copy of the letter – so I write one by hand – all typed copies used.

Wanted to get to Hamburg – as the Nordenflychts cannot have me – the room they promised taken by a sick friend from the front.

Wrote Mrs. Behrens at H'burg saying wd. come to her. But got a 'phone reply asking me to wait her letter sent in answer.

Told Blücher all my doubts & difficulties.

Wrote C'tss Hahn who called on me at 4 and told her the whole story. I called at Norwegian Legation at 5.20 p.m. & left my card.

Berlin, Sunday, 7 February 1915

Finished copy of letter for Larisch & took it at 1 to 11 Hildebrandstrasse and stayed to lunch there. A Count & Countess Hahn (I think) the mother apparently of Countess Larisch there too. Larisch very friendly – but not very intelligent I fear.

Wire from Adler at 7.50 to say arriving at 10. So went to meet him & took him to Excelsior Hotel. He reported all well at home. Had told his father all – & the schoolmaster, who is so afraid of being pulled into a 'State trial' he pretended he did not remember Adler telling him before in Decr. all about it.

Berlin, Monday, 8 February 1915

Mrs Behrens does not want me yet in Hamburg – says Ballin in Berlin & weather there terrible.

Adler wrote a brief note to the Norwegian Minister, on my advice, & left it in person at about 1 p.m. at the Legation. He offered to call whenever the Minister wished to see him. He wrote (with difficulty) in Norwegian.

Berlin and Potsdam, Tuesday, 9 February 1915

Adler called at Norwegian Legation & asked for Minister – not in.

I & he to Potsdam in afternoon where I thought of staying over the press row. But it was wretched & at the Palast Hotel where Klicks the manager of the Continental told me to stay, I got such a rude reception when they found I spoke only English that I returned to Berlin in despair. Called on Mrs. White & told her all about Christiania – also on Fräulein Meyer – but she not in. Mrs. White very friendly and wants me to go to Vienna. She recommended me to go out to the Sanatorium in the Grunewald (where I now am) and stay there over the row – I decided to do this.

Got a very courteous reply from the Swedish Minister by this morning's post – & tonight a very discourteous one from the Portuguese Minister. Latter refused to send my letter to Lisbon as it 'exceeded the legal rights of his Legation' & he returned it to me. The Swede wrote a charming note saying he had not failed to send my letter to Stockholm.

Berlin, Wednesday, 10 February 1915

Meyer came at 11 & carried off the letter of the Portuguese Legation to show to Zimmermann. He said the P. Minister was a 'cochon.' I agreed.

He said he thought no other Legation wd. treat my request so rudely. He further says he fears publication of my letter in Rome is impossible! They have doubtless heard by wire.

He says <u>all</u> the 'neutral' papers in Italy are 'pro-ally' & will say nothing against England.

He thinks, however, that the letter will be out 'by Friday' & I gather in Vienna. But Meyer is so secretive and lacking in frankness that he tells me nothing. I am treated by him as a sort of tool or agent – to be directed & used – but never kept informed or referred to – or consulted. Only directed. He now wants me to arrange to have Aubrey Stanhope, Karl Wiegand and Conger out to interview me on <u>Friday</u> (but not before!) and tell them all. I said much better do it before, so that they might be <u>ready</u> by Friday, not merely told on Friday. The wretched suspicion and mistrust of everybody that characterises all their conduct of public affairs again revealed here. I decided to go out to the Sanatorium at Grunewald – as 'Mr. Hammond' once more. This latter on Meyer's advice. He said he would arrange all with the police. Arranged with the Continental Hotel to forward letters for '<u>Mr. Hammond</u>.'

Meyer will make a mess of everything I am convinced. He & his department are the acme of <u>stupidity</u> & <u>blight</u>. I have lost all faith in their good sense & action. They are either always too late or else do the right thing in the wrong way.

I went out to the Grunewald Sanatorium at 3-4, calling on Mrs. White on the way and telling her and asking her to lunch and bring A. Stanhope and Karl Wiegand to lunch.

Then on to the Sanatorium & took a room there – Adler with me but he returns to stay with the head waiter of the 2nd floor of the Continental Hotel.

I spent a wretched evening in the Sanatorium. The people there largely military – & all very friendly and polite – but I feel so lonely & abandoned & want only to get away from police spies & military and all the rest of it.

Meyer telephoned at 5 to say '<u>not before Friday</u>' to see the U.S.A. correspondents. Meantime I have asked Mrs. White to bring them! I'll adhere to the invitation.

Especially as today's news is that England has prohibited <u>all cables from the Continent</u>!

This is a fine measure of freedom of communication! My God! How much more will the world have to stand from that Bitch & Harlot of the North Sea!

This measure is <u>asserted</u> to be in connection with the transport of Kitchener's army to the Continent. That may be – but if so it would be the <u>other</u> way about & no cable communication <u>to</u> the Continent from England – whereas it is from the Continent to the outside world they have interdicted.

It is much more likely that the measure is a part of their d....d. conspiracy against me. They fear mightily my charge coming out in U.S.A. <u>first</u> & before they have arranged their version & publicly branded me as a 'traitor' before I get the public charge brought against them. This will surely be their game.

And while they are arranging that, here I am a semi-prisoner at the Sanatorium under a false name, with a wholly false entry of my name &c. &c. & depending on Mr. Meyer to make all right with the police.

After the various proofs I have had of their hopeless ineptitude I should not wonder if I were arrested in the morning.

Berlin (Grunewald Sanatorium), Thursday, 11 February 1915.

I am in my room at the Sanatorium writing up my diary & eating my heart out. An agent of the secret police has just called (11.20 a.m.) to ask for my 'military pass'. I have none – I gave him the old police card of Mr. Hammond which I happily still have & referred him to the Auswartiges Amt for further information. It is highly possible they will bungle things there & I may be hauled off to jail.

BRIDGING ENTRY,
MARCH TO DECEMBER 1915

Berlin, 28 March 1916

My 'Diary' ended here.

I was so disillusioned & miserable from this on – so utterly out of touch with the monitors of the German F.O. that I saw the whole aim & object of my journey was a failure. The <u>only</u> thing I had to show for all my sacrifice (& folly) was the Treaty. <u>This</u> was a historic fact.

Here, in a formal agreement signed with the Seal of State, the Imperial Govt. had pledged itself to take certain steps to assist Ireland to gain complete independence & in the event of these proving successful to recognise publicly and support the independent Govt. so established.

All that I stayed on in January for was based on this Treaty. I hoped that, even while I saw the futility of the Treaty since a possible German victory faded away further & further into the limbo of the lost. Still this Treaty justified <u>me</u> – & it did more.

It was, in itself, a recognition of Ireland in the world – of Ireland a Nation – an extraordinary admission to have obtained in such set official terms from the most arbitrary of Govts. My <u>only</u> hope was to have it published.

If that could be done, I saw its value to the <u>cause</u> of Irish liberty in the future & to the inspiration of those holding up the flag today. Moreover it was the surest means I possessed or could invoke to keep Irishmen out of the war.

Once it was proclaimed <u>urbi et orbi</u> it was clear that the real Nationalists of Ireland would have an answer to England & Redmond that no one had dreamed of. It became then, to try & get the Treaty published.

I sent copies of it to U.S.A. – but only in March – as I had been asked by the F.O. to 'keep it quiet'. But it was obvious that if Irishmen in the

U.S.A. were to be moved to great effort they must be informed of the basis on which our hopes rested. So at length I got the Treaty sent over & I subsequently learned it had arrived safely – not the original of course, but a copy.

I was almost completely cut off from communication with America. On one occasion nearly four months passed without a letter coming thro'.

And I could not say all I thought or wanted to, because I did not know who would read my letters en route. Thus we were often at cross purposes.

I knew the German offensive had failed on the West[ern] front.

It was really broken in Nov. 1914 by Ypres & broken by the English!

This fact I realized in the beginning of 1915 – gradually. I saw that all the talk of 'getting to Calais' was talk & that the German lines on the West front wd. remain (at the best) where they were & that the war would gradually take on an attitude of 'stalemate' unless one thing happened – viz – the defeat of the Br-French in Turkey & a successful Turkish advance on Egypt with a possible later movement on India. I had never changed my fixed point of view that England was the enemy & that unless England could be really & vitally threatened Germany must, in the end, be forced to her knees.

I always preached this. My whole German-Irish policy was founded on this perception.

At a luncheon at the very end of March or beginning of April 1915, given in my honour by Graf Henckel [von] Donnersmarck (brother of my friend Ctess 'Tessa' Hahn) there was a Baron von Schröder, a brother of the Baron in London. This German brother had expressed much earlier a wish to meet me – to the von Roeders.

At length I met him at Haenckel-D's luncheon party in the flat in Kurfurstendamm. I sat between Princess Reuss and Princess Hohenlohe – the Hohenlohe who was daughter of Count Münster I think – a nice woman, the Blüchers called 'Baby Hohenlohe.' Princess Reuss I had met more than once before.

Baron v. S. talked about the Findlay affair before we went in to the dining room – & also about Ireland. I saw clearly he had no opinion at all of the Irish question – despised it & he almost frankly said so.

I remarked 'if the German Govt has no sympathy at all for Ireland or any aim or policy in respect of it I wonder why they issued their Declaration of 20 Novr. last year.' He smiled & shrugged his shoulders – I

went on – 'That being so as I perceive also – I see no reason w/
remain in Germany.'

The trouble was & has been always that I <u>had</u> to stay in Germany. I
have been virtually a prisoner from the first day I landed. Ringed round
by the Br. Fleet!

Once the 'Findlay affair' arose there was no return for me. I should
have gone back to the U.S. on many occasions – for I saw again & again
in the late winter and spring of 1915 that the German Govt. had <u>no</u> policy
at all about Ireland. No hopes, aims or plans.

They fully justified Findlay's statement that 'The German govt. don't
care a rap about Ireland but they will welcome Sir Roger in order to make
trouble for us and use him for their own ends.'

That I had long since found out was true – & that (except for the Treaty,
where I had completely beaten them at their own game, & committed
them to an Irish policy) it was useless for me to remain in Germany. My
heart was breaking. I knew I was being fooled & I did not trust a word
they said to me.

With the failure to recruit the Irish Brigade & the exposure of the
Findlay affair they had got, as they thought, all they could out of me &
'the German-Irish Alliance.'

They wanted to drop it.

This was amply proved later on, by John Devoy's letters to me. They
had squeezed me dry, & they did not want to be committed further.

In April 1915 came [Joseph Mary] P[lunkett] from Ireland with his
great tale of the planned revolution there. I discounted all that – & sat on
it and him as vigorously as was possible.

I told him just what I had often told Wedel at the F.O. that no rebellion
or rising in Ireland could possibly succeed of its own unaided effort. The
<u>sine qua non</u> of a successful military movement in Ireland, today far more
than in 1798, 1690, 1641 or 1598-1601 was the military (& naval) support
of a great Continental power.

To attempt a rising in the streets of Dublin in 1915 I held was worse
than folly – it was criminal stupidity. ,

But I said 'if you do it – if you if you are bent on this act of idiocy I
will come & join you (if the Germans will send me over) & stand & fall
beside you. Only I deprecate it wholly and regard it as the wildest form of
boyish folly – I am not responsible for it and while I strongly disapprove
it, if these boys break out I could not, in honour, refuse to stand beside

167

them, since however vain & futile their fight might be, it wd. be a fight –
an act, a deed – & not talk, talk, talk.'

I who had always stood for action (but not this action & certainly not
in these circumstances) could not stay in safety in this land while those
in Ireland who cherished a manly soul were laying down their lives for
an ideal.

Just before P[lunkett] arrived in Berlin – it was 16 April he came
from Switzerland – Fr. Nicholson, who had been at Limburg since end of
January 1915, came up to see me.

He said there was a ray of hope of the Brigade being formed after all
– that quite a number of men in camp were listeners & that, in addition
to Quinlisk (the young corporal of the 18th R.I. Rgt. who had stepped out
the first day) there were two very good men.

Keogh and Dowling, who had been backing up his, Fr Nicholson's,
propaganda with great hardihood.

He asked me to see these men, & if I thought it well to then come
down to Limburg & perhaps I'd succeed in enrolling enough men to have
the treaty proclaimed.

I sent for the men – Quinlisk, Keogh & Dowling.

They were brought to Berlin by order of the Kriegs Ministerium.
A Hauptmann van Lübbers was the intermediary – I was then at the
Baroness von Nordenflychts with a threatened lung attack, her brother Dr
Muhlig said. They were kept for ten to 12 days at the Hotel Prinz Wilhelm
in Dorotheen Strasse <u>with no one in Berlin knowing</u>!

I asked repeatedly at the F.O. where they were – no one there knew!
Finally, by chance, I learned they had been for two weeks at the little hotel.

Meantime I had left the Baron von N's & was at the Eden Hotel (once
more). The three young soldiers were brought to me (in plain clothes of
course) by the soldier guard who had come up with them from Limburg.

I saw them several times at the Hotel and introduced them to P[lunkett]
('Mr Petre'). They begged me to come down to Limburg, saying they felt
convinced that some 200 men at least could be induced to come out.

I explained pretty plainly the position that I did not believe now any
military help for Ireland was possible – the seas were closed & held tight
by England – but the political value & importance to the Irish cause of
the Treaty remained & if I could succeed in having it published based on
the live fact that a body of Irishmen were in arms, under our flag, it would
uplift the Irish heart all the World over & revive & restart much of the

true national spirit we had been steadily losing under the demoralization of the Parliamentary campaign.

They saw the truth of this & begged me to go down to Limburg & make a final effort.

I agreed.

I told the G.G.S. & F.O. of the hopes of the three young soldiers & Fr. N's hopes & asked for Captain Boehm to be placed at my disposal to take the three young soldiers back to Limburg & get all the liberties c ... &c. &c. necessary for a fresh recruiting effort.

This was at length agreed & I asked P[lunkett] to accompany Boehm & the three young men. This I did with the following in mind.

I had more & more come to the conclusion that the German govt. were wholly insincere in their pro-Irish professions – & I hesitated more & more at the thought of getting a body of Irish soldiers to commit treason just for an ideal.

I told many of my doubts & fears to P[lunkett]. I said I wanted him really to be a check on Boehm & to see for himself how things went. I wd. follow in a very short time, but I did not want Boehm to have a free field & no check. And yet Boehm was far the best, more friendly & more capable for the purpose of all German officers I had met.

The G.G.S. & F.O. again wakened up – the mere prospect of getting 'the Irish Brigade' formed stirred the dry bones to life.

The Under Secretary of State Zimmermann said he would see me! Assessor Meyer who had not been near me since 1 March called furiously & asked if there was 'anything I wanted.'

Once again I had become useful – or possibly useful.

I went down to Limburg on 12 May, a day or two after the others had arrived there. They had got 53 men the first few days – & there things stuck. A 'circular' had been sent out by Boehm off his own bat (which I have never yet seen!) that Keogh told me (long afterwards) had done harm. I don't even now know what was in it, but I fancy <u>it</u> may be the origin of 'a German farm' and 'a German wife' the *Graphic* of 26 February attributed to me! I knew by long experience that in underhand or stupid acts of this kind, off their own bat, the German officials all excelled.

I had seen in March, or the beginning of April the batch of printed questions Wedel & Co had sent out to the men at Limburg without even consulting me. Indeed it was only by chance I heard of this gross act.

The Graphic, 26 February 1915: the front page cartoon by William Hatherell, the Edwardian newspaper illustrator, was captioned 'The Voice of the Traitor!'. He imagined Casement speaking to a group of Irish POWs at Limburg. Casement was outraged by the image and initiated legal proceedings against The Graphic. [Angus Mitchell].

I called one day on Wedel & found him with a pile of printed papers before him, which he was looking through. He showed me them – saying – 'It is strange Sir Roger how the answers to these questions seem to be stereotyped' – handing me a batch of the papers. They consisted of a printed series of questions addressed to the Irish prisoners of war in Limburg – such as 'What was the political feeling in Ireland when you left?'

'What was the sentiment in your Regiment to the English Govt?'

I was staggered – dumbfounded. I turned on him & said: 'Is it possible you put such questions to the Irish prisoners? Why, no wonder you get these answers. What could the German Govt. have been dreaming of? The men, practically all answer you alike – that it is none of your business & that they don't admit your right to put such questions to them? They are perfectly right. I might as an Irishman say things to them – but you can't. You have here done your best to convince them that I <u>am</u> a German agent, as the opponents of my movement assert.'

Wedel was far too stupid to understand. I think – I presume he, Meyer and the great luminous mind of the G.G.S. or Kriegsministerium had decided that they knew much better than I did the mind of the Irishmen & they would find out themselves the possibility of the movement by this <u>adroit</u> series of questions.

All these things – I can touch here on only a few of the causes of my ever growing want of faith in the authorities – convinced me that while it was vitally desirable to proclaim the Treaty & its publication depended on a certain number of men being enrolled, I should not be justified in doing anything more than I had already done to induce men to join. No temptation was to be offered. P[lunkett] was far less scrupulous. He said once – 'We'll have to get them, if we kidnap them'. I said, 'No – we must continue only & <u>solely</u> to appeal to their patriotism.'

On reaching Limburg, Boehm, P[lunkett] & the three young soldiers met me. I had got them uniforms during their stay in Berlin & these they wore in the camp only.

It was arranged I should address a Company of men called 'B Company' – & this I did on May 15. I got the gist of my remarks – they were delivered without prior notes or writing – printed & circulated.[49]

---

[49] Later published as *Objects of an Irish Brigade in the present war: Text of an address by Sir Roger Casement delivered on 15 May to B Company of the Irish soldiers at Limburg.*

The Gaelic American.

A JOURNAL DEVOTED TO THE CAUSE OF IRISH INDEPENDENCE, IRISH LITERATURE AND THE INTERESTS OF THE IRISH RACE.

Vol. XIII., No. 9. Whole No. 909.   NEW YORK, FEBRUARY 27, 1916.   PRICE FIVE CENTS.

NEW YORK DEMANDS GENUINE NEUTRALITY.

Great Mass Meeting Fills The Hippodrome And Voices Strong Protest Against The Administration's Lax Performance Of Its Duty And Tame Submission To England's War On American Commerce—Governor Colquitt Of Texas, Representatives Parker Of Pittsburgh And Martin Of South Dakota Deliver Vigorous Speeches And Judge Tiernan Presides — Resolution Call For The Assertion Of This Country's Rights, Impartiality Towards All Belligerents And Condemn England's Misuse Of American Flag.

ENGLAND'S HIRELINGS ASSAILING CASEMENT.

Torrent Of Abuse And Lies Flung At Ireland's Envoy To Germany From Both Sides Of The Atlantic Attests The Value Of His Services—British Government Realizes The Danger and Sets Its Horde Of Salaried Scribes, Placemen And Emissaries To The Work Of Defaming His Character—Real Importance Of Shameless Lies Of The Dirty Lot Is A Disgraced English Diplomat In America—Gaelic-Gwin's Times Of Falsehoods. A Disgrace To American Journalism.

VILE ENGLISH LIE NAILED

Joseph McGarrity Refutes a Foul Libel on Sir Roger Casement Published in Many Papers by the "Marquise De Fontenoy" Syndicate and Written by a Discredited Englishman.

One of the stumbling blocks was the oath of allegiance – & there I said every man must decide for himself. I only pointed out that Kings owed a duty to their people quite as much as a people to them. Kings – & I emphasised how false all <u>our</u> sovereigns had been to their trust as Kings of Ireland, no less than of Great Britain.

I was in a very difficult position. In my heart I felt much with the men – & I understood their point of view – on the other hand I saw the great importance of the Treaty to Ireland & the vital need of getting a small force together so that we should be able to publish it. So much might hinge on its publication. Not only in Ireland, where furious efforts were being made to get Irish men into the Army – but in America. So I tried but only within limits I felt to be honourable (for an open rebel).

I refused to bribe or tempt with money offers, beyond the compensation offer 'up to say £10' – for any monies a recruit to the Brigade would forfeit. Indeed I failed really just because I would adopt English methods. England was bribing, corrupting (& intimidating) Irishmen into her army of aggression & plunder – I could only offer the hope of striking a blow for Ireland – & that, too, a problematical one.

When it became clear that no more men would join at present, Boehm decided to take the 53 away to Berlin as a beginning. The promise made was that they should be put into uniform at once, armed – & trained, in all respects, according to the Treaty clauses. This done & assurances thus conveyed to the many waverers in the camp that the thing was serious – photos were to be sent down of the men in uniform – then we might hope for more – possibly up to 200.

On 200 recruits the Treaty could be published.

> **Objects of an Irish Brigade in the present war.**
>
> **Text of an address by Sir Roger Casement delivered on 15. May to B company of the Irish soldiers at Limburg.**
>
> Sir Roger Casement speaking to the men said, roughly as follows:
>
> ‹You have been told, I daresay that I am trying to form an Irish Brigade to fight for Germany; that I am a German agent; and that an attempt is being made to suborn you, or tempt you to do something dishonest and insincere for the sake of the German Government and not for the welfare or Ireland.
>
> Well you may believe me, or disbelieve me (and nothing I could say would convince you as to my own motives:) but I can convince you, and I owe to yourselves as well as to myself to convince you that the effort to form an Irish Brigade is based on Irish interests only, and is a sincere and honest one, so far as my action with the German Government is concerned and so far as their action in the matter goes.
>
> An Irish Brigade if it be formed today, will rest on a clear and definite agreement wherein the German Government is pledged to aid the cause of Irish independence by force of arms, and above all, to aid Irishmen to themselves fight for their own freedom.
>
> The agreement that is the basis on which an Irish Brigade can be formed is one now in my hands, and which I will read to you.
>
> – 1 –

The 'Text of 15 May address at Limburg' was printed up and circulated to Irish prisoners. [National Library of Ireland]

I asked P[lunkett] and the three young recruiting soldiers to stay on at Limburg & keep the fire warm while the 53 were being put into uniform &c. &c. 'at Berlin.'

I told P[lunkett] this was to me a test case. If the G.G.S. agreed to treat the 53 'as soldiers' & carry out the provisions of the Treaty strictly & honourably I'd feel justified in going on with the attempt to get 200 men. But if not, then I should not feel justified in trying to persuade another man.

I would not lift a finger until I saw what was going to be done in this respect.

I wrote to Wedel urging the importance of getting the 53 into uniform &c. at once & then I went to Munich to see Gaffney. This journey I had long contemplated.

It was not merely to see Gaffney but to make enquiry on the spot as to an offer to get me back to America that had come from a friendly American there. If the plan was workable I might accept the offer & go.

Meantime I could do nothing at Limburg until I saw which way the War Office lot wd. jump over the 53 first fruits.

After about a week in Munich when the proposed U.S. journey was discussed & the means exposed – I returned to Limburg & found two fresh recruits there & P[lunkett] anxious to get back to Berlin. I sent him there & stayed on a day or two longer at Limburg – writing Wedel more than once & urging that the Treaty be sent to Bernstorff with instructions to publish on receipt & a cable.

Finally I returned to Berlin early in June – about 6th or 7th I think. I went to Wedel first. He agreed to all my proposals & said he had already sent the desired instructions to Bernstorff. Then to the G.G.S. with P[lunkett] – who was getting ready to return to Ireland via Switzerland. I wanted P[lunkett] to see for himself the dead wall of obstinate stupidity one was up against.

The G.G.S. (Nadolny & Frey) were furious at the poor results obtained. 'Only 53 men & we had ordered 100 uniforms!' was one of the chivalrous remarks by Nadolny. I very nearly said 'Send me the bill.' I urged the vital importance of going on with what had begun – & convincing the men in camp that the Govt. were serious & could be trusted – but the petty mind prevailed.

There were furious interviews at the F.O. between the military and the F.O. people. I will not go into the particulars here. P[lunkett] was present (in an anteroom) at one of these altercations & began (slowly – I fear) to understand. He asked at the G.G.S. for arms for Ireland. These were contemptuously refused by Nadolny who said that they had plenty of goodwill for Ireland (in his words!) but would give no arms. Arms must be provided by the Irish in America.

P[lunkett] was raging – & asked me if I could obtain him an interview with the Minister of War!!! I laughed & said you might as well ask to see the Emperor.

P[lunkett] left for Switzerland (with a photo of the Treaty in a hollow stick!) towards end of June. As I saw him off I felt the last link with hope was going from me for ever. I knew I was now & henceforth face to face with absolute failure, ending only in death – or contempt & derision & utter failure to understand all the difficulties around me. I was alone. I had practically ceased to have any hope of the F.O., the German Govt. or anything. The 53 were out at Zossen in a sort of convict garb – mixed up with the Mohamedan prisoners.[50]

I kept on urging the fulfilment of the Treaty promises to them – mindful and all as they were – the obligation could not be gainsaid. I insisted on its fulfilment.

Wedel wrote me at very end of June a letter, evidently a sort of severance of diplomatic relations, pointing out that the Irish in America had failed to show sufficient interest in the cause of Ireland & putting the blame on their shoulders. I replied very courteously rebutting the statement & pointing out that I should be very pleased if I could find in Germany any public expression of opinion about Ireland half so useful as Irish sympathy for Germany had been in America.

I sent copies of both letters over to America & packed up & left Berlin on 2 July – I hoped perhaps for ever. If possible I would get over to America. I was torn in two of course – for there were always the 53 at Zossen to be provided for & faith kept with them. But I saw that the best way to compel the Govt. to do its duty to them was to get out of Germany first – & once I was free to say just what I thought, then to send them an ultimatum & demand the strict fulfilment of their promises to the men. In any case I could do nothing by staying in Berlin. I could not advance anything there – for I could scarcely keep my face before these people – and there was nothing, absolutely nothing to discuss,

---

[50] The volunteers of the Irish Brigade were relocated to Zossen, a camp near Berlin. It was known as the 'Crescent Camp' because Muslim prisoners-of-war were held there.

The house where Roger Casement stayed in Riederau, beside Lake Ammersee, southwest of Munich.[National Library of Ireland]

I knew for an absolute certainty they had no care or thought about Ireland – only for themselves & that when they saw they could get no more out of me – & the poor betrayed 53 – they had no use for us. I was determined to do all I could to make them keep faith with the men at Zossen.

Throughout July & August I was out at Ammersee[51] – writing sometimes to urge the action as I desired for the men at Zossen – once I asked for my passport – & within a few days I learned that (on 4 Sept.) the men had been put into uniform & moved to new quarters.

Keogh wrote & begged me to go & see them – I did so – & as money arrived from U.S. at same time I was able to make financial arrangements that were satisfactory for paying them.

The difficulty was that there was nothing for them to do. When I gave up the attempt to (or thought rather) of going to U.S.A. then I returned to trying to do something with the handful of men at Zossen.

I told them of my idea – viz – of going East with them as provided in two of the clauses of the Treaty.

I began urging this on the German authorities & rec[eiv]ed assurances from Wedel that as soon as they had opened the road thro' Servia I might get underway. And so the thing went on. Always promising – always delaying. The want of officers was raised – no German officers available. Meantime no attempt was made to arm the men. They were only in uniform & behind barbed wire in a cage.

---

[51] Ammersee was a lake, southwest of Munich, and a popular resort during the summer.

Postcard showing the location of the house in Ammersee. Casement has written in pen 'I spent Summer of 1915 here'. [National Library of Ireland]

Finally, when I was again falling into deeper despair, one fine day Adler Christensen turned up bringing over Lt. Monteith from America – a fine piece of smuggling – Christensen had returned to America after I left Berlin for Munich. He had carried messages over from me to J[ohn] D[evoy] & Joe McG[arrity] & had behaved well at first & J.D. got him to smuggle Lt. Monteith back safe & sound to me. Monteith arrived about 22 October & after getting him 'recognized' I sent him down to Limburg – once again – to see if there was any chance of beating up more recruits. The military authts there wd. not allow him to wear his uniform!

That helped more than all else, I fancy, to convince the men there that the thing was a sham.

After two weeks at Limburg, I had to send for Monteith to maintain discipline at Zossen as things were getting worn there. He returned in Novr. 1915 & went out to Zossen to take on the command there. He has been there ever since – an invaluable man. Loyal, brave, untiring & of a great fidelity. What I should have done without him I know not. With him in charge at Zossen I was greatly relieved – but the wish to get to work & to get out of Germany & to justify "our treason" was strong on us. I urged again & again the march to the East.

Early in December I again saw Nadolny – 8 Decr – the first time since the stormy interview with P[lunkett] assisting towards middle of June. Frey, too, was there. Nadolny said they were doing all they could to get us down to Turkey. That Enver Pacha agreed – but the (German?) Commander-in-Chief at Bagdad refused. He was trying again – in another direction in Turkey.

A LAST PAGE

Berlin, St Patrick's Day, 17 March 1916

I write this beginning of what I feel is a last chapter on Patrick's Day in Berlin this year of war 1916. Last year on Patrick's Day I was also in Berlin, ill in bed, in the house of the Baroness von Nordenflycht.

Even then, hope had gone from me – for I realized then, already, that those I trusted here were little to be trusted and that their only interest in me lay in exploiting me, and the Irish cause in their own supposed interests.

Since then a hundred proofs have accumulated – and yesterday the climax came, and as now but little is left I begin, today, a hurried record of things that must be stated in order that some day the truth may be known.

In three weeks I shall probably be at sea in the maddest and most ill planned enterprise that the history of Irish revolutionary efforts offers. But it is not of my choosing, of my planning, or undertaken with my approval. I go because honour calls me to go – and because to stop it now (even if I could stop it) would involve others and perhaps bring greater grief. Moreover by going with the tiny band (12 men probably) that is to sail on 8 April I *may* save them – and perhaps Ireland too from a dreadful fate. To stay here, in safety, while those others go would do no good to Ireland – and would leave me a prey to eternal regret.

Thus while I strongly disapprove what is being attempted, and so wretchedly attempted with a foregone assurance of failure, I *must* lend it my countenance and accompany the forlorn hope.

And now to make a little daylight for the hereafter.

I will confine myself today to dealing with events only since the beginning of this year, trusting to the few days of quiet I hope still to get at Riederau am Ammersee[52] to put down earlier happenings, since

---

[52] The name of the resort town on the banks of lake Ammersee where Casement resided.

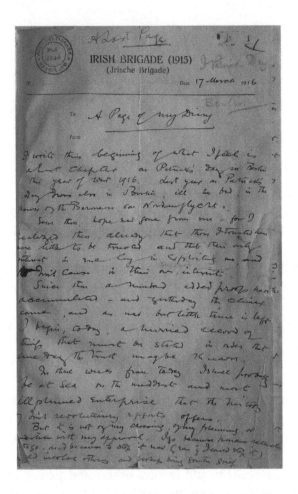

I stopped keeping a regular diary at the beginning of February last year.

I stopped that Diary when it became clear that I was being played with, fooled and used by a most selfish and unscrupulous government for its own petty interests. I did not wish to record the misery I felt or to say the things my heart prompted. But today it is my head compels me to this unwelcome task.

At the beginning of this year I was staying out at Zossen, the most wretched of men.

The small band of Irish soldiers who had volunteered in May last were there [...] in uniform, but still kept practically as prisoners of war, and Lt. Monteith in command of them. I had gone out to Zossen on 4th

December 1915, to be near him and the men, to encourage and cheer them in their bitter disappointment – and always in the hope that our long-urged journey to the East, to get into action, might be sanctioned. The General Staff here had promised me repeatedly, in December 1915, that the 'Brigade' should be sent East.

Enver Pasha had agreed and it only lay with the German ships in the East to accept the men. The final assurance was given me explicitly on 4 January 1916 (on return from a hurried run to Dresden) at the German General Staff [G.G.S.] that the corps would be sent to Syria, and that they would 'at once' be trained in the use of machine-guns. This promise, like all preceding promises – was not carried out.

Day by day I got worse. I had been ill for long – sick at heart and soul, with mind and nerves threatening a complete breakdown. No man was ever in a falser position. The truth I could not tell to my friends in America. I had no means of communicating with them, except by letter that had to pass through the hands of those I felt sure would read it – and to expose *their* perfidy thus would scarcely work.

MÜNCHEN   Kuranstalt Neuwittelsbach   Gartenansicht

Kuranstalt, Neuwittelsbach, Munich: The sanatorium where Casement stayed in early 1916 to recover from nervous exhaustion. [Angus Mitchell]

Finally I broke down and acting on the advice of a great doctor I went to a 'nerve rest' at the Kuranstalt, Neuwittelsbach, Munich. This was on 19 January 1916.

I was very ill on arrival – but I gradually got better. Then, while there, came the return of my friend Gaffney from America. He stayed in Berlin, but wrote me often, and imperatively begged me to go to Berlin, as there was a matter of 'great importance' to discuss with me.

After days of delay and doubt I came here to Berlin arriving on 16th February & coming to this Hotel Saxonia, Gaffney & Lt. Monteith meeting me at the station at midnight.

I was ill and unfit to travel – and got worse here.

I stayed here until 26th February, returning again to the Kuranstalt on 27th where I was ill in bed for some days on my return.

[...]

On Friday, 3 March, while in bed I got a letter from Lt. Monteith dated 1st March urging my immediate return to Berlin. No reasons were given. I answered that I could not travel then & begged him to explain the reasons that called me back so hurriedly.

On 6th March a letter from him of the 4th came, telling me there was 'a move on' that he could not write, or tell to anyone save myself, and that he would come to Munich to see me, arriving the next morning. I was then much better and on the following day, Tuesday 7th March, he arrived and spent the forenoon with me.

The 'move' was this.

On the 1st March he had been asked by the G.G.S. to call where he had seen Lt. Frey. Frey said a 'telegram' had come from Devoy asking for rifles &c. to be sent to Ireland, as 'something' would happen shortly of 'great importance'.

The military here at G.G.S. were willing to give *up to 200,000 rifles* *with ammunition* Frey said; to land them in Ireland by a given date, probably in trawlers—and Monteith wanted my counsel and help as to what to do.

I said first – 'My difficulty is that I don't trust these people in anything they promise – they lie always – they may or may not keep faith today – but I have no reason to believe that in anything they do they ever think of us, or of others – but only of themselves. If then they promise today to give just *200,000 rifles &c.* I am forced to seek their real reason. It is *not* to help us – rest assured of that. They have shown me, so repeatedly, that they cannot keep faith and that they have no feeling about Ireland at all, that in anything they promise now I seek only their real motive and what end of their own they are after.

However, as they offer us this large armament we should be fools not to take it if we can get it. Let us get what we can.'

I drew up a Memorandum for Monteith to take back with him that night & hand to them the next day in Berlin – promising to follow it, in person, in a few days.

Time was precious. Monteith said he gathered the 'something' in Ireland would occur in April – & the arms were to be there in good time. Devoy's telegram had been in a cipher arranged with Bernstorff & said that a letter coming over by first mail would explain details. This letter was due to arrive, Monteith said, in the course of the present week – 13 March to 18 March – and he begged me to try & come to Berlin in good time.

[....]

I left the Kuranstalt on Monday, 13th March – & went to Riederau am Ammersee. Next day I tried to see Dr. Curry but missed him & had to wait over till Wednesday 15th – when he hurried back to Munich to see me.

[...]

I arrived here yesterday morning at 8.40 a.m., being met by Monteith at the station and he told me he had arranged with Captain Nadolny (Abteilung IIIb)[53] to receive me at 10a.m. at the G.G.S.. We went together to the Staff & spent over an hour with Nadolny and two other (junior)

dolf Nadolny: a senior German intelligence officer in Abteilung b; he created an independent political operation known as 'P' olitik) and became a spymaster, directing covert support for rious anti-government groups in Russia, Ireland and elsewhere. dolny's negotiations with Casement turned increasingly rimonious. [Auswärtiges Amt]

---

[53] Abteilung IIIb is the name of the German military intelligence division of the G.G.S., formed in 1889 and directed from 1913 to 1918 by Colonel Walther Nicolai.

officers, Hauptmann v. Huelson and Graf von Haugwitz (Ausbacher Cuirassiers).

The proposals <u>now</u> made were the following:-

1st. The Admiralty refused to send me or anyone ahead on the submarine. Their reason was that it was 'too dangerous'! Too dangerous for our project. The Irish coast was so closely watched the submarine would be seen & thus the whole project 'blown open'. I pointed out that this by no means followed. Submarines had often been seen off the Irish coast & nothing followed & it was absurd to say that if one *were*, by chance, seen it would reveal our plan. But if my advice were followed, she could not be seen & no risk incurred for her – only for us who landed & that was our affair. Moreover if the watch was so close that a submarine could be seen then how did they hope to land arms from a big steamer?

All the arguments were brushed aside with the statement that the German Admiralty *would not agree & there was an end of it.*

So then we advanced to the 'project' itself. It was this:

The G.G.S. would load up twenty thousand rifles (not 200,000!) with 10 machine guns & 5,000,000 cartridges in trawlers or 'on a steamer' & dispatch them, with our Irish handful at Zossen by 8th April at latest. The 'rising' in Ireland was arranged for Easter Sunday & the guns were to be 'in hand' before that date. They reckoned here to allow ten days for the journey – so that this armament should reach the appointed spot (wherever that might be!) by say 18th April.

Devoy would be informed by wireless & he would have to make the connection with Ireland, to arrange from New York, all details with the Revolutionary Committee in Ireland for reception of the rifles & guns. *No prior word could be sent from this & nothing done from here save inform Devoy in this way.* I pointed out all the grave objections to such a very limited, uncertain and roundabout way of arranging with the men in Ireland – but all in vain.

Nadolny suggested that *all* the 55 Irish soldiers at Zossen should go, but I said that all could not be trusted, and the selection must be left to Lt. Monteith to pick out the men he believed in. These, I said, must *at once*, without an hour's delay, be trained in machine gun practice, so that on landing they could use the guns (or some of them) if needed to ward off police attack or rifle fire. As the proposals developed I saw how hopeless and inadequate they were – and I saw how false were all the professions accompanying them. Nadolny said that with this 'help' we should surely be in a position to dictate our terms to the British government and secure '*at least autonomy*'!

The 'war' in Ireland would compel England to 'surrender' to us!! Was there ever such a Mind in the World! If sincere & he believed what he said, he was a bigger fool than any I had yet met – & if not sincere he must have taken me for that man.

I could not say what I thought of it all. I listened, smiled and looked at Monteith across the table. I even pretended to concur in these manifestations of lunacy, or at least I did not say 'you are an ass or a rogue'. What else could I do? The guns were of service. If we could get them to Ireland they would be a reinforcement to the armed men there who had already with such inadequate weapons, compelled Great Britain to exclude Ireland from the Conscription Act.

Twenty thousand more armed men & 5,000,000 cartridges would be an added security to keeping Ireland out of the war – all I was now hoping for. Besides I saw it was *all* we were to get. If I refused this offer – & pointed out all the absurdities of the plan and the grave risks, I should rob Devoy & the Irish in America and my Volunteers in Ireland of the *only* chance of external help that would ever come from Germany.

The Germans would throw the refusal on me – the Irish in America & at home would do the same. The facts, as I knew them, could never be known – all that would be said or seen would be that this government had offered 'generous help' in response to our request & I had stood in the way & opposed. So I was bound to seem to agree to what was patently the most despicable offer. I asked for the documents they had got from Devoy to see what he had actually asked for. They produced *at length*, a typed copy of a letter dated '*16/2/16*' & signed by him as secretary.

This letter stated what he believed to be the situation in Ireland both as regards the Government forces available, & the number of Volunteers to be counted on. The former were put at 40,000 men (30,000 troops & 10,000 police), the troops inferior men with little artillery.

The Volunteers were put at *10,000* already armed, but with only some 200 cartridges per rifle, and many thousands available if arms could be supplied. Devoy asked for these, saying that if *100,000 rifles and artillery and German officers* and artillery men could be landed, there was no doubt of our ability to defeat the British forces.

He suggested Limerick as the best place for landing – and said that the 'rising' would take place on *Easter Sunday*. The final paragraph of the letter was a request that I should remain in Germany as the accredited representative till the end of the war of the Irish Revolutionary Body!!! Poor, good, brave old man – & it is to get rid of me, him, Ireland, the Treaty and all their commitments they now send out this shipment.

I pointed out to Nadolny that Devoy laid stress on the presence of German officers & some trained artillerymen, & that they were not sending any but only Lt. Monteith and some 20 men of ours at outside *not trained* in gun practice.

I said no more. I added that the final paragraph it was my obvious duty to disregard and that I should have to accompany the men. He said '*of course, it is impossible* for you to remain behind. You must be there with them. Everything forces you to go'.

I again urged the dire importance of first sending messengers from here to let the 'Supreme Council' in Ireland know exactly what was going to be done.

He refused, and put it all on the Admiralty – pointing out that if we raised difficulties on this score they might refuse the ships &c. & the whole enterprise collapse.

The trawlers would be accompanied by a submarine – that was all! He would cable Devoy & he, Devoy, would have to arrange everything with the men in Ireland. Meantime he would go to the General at the War Department and get the men Lt. Monteith should pick out *at once trained* in machine-gun exercise. I pointed out this would take some days – to get the permission &c. &c. &c. that the training could not begin for perhaps a week. He agreed. So that the invasion of Ireland in 1916 is to be with 12 or 20 men (who are not to be told in advance a word!) & who are to have perhaps a week's practice with a machine gun at Zossen!

We are all to go on the trawlers (dressed as soldiers in English-made clothes, got from some of the interned British prisoners in Germany – (this was my idea) – 'accompanied by a submarine', round by way of Norway &c. &c. to the West coast of Ireland – or possibly in 'a steamer'. What a fine party! Was there ever seriously put forward by a great military power in the world such a proposal!

And if I point out its stupendous idiocy, its fundamental falsity, its foredoomed failure, I shall be held to all ages in Irish history, as a 'traitor', as the man who, at the moment of destiny, failed his country's cause & prevented the great German empire from extending 'military help' to revolutionary Ireland. My God! Was ever sane man in such a position!

I left the G.G.S. with Monteith at about 12.10 and walked back with him across the Tiergarten by the pond, [...] I told Monteith all my fears – but how I saw clearly I *had* to go. He agreed that I could not stay behind. He also agreed with me that in any case, without a German army corps, any 'rising' in Ireland by ourselves alone is hopeless – worse than hopeless.

But to attempt it with this meagre 'help', under such conditions is madness and criminal. He agrees to it & sees the hopelessness, but feels with me it is our duty to try & get the rifles into Ireland. We have no right to stand in the way of that attempt. I explained to him that my only hope in going is to arrive in time to dissuade the leaders at home from the attempt. That if I can only get ashore a little ahead of the rifles I may be able to stop the 'rising' and arrange only for the safe delivery of the rifles. If this can be done *then* (& then only) would the thing prove useful. Otherwise it is an awful danger. Of course the chances are that we shall never get near the shores of Ireland. If it is too 'dangerous' for a submarine to go off that coast, how do they expect 'the steamer' or the trawlers loaded up with rifles &c. to escape observation? The thing is worse than mad – it is dishonest.

The more I think of it, the more do I believe it to be an act of dishonesty. It is to get rid of us – 'the Brigade', me, the Treaty with Ireland, & all their responsibilities to us, founded on their past dealings with me and with the Clan in the USA – on the cheapest possible terms to themselves, under the pretense of complying with our request and furnishing us with the very aid we asked for.

[...]

The only object *this* Government (the German Govt) has in *now* offering us this meagre & belated help is to continue the fooling of the Irish in America & a possibly far-off hope that we may create some little complication for England in Ireland. They know *nothing* about Ireland – & not much about England. They are incapable of understanding the minds of other men – or of dealing with free men. They have no conception of personal freedom or of how men used to free action & free thought think. Their sole method of dealing with other people is to apply the methods used at home to their too obedient, servile, drilled and disciplined population.[54]

Certainly from the point of view of foreign government, Germany does not deserve to win this war. Her people do deserve to win – for they are innocent and victims – and England is certainly attacking them not because of Prussian militarism but because of German commercialism. Still, the Emperor and the gang around him are a hard nut for the world to deal with.

In some ways I have acquired sympathy for the English standpoint when I contrast the individual candour, truthfulness and straightforwardness of the Englishman with the absence of these qualities in the governing classes here – or indeed in almost any section of the people. Collectively a great nation – individually an undesirable one.

Here comes Gaffney – so I must stop for the present. I have written all the morning nearly – and shall try to go on here & at Munich between this and the 4th or 5th April when I must return to this horrible city to go to my doom. I don't mind that, if only I could feel there was some way out for Ireland & those at home, who are so misled into believing that 'help will come from Germany'.

I see no way out. There is nothing for it but to go to what I know leads only to ghastly failure.

[...]

Munich, Monday, 27 March, 1916

It is ten days since I began my 'final page' at Berlin on 17th March. That afternoon, at 3pm, I went to the Reichsmarine Amt[55] & saw Captain Heydell & two other Captains in Room 763 who had charge of the project. [...]

I learned much more. First, I renewed the appeal for the submarine to take me & two men ahead. They rejected it – peremptorily. I pointed out the grave importance of this step – they met it with alleged naval

---

[54] Casement added a note on 8.4.16: ('I was wrong here – they had & have a far worse object – viz, bloodshed in Ireland. The guns are to be a real gift of death. I have seen for days now that no action of mine can stop the guns. They are determined to send them as they have arranged for bloodshed as their price.').

[55] The Imperial Naval Office.

reasons, the chief being that the Irish coast was very closely watched & the submarine would be *caught*. How then about the steamer or steamers with the guns? And they said the shipment would be in a 'small steamer of 1,000 tonnes under the Norwegian flag'. She would have false papers of course. *She would not be accompanied or convoyed by a submarine.* I insisted on this, but Heydell said it would give the thing away. The submarine to keep up with the steamer would have to steam on the surface & then the British cruisers &c. on look out would see the smoke of the submarine alongside & that would damn the steamer & draw close attention to her. Nothing I could say would change their obstinate refusal to either send anyone ahead by a submarine, or to convoy the gunship by a submarine! This being so I said I should then rely on trying to get a messenger sent over ahead, & I asked them if they would pass John McGoey over the frontier for me. They sent for Captain Isendahl (of last 1915 February reminiscences!) who at once agreed to get McGoey off whenever I brought him in. I said I should have him there at the Admiralty next afternoon – 18th March. They had a chart (an English Admiralty chart) of the coast of Kerry & pointed out to me where they proposed to land the rifles.

It was to be at Tralee Bay, at Fenit Pier. The steamer with the rifles would come to 'Inishtooskert' (the N.W. of the 'Seven Hags' Rocks north of Rough Point), between 20–23 April – & we (the Irish) were to have a pilot there to bring her into Fenit. The pilot boat to show 2 green lights (after dark) only for a short time. This information they said had been cabled over to John Devoy and his reply 'All right' *dated 14 March* was shown me!

[...]

I left the Admiralty even more hopeless than the G.G.S. the day before. The thing gets plainer and plainer. It is a regular plot to get rid of their Irish obligations on the very cheapest terms to themselves, with the least risk and least publicity.

And what will the Clan be doing? They have been told that there will be a ship at Fenit on a certain date (20–23 April) but have they been told she will have only 20,000 rifles & 10 machine guns & *no* German officers or artillerymen?

I feel sure not. They have been led to believe that Devoy's letter is being favourably considered & the 'goods' supplied – while, in truth, they are avoiding the fundamental issues raised by Devoy – our lack of officers in Ireland & of trained artillery men &c. &c.

I went back to the Saxonia Hotel, in a very despondent mood and sent for John McGoey to be brought in next day.

[…]

John McGoey had come over from the US as a Volunteer, to help me in any way, with strong recommendations from J. McGarrity. As I could do nothing else with him at the time, I sent him out to Zossen to the 'Brigade' on the conditions prescribed in the undertaking he signed on 2 December 1915 which provided for him 'immediate' release whenever I should need him for other service. In February I wished to send him back to US to warn our friends there of the double dealing & faithlessness of this government – & how little reliance we could place in anything they said.

Now, as the letter for his release had been ignored, I told Monteith just to bring him in to me without anyone being asked good, bad or indifferent. I would arrange for the War Office being told once I got him out of the country.

McGoey was brought in next day – I explained all the situation to him very fully and pointed out the imperative need of trying to get some one into Ireland to warn them there of the wholly inadequate help being given & to say that I strongly urged no 'rising'. He (like Monteith) was with me here. McGoey said it would be criminal & that he had long suspected the Germans of playing a double game. He would do anything I asked him to. I told him it was necessary for me, to keep silent as to my real opinions before the G.G.S. and that when I took him to the Admiralty he must do the same.

We went at 11.30 o'clock and found the three Captains again – all was explained to John McGoey. He is to go as an added string to our bow (in addition to the telegram to Devoy) to tell the Dublin Council to have the pilot boat ready at Inishtooskert, &c. &c. but he goes really to get the heads in Ireland to call off the rising & merely try to land the arms safely & distribute these.

[…]

The chief satisfaction I have is to think that I am successfully getting John McGoey out of the country over the heads of the War Office & the others – who have been so ill-mannered. If he gets safely through to Dublin he is to seek out Tom Clarke, & through him B. Hobson & try to 'call off' the rising & get them to concentrate only on the successful landing of the guns.

The name of the steamer not yet known. They could tell me on Tuesday, but I said it was more important to get John McGoey off *at once* than keep him two or three days just to learn the name.

He left Sunday morning 7.30 with the Detective – and I can only pray and hope he got across the frontier all right & that he may be able to get a ship at Copenhagen to Scotland. I gave him (against his will) 300 marks in Danish money – the hotel porter got it changed for me – and then 30 marks in German money – I saw him off at 7.30 on the stairs of the hotel with a last blessing & greeting in Irish.

[…]

The English have a ring of patrol boats right across from the Orkneys to Norway & I don't think there is the ghost of a chance of our getting thro'.

The more one considers the whole thing, the more certain it is that the chief aim of this Govt. is to 'cut their losses' & shuffle out of all dealing with Ireland.

The Emperor had doubtless again changed his mind – or those round him. Just as he once played with President Kruger – so he is now trying to do with Ireland – blowing hot & cold. But this is more than the abandonment of Kruger – because this *is* the *betrayal* of me into the hands of the English.

They know well we shall be taken – & they know the fate that means for me surely & perhaps for the poor young soldier boys.

The only thing I can see is that by going with them I may save them— as the English will be content with catching me & putting the blame all on my shoulders. But I can not imagine a more cowardly proceeding by any Govt. than this one arranged by three Departments of State to get rid of a handful of poor men they have deceived & of an obligation that has become hurtful to them.

If I live to make all clear – someday – but there is no chance of that. And yet it is only right that the truth should be known and told – for history is history, however Govts and rulers change their minds – & it is historic fact that the German Govt. made a Treaty with Ireland & promised recognition of complete independence following on the attempt they were pledged to of conveying military aid. And this is the way to try to fulfill their pledge! To invade a great Kingdom with 12 men! – dressed as sailors. Was ever such a thing seriously put forward! They are really beneath contempt.

[…]

That Sunday afternoon (19 March) Gaffney and I went out to Zossen to attend the funeral of poor Holohan,[56] the first member of the Brigade to die. He died on Patrick's Eve – & the priest Monteith had got down to confess the men on Patrick's Day arrived 20 minutes before his death – God be praised.

All the poor lads fell on their knees & recited the rosary when they heard of Holohan's death.

Today the funeral was well done, & the priest who had been in Ireland, preached a fine sermon over the grave. Some of the boys cried. Then Gaffney, Monteith and I went out to the camp and Gaffney sang a stanza of 'The Boys of Wexford'.

We returned at 7 to Berlin.

Of course Gaffney knows nothing. Nadolny impressed (on 16th March) on Monteith & myself the absolute necessity of 'secrecy' – and here is the second part of the proposal. As soon as we are gone with our party, the rest of the Brigade are to be locked up – 'in prison' Nadolny said, until it is known we are safely across. A fine fate! And who will ever see them out of prison? I said, in answer to this proposal that of course they remembered they were committed to sending the men to America and he said 'of course, of course'. It is all 'of course' of a course with much else that I have found at their hands.

How can I go on with it? What am I to do? Whatever way I turn, misery, failure, degradation & no way out. I know not what to do. I have told Monteith the acute fear I have – not physical or for myself, but for Ireland & our national cause. We are being put in an abject position – and this by this great almighty power.

I left Berlin again on 22 March for Munich intending to spend some quiet days and write my Diary up at Riederau – but I cannot!

I went to Riederau on 24th & stayed over to 25th walking in to Diessen. I returned on Saturday 25th to Munich & decided to go to Berlin on Sunday 26th. Took tickets & packed & at 8.45 – when about to leave the hotel, a feverish attack came on. I knew it would get worse in night – so at last moment I decided to stay. No use arriving at Zossen ill, with high temperature to go to bed. My last week in Berlin will be a very busy one.

---

[56] Patrick Holohan died in Zossen.

So here I am in bed this Monday – better & determined to go in morning by first train.

I shall be in Berlin tomorrow night 7pm & go to 'Saxonia' & talk things over with Monteith. He only got the machine gun to begin to practice on 25th March – nine days after Nadolny spoke of getting it. They will have a little over a week's training – and it is *ten months* since they were taken from Limburg with the promise to be 'at once' trained & equipped.

I am getting more & more disposed, as I lie in bed here in Munich (with 6 grams of aspirin in me) to put my foot down & call off the whole thing – so far as I can.

Unless they agree to send a submarine with us – then all might be different. I shall talk it over with Monteith tomorrow night.

Berlin, Wednesday, 29 March 1916

I arrived here last night at 6.50 from Munich. Monteith came. He agreed with my view that the thing is worse than mad. 'Dastardly' is his expression, mine too.

He is training the whole 38 men at the machine gun in Zossen but says only about 12 'at outside' can be counted on. I told him my last idea, arrived at yesterday while lying ill in Munich waiting for the doctor – viz – to point out the grave wrong (and risk to Germany too) of sending the men. That to do so is a break of faith of the kind to them & a flagrant breach of the agreement of 28 December 1914.[57] Moreover, it means that once we are captured the men would naturally & rightly point out the falsehood and the trick played on them by the German Govt. & recount too, many breaches of faith perpetrated on them. The English Government would be pleased, perhaps, to pardon the men to make the perfidy of the German Govt. stronger & plainer.

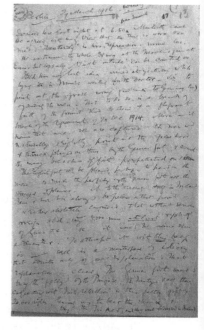

---

[57] This refers to the agreement or treaty signed at the end of December 1914 between Casement and the German Government determining the organising principles of the Irish Brigade.

As to the 'rising' itself in Ireland I am & have been always hopeless on that point, or rather absolutely convinced that without serious foreign aid, say 5,000 men *at least* & plenty of guns &c. &c. it would be worse than a disaster. To attempt it with *this* help – well [it] is a masterpiece of idiocy that admits of only one explanation. That explanation is clear. The German Government want to bury the 'folly' of the Brigade, the Treaty & all their coquetting with 'Irish rebellion' in this paltry gift of 20,000 rifles, leaving us to bear the shock & pay the piper and they want bloodshed in Ireland.

My view is still we should try & get the guns across. If we don't do that we run counter to the strong wish of those at home and in America who are counting on this at least. The guns, if landed, are an asset & to merely land them need not necessarily involve any bloodshed, or serious trouble, if the men in Ireland can act well.

[…]

Devoy asked on 16 February for 100,000 rifles, trained artillery-men, officers and plenty of cannon & suggested Limerick as place of landing. They replied to that request (I have never been shown their reply yet 8/4/16) saying a ship, or ships, would be at Fenit by 20–23 April to which on 14 March he is said to have answered 'all right'.

[…]

Now today 29/3/16 I am sending a note to Captain Heydell to say I wish to see him & I shall go round & tell them there, first, that I object to the soldiers going at all – but am willing to go myself. That I regard the thing as quite hopeless & wish to limit the number of victims to myself.

I will draw up a Memo giving all the overmastering reasons & send it to the Admiralty once I have discussed it with them.

They are much franker & straighter than the G.G.S. or Foreign Office & are far more likely to speak the truth. They are merely innocent agents in the matter, carrying out as well as they can the wishes of the German Government as represented by the G.G.S. & Foreign Office – whose object is to get rid of us all under pretence of complying with Devoy's request – & above all to ensure bloodshed in Ireland.

I shall not say anything of this to the Admiralty – but merely express my personal objections to sacrificing the men who trusted in me and the Treaty of 28 December 1914.

Monteith agrees entirely. He would go further & stop the rifles too – as likely to provoke bloodshed in Ireland, even if successfully landed.

194

I reply to that, that we are ignorant of all the plans & methods in USA & Ireland & it is not right to rob them of this tiny offer of help which would not *necessarily* involve more bloodshed than Howth if the parties to get the guns do their duty. At any rate, as things are I *dare* not accept the responsibility of stopping the guns (even if I could do so!) & leaving the men in Ireland in the lurch.

I am sending this note to Heydell.

29 March 1916

Dear Captain Heydell,

I arrived last night (having been detained two days by a return of the influenza attack) & shall be very glad to see you today whenever convenient to you.

There are some things of importance to discuss and I will call at any hour you name.

Yours sincerely,
Roger Casement

The things I jot down for this interview are the following:-

1. To show me the *exact* text of the cablegram they sent to Devoy to which he replied on 14 March 'all right'.

What was the exact offer they made? I know his demand – what have they told him they are doing?

2. To point out the grave risk of sending Lt. Monteith & the men – how it may fatally compromise German honour before the world – & how it is really in direct contradiction with the solemn promise of the German Govt. in the Treaty.

If the men are captured, as is almost inevitable, they would be regarded as victims of German duplicity & the case against Germany would be overwhelming. I shall not *say* all this out brutally – but let them see the danger – I shall insist that I go with my eyes wide open, knowing I go to a dreadful fate & that I don't intend to have my innocent young countrymen risk their necks too so hopelessly.

I shall tell them, too, I mean to have poison with me – & that I go really so that they here in Germany shall not say I was a coward.

3. To get the name of the steamer, the port she goes from, the date and hour of departure – & when I must go and be on board, if it is still decided that I go after I put my foot down on the shipping of the men.

It is probable, highly probable, I think, when the G.G.S. & Foreign Office learn that I am resisting the shipping off of the 'Irish Brigade' they will recall the whole thing and give up the attempt even to land the arms – putting the 'blame' for the abandonment on my shoulders. (I was nearly right there! R.C. 8/4/16)

4. I will ask to be allowed to communicate by wireless with John Devoy. (I did not know until Monteith told me in Munich on 7 March) that J.D. had any means of communications with German in cipher or they with him. Another proof of their double dealing! They never told me they could send messages for me to him in cipher & never once offered – & from the first day I landed they have always had some card up their sleeve and have never been frank or straightforward. It is a vicious bureaucracy indeed!

At the Admiralty I was sent to Captain Stültzer. Heydell came & brought in the chief naval officer [...]

I told them then that I feared to take any of the Irish soldiers – on political grounds – that if captured they would surely turn 'King's evidence' & rightly & the blame would be on the German Government.

They saw the gravity & said I'd better go to the G.G.S. at once. The *whole* scheme was controlled & directed from there. [...]

At the Abteilung IIIb of the G.G.S. I found Nadolny and his two aides – von Hülsen and Haugwitz. The Captain explained my fears about taking the men, & I added some remarks. Nadolny became very angry & exceedingly rude – & Von Hülsen glared at me with bleary eyes and whispered to the Naval Captain.

Curt von Haugwitz: worked as a liaison officer between the German F.O. and the Emperor's Military HQ. Haugwitz was in charge of organising the shipment of arms to Ireland. Casement thought highly of his abilities. [Auswärtiges Amt]

The only one who behaved well & is a gentleman is the young Count von Haugwitz. It was a most unseemly exhibition of German military culture.

I gave back as much as I got & insisted on the whispering stopping & the conversation being conducted in a language I understood, either English or French. The chief cause of the fury was my having sent John McGoey to Ireland! I nearly laughed in Nadolny's face. He said it was a gross breach of faith. I told him he was a liar. He said he would cable to J. Devoy & say that owing to my action the German Government now refused the rifles. I said he might do so if he pleased – but that his statement would be an obvious falsehood.

I asserted my absolute right to send a messenger to Ireland – that McGoey had come for this *very purpose* – sent by the Clan – & that unless I was to assume, which, with a shrug I said I clearly was – I had entire freedom to communicate with my countrymen in Ireland or America.

If Nadolny cabled I presumed I should be permitted the same action. 'No', he roared – 'I will tell your countrymen it is you have robbed them of the guns they asked for.' The Naval Captain, having had his ears filled by Hülsen, got up & scarcely looking at me, went out. I stayed on & talked more with Haugwitz than the others. Nadolny went and came – so did Hülsen – Haugwitz stayed by me – a gentleman. Their fear was that I had sent John McGoey to stop the rising! They asked again & again if I had given him instructions to that effect. I said I was not the master of the Irish Revolutionary body & whatever I might say would only be advice or suggestion. I avowed that John McGoey himself was dead against a rising, & the fury was uncontrolled. How had I dared to send such a man to Ireland without letting them know!

I saw in a clear sharp light, the whole devilish game – Devoy was being fooled too – had been fooled I felt convinced by the ass

Bernhard von Hülsen (1865–1950:) a German general who formed a paramilitary group after the war heavily involved in the suppression of the Spartacus League. [Auswärtiges Amt]

197

Von Papen. Devoy, an old man of passionate feeling against England, burning for *one* brave fight before he dies, had been assured of the entire good will of Germany & of strong military aid.

[....]

These people wanted only bloodshed in Ireland for their own ends – & the fatal steamer was to be the price of the rising. I was being shipped by her, merely to get me out of the scene, tear up the Treaty, & having had their 'rising' in Ireland, for what it might be worth to them, then they could wash their hands of all further connection or contact with 'the Irish'. I had, possibly, spoiled the game by sending John McGoey across, & at any rate gravely imperilled the 'rising' coming off – or '*the War in Ireland*' as Nadolny termed it!

[....]

Finally – it was two hours or more I had been there – Nadolny who had been going & coming to his other rooms, came and sat down and said, 'Well, Sir Roger Casement, you must promise to do nothing – to move no hand or finger in this matter & communicate with no one – we shall decide what course we'll take'. I said 'I *can* tell no one – you take good care of that – you have me here virtually a prisoner'. He laid stress on my not communicating '*with America*'. I said 'How can I? You hold all the channels of communication with America & anything I send there is read by your people. Let us talk sense. I shall certainly communicate as I choose with Lt. Monteith – my officer'.

He started & I saw a look in his eyes – 'How can you forbid me to do that? He is here in command of my men, with the sanction & recognition of your government under my orders – & I shall tell him anything I choose. The only thing I regret is I have not twenty faithful John McGoeys!'

He gulped with rage. 'Very well,' he said, 'tomorrow we shall decide what we shall do and act as we think fit.'

I said, 'No one can prevent you.'

Coming back from this revelation of depravity and cowardice & of worse – of attempted blackmail – I met Gaffney & he said Noeggerath wanted to see me, so we went together. There—in great distress of mind, I made both promise to keep silent & told them all. I did it to enlist Noeggerath's action with F.O. to see if pressure could not be exercised there to see that I got a fair deal and above all that the men at Zossen were spared the ordeal I had to go thro'!

Noeggerath promised to act at once & telephoned there & then to Under Secretary Zimmermann to seek an appointment for tomorrow. Z. gave it by phone while I was there for the morrow 'between 12 and 1' in the Reichstag 'to come by the Tiergarten entrance'.

I told him what I wanted – to impress on Z the grave danger of taking the men on board the ship – since they would assuredly be bound to give the German government away under question and expose how it had not kept faith with them. My true reason is to get the men saved as Monteith implores me to do.

They came back to dinner with me at Saxonia & we talked till late.

Berlin, Thursday, 30 March 1916

I did not sleep all last night. I had fever & tossed in misery on my bed.
[…]

I went on to the G.G.S. at 10.30 am & found Nadolny alone. He said as follows:

'The plan of aiding your countrymen in Ireland was proposed to us from your friends in America. We had & have no responsibility in it, beyond trying to the best of our ability to comply with *their* request. It is not our plan. Your countrymen in Ireland are determined, they assert, to rise on a given day – your friends in USA appeal to us for help. We knew nothing of it before Mr. Devoy's telegram came & all our subsequent action has been based on that. You know our proposals & we have sent them to Mr. Devoy. He agrees.'

He said much more. He said, 'We have no idealistic interest in Ireland and no revolution, no rifles. If it were not that we hope for a military diversion there we should not give the rifles.'

I said I could guarantee no revolution and that I sincerely hoped there would be none! I was profoundly against it unless there was great military support & they were giving none – practically three men in a boat to invade a kingdom. The thing was an insult to my intelligence & either he was a fool or thought I was one to speak to me as he had about 'autonomy'. But as things were, I was forced to try & get the rifles to Ireland since they had so planned things that the 'rising' seemed certain through their promises & these promises I did not know but could guess.

'You oppose the project – or you are hindering it. The soldiers are an essential part to its success. The naval men say so. The machine guns

199

must be ready to come into action as soon as their steamer arrives. We have no other men to send. If they don't go the whole thing may collapse. I shall cable Mr. Devoy and say owing to your action we are compelled to withdraw from the matter at the eleventh hour, & leave your countrymen in Ireland in the lurch – and all the responsibility falls on your shoulders.'

I protested this was gravely unfair – that they were not, to begin with, complying with Mr. Devoy's request at all – in sending a far smaller consignment of arms than he had asked for & *no officers* on which he laid such vital stress. He had never asked, either, for me or for the Irish soldiers. I personally had to go – that was evident and required no further word. I had to stand beside my friends in their resistance whatever it might be & take all the consequences, since I was so largely responsible for the whole situation, although not for this wholly unexpected development. As to the men I felt a peculiar personal responsibility for their not being captured by the British Govt. That was my objection today. As to the ship, she must go at all costs – I would go alone – but he insisted on the men.

I left him in despair & saw Noeggerath after his interview with Z. He said that Z. had listened very attentively & would act. Also submarine essential.

Monteith had come in to see me before I went to the G.G.S.. I told him to do so, by 'phone, by telegram & by special letter. He reported Haugwitz had been out there at 9.30 a.m. ostensibly to see how the men were shooting—really to try & get him, Monteith to take the men to Ireland over my head. Monteith said it was a clear 'try on'. He even offered money in shape of 'funds for propaganda'. Monteith replied he was here absolutely & solely under the orders of Sir Roger Casement.

[...]

I was in despair – and my fever on me worse than ever. That evening before Monteith returned to Zossen we talked things over. I told him that I should play a last card & write Count Georg Wedel, one of the few men here I had any regard for and tell him just how I saw it all. This with a view to save the men at all costs – that idea was growing firmer and firmer – that they at any rate could not be taken. Monteith begged me to do this – that he thought it infamous to take the men – in any case & especially with the absurd training of only 2 or 3 days already at the machine guns.

He urged me to haste – & I said I'd write that night. I lay awake for hours in despair and at 1 a.m. or 2 a.m. got up and wrote a rough draft of a long letter to Wedel – I did not lie down again until near 5 a.m. and was awake again at 6.30 a.m.

Von Haugwitz on his return from Zossen apologised to me for going there – saying he had not wished to do anything behind my back.

I absolved <u>him</u>.

He is the only decent man I have met at the G.G.S. the rest are all cads, scoundrels or cowards – & invariable liars.

I have detected Nadolny often, (v. Lübben once!) Boehm more than once, a Herwarth v. B. &c. &c. There is not one I'd trust out of my sight on *anything*.

Berlin, Friday, 31 March 1916

I was ill in bed all day with the Doctor – congestion of lungs threatening – I finished as well as I could the long letter to Wedel.[58] I emphasized so much – and repeatedly the danger of capture to myself because I wanted to excite their fears for themselves. If they could be brought to see that my capture by the British government would reflect on their honour, possibly they would begin to appreciate the importance of my request for the submarine & if I could get that and land in Ireland before this d--d ship & her guns arrive I may stop the whole dreadful thing.

It is for this I still play, but I am so sick and utterly wretched beyond expression. Doctor told me to stay in bed and prescribed usual stuff.

Berlin, Saturday, 1 April 1916

Finished my letter to Wedel – softening down some of the rougher passages. Gaffney came & I read it to him & Lt. Monteith took it (after hearing it) up to Wedel & gave it to him in person. He saw Wedel who said it should have his 'immediate attention.'

---

[58] This letter, which survives in multiple forms, was a précis of the diary for the last few weeks and sought to explain to von Wedel the impossible situation in which Casement found himself. For a draft of the original see NLI MS 43,227 (1–4).

I was in bed till afternoon when on Drs advice I went out for a very short walk in blazing sun to Thiergarten & then to tea at the Esplanade Hotel with Emerson & my translator Fromme.

The Zerhusens came – she a dear, kind-eyed Irish woman – Gaffney dined with us.

I wrote Wedel again today – a short letter pointing out the *sole* justification I could see for any armed attempt in Ireland – and I was told he had 'gone on leave of absence till Thursday.'

[…]

Berlin, Sunday, 2 April 1916

This morning I sent a letter (No. 2) to Count Wedel following on that sent yesterday morning (No. 1 of 30 M'ch) – see both.

The messenger reported that Count Wedel had gone away on 'Urlaüb' [leave] until Thursday next. Gaffney was with me at the time. We both hope that this meant he had gone to the Hauptquartier to try and arrange things as I decided.

Auswärtiges Amt: The German Foreign Off
in Berlin where Casement had ma
meetings [Auswärtiges Am

I decided to stay here all day, instead of going to Zossen, and now at 6.35 p.m. I get a telephone call from the Auswärtiges Amt from Assessor Meyer. I record it instantly. He said:

'Count Wedel left yesterday for some days leave of absence, and before going he handed me your letter. He reports he can not do anything in the matter. This has been arranged entirely between the G.G. Staff and the Irish organization in America and we cannot interfere or bring any pressure to bear on them. You must arrange everything with the G.G.S. and I suggest you seeing Captain Nadolny.' I said – 'I have written very plainly my standpoint and I must abide by it – I cannot and will not be forced into a false position by Captain Nadolny or the G.G.S. and do what I feel to be wrong.'

Mr Meyer said. 'We cannot discuss the matter in detail over the telephone' – I agreed – and went on 'perhaps you will come here tomorrow and see me?' – I said 'What use is there in that, if you the Foreign Office cannot interfere?'

I then asked if he had seen the letter I had written to Count Wedel today – and he said 'No – that must be the one lying on his table – I will read it – and then, perhaps I may ring you up tomorrow, but in any case the matter must be settled between you and Captain Nadolny.'

I said again that 'I am not going to be forced into a wrong position by the G.G.S. and my last word, or at least my last fixed opinion is expressed in the letter sent to Count Wedel.'

So there it stands.

This is the climax of their cowardice and infamy!

The whole thing, so far as they are concerned, is a put up murder plot (in which I am to be one of the victims) and Ireland the chief. Anything more atrocious is hard to conceive.

The war party here – who are supreme, evidently think they had a chance of reaping some military profit from bloodshed in Ireland – and at a very cheap price! (Twelve men in a boat!) – '£200.000' as Nadolny priced it!

The 'Irish Brigade' is to be got rid of – & the Treaty with me buried.

The Germans are to have their pound of Irish flesh at all costs.

A more infamous form of blackmail it is hard to conceive.

Wedel runs away on purpose till Thursday! Knowing that by Thursday I shall be 'dealt with.' What *shall* I do?

If I go and take the men as the Staff wants me to do – shall *we* seize the ship and give ourselves up? That is one thought. Anything to punish these scoundrels and ruffians and base, dastardly cowards.

I must see Monteith and talk things over with him tonight.

It is the most damnable position a man was ever put in – and this is the Great German Govt!

My God! What curs and cowards and infamous scoundrels – and these are the ruffians I thought might help Ireland. English rule in Ireland has indeed been a curse – but the English man is a truthful man and a gentleman & his word is sure – and here no one of these men is a gentleman. They don't know the meaning of the name.

11.30 p.m. I saw Monteith & kept him till 1.28 train when he went out to Zossen. We don't know where we are – but we agree that under no circumstances am I to consent to the men going – that M. will accompany me – but we go alone. That is all I can decide.

Tomorrow Meyer will 'ring' me up again & say I must see Nadolny &c. I shall decline – & say that they must come to me – that my mind is made up & I go forward on *my* terms alone – & part of those are that they come to me to discuss the minor details left. Or if I go to the G. Staff that then I take a witness with me! One or the other. But *in no circumstances* shall I take any of the soldiers or allow them to go. On that M. & I are fully agreed & beyond that I can dictate nothing. I am already a 'dead man' – but not yet a wholly dishonoured one, despite all my mistakes. God knows they were not for self. R.C.

Berlin, Monday, 3 April 1916

A very bad night.

[…]

This morning I wrote a letter more and decided to see a certain lady in whom I could trust. I met her early & told her enough – not anything of the inside matter, merely my awful doubts and the hopeless position in which I was and the use they were trying to make of 'the others'. I did not say who the others were, and she does not know or guess – but I said I had made up my mind not to budge from my position on that point – and I asked her to keep the two letters (copies) of 30 March & 2 April to Wedel I handed her these & she promised faithfully to keep them until the end & then to hand them over to the person whose name I gave her & wrote on the cover.[59]

Also I am going to leave my 'Diary' as far as it goes with G[ebhard]. I may be arrested, I think, at any moment! The lady said that the Emperor himself was powerless today – he was in the toils too – and was being accused of being 'pro-English' – that the whole power of the land was in the hands of Falkenhayn & a small clique and everyone trembled before them. That Falkenhayn *was a* scoundrel and swayed by 'finance' – whatever that means!

She agrees with me that this curse of Prussian militarism is an internal evil that must be fought by the German people themselves & broken from within.

I then saw G[ebhard] at his quarters – & told him I wanted him to keep papers for me until he could get them in a safe place – if such be in this land today. Everyone is spied on. That is certain. They have had spies on me ever since I came here. She told me of some of the stories circulated against me! She doesn't know half of them.

She does not know the situation I am in – poor lady.

I got at 12 a telephone from Count von Haugwitz begging me to come to the G.G. Staff at 3 p.m. this afternoon.

I demurred & asked him to come here. He said he could not leave the place – someone was away & it was very desirable we should meet and Captain von Hülsen was not there. I think he said not there. This Captain V.H. is a bleary-eyed pig who has the papers in hand & the whole business is his particular show. Nadolny is the presiding chief of the whole 'Political' Department – which is really the Spy Department of the G.G.S. – as things are going and as the time is so short now, I have consented to go at 3 but I feel it is a mistake – yet what can I do? At any rate I must at all costs stick to my guns and help the soldiers here.

Today settles their fate sure – or rather as far as I am concerned that is settled. It settles mine – for ever.

I arrived at 3 & found him & von Hülsen there. The first thing they did was to show me a typed paper with the names cut out signed John

---

[59] Presumably, Princess Blücher.

Devoy recording Christensen's perfidy in U.S.A. dated 20 Decr. 1915.[60] It had been brought by von Papen they said. I nearly laughed – and asked why they had not shown it earlier. What their idea was in now showing me this paper I can scarcely conceive, except that they stupidly thought it would intimidate me to see that Christensen, the man I had trusted & sent to America, had turned into a ruffian & was found out by Devoy. I read the paper smiling & told them I was already perfectly aware of the whole of the facts there recorded. This preliminary settled, they began telling me of the plans made and what had already been done in the way of getting the rifles, ammunition &c. ready.

Finally there was a lull and it came my turn to say that I had made up my mind <u>not</u> to take the men. From the way they received it I could see that they were perfectly aware of my letter to Wedel & knew well my whole point of view. They argued & expostulated civilly & nicely, pointing out the need of the men until about 4 p.m. Nadolny came in. They explained to him my 'new departure' over the men, and immediately the issue was joined. Nadolny began by disputing entirely my right to regard the men as in any way under my power, and said he quite refused to recognise my right to interfere as the Agreement was 'dead'!

The conversation this afternoon on Nadolny's part was even more infamous than before. He insisted first – that the Agreement of 23–28 December 1914 was now null and void – and he declined to recognize my right to interfere in any way in regard to the Irish soldiers at Zossen. The 'Irish Brigade' had not materialized and therefore the agreement had not come into existence! He could do as he pleased with the soldiers at Zossen and send them to Ireland if he chose and they agreed.

I said laconically 'try it.'

I pointed out that while the purpose of the Agreement had not been attained the pledge to the men certainly held good, if the German govt. regarded its honour.

He called the agreement a contract – very well, a contract between two parties. One party could not interpret it as he pleased. I had as much right as the German govt. in the matter to put my interpretation on it – and this was clear that the pledge of the German govt. applied as fully to

---

[60] The information concerning Christensen had been relayed to Casement in a letter from Devoy dated 19 December 1915, see NLI MS 13,073/44/viii. Devoy described how Christensen had been trying to swindle money from him in order to support his wife and new-born baby.

<u>one</u> Irish soldier who had come at my call, on faith of that agreement, as to 500 or 5,000. If the Agreement were dead, non-existent, I asked him what then was the status of these men at Zossen?

'Oh!' he said – 'Deserters!' 'Deserters!' I exclaimed – 'and <u>who</u> made them desert, you? I? – did the Imperial German govt. actually descend to tempting men to desert? and does it now propose to despatch deserters to Ireland against their will – or with their will for that matter?

'And if they are "deserters" – *what* is Lt. Monteith the officer in command, with the sanction of your war office?'

I had the cad there. He blushed, looked down & stopped.

'Oh well' he said: 'Let us view it this way – those men are Irish patriots, they wish to fight for their country, we offer them a chance, we are sending help to Ireland & they are *vitally* necessary to the success of the undertaking to have the machine guns ready for instant use on landing. You are not a soldier. You oppose this vital military requirement on a theory, a doctrine – we shall appeal to the men direct over your head and ask them if they are willing to go to Ireland under these circumstances.'

I said I could not prevent him doing so if he insisted, since I was so obviously a prisoner here in Germany (I did not say in the coils of a serpent!) but that I could and should still prevent him getting the men, unless he took them by force & as prisoners on board.

He said '*How?*'

I said 'because you do not understand the minds of free men! The men will respond to your appeal to fight for Ireland with alacrity, I know – & then they will ask – the first question – what about Sir Roger Casement and Lt. Monteith, our officer – *Where are they? Are they not coming?*

And if you do that, and try by this method to entrap these men against my will, then I don't go – and Lt. Monteith does not go – and once the men know our view, *they* will not go – unless you kidnap them.'

He glared, & bit his lips – 'Then,' he said, 'I shall telegraph to the Irish Committee in America and ask them if they will require the men to go?' I said again – 'You may do so – but I should demand the right to telegraph too & put my views forward.' 'No,' he said – 'you shall not telegraph.'

'Very well,' I said 'try that course if you like but don't think it will succeed either for you will surely find that in anything you try to do with these men you will have to come back to me, and my mind is made up. Nothing you can say or do will alter it, or budge me one inch. You may take me out there and shoot me,' & I pointed to the Spree bank outside the window of Zimmer 178III – 'but I'll never agree to those young men going. They trusted in my honour & good faith – as I in yours – or that of the German govt. – and while I am not responsible for your point of view, I am for mine.'

The only gentleman on their side was young von Haugwitz. He agreed with me on all points except that the military necessity of the case required the men as gunners.

I said I should let no plea of military necessity or any other necessity override my sense of honour. They said – collectively – 'you argue for a theory – a principle – we, as soldiers for a vital military need. Do you wish the thing to succeed or fail?'

I said I should not wish for any success founded on a dishonourable and cowardly act and that I feared we had 'been brought up in two different schools of thought.'

I said this to Nadolny. It was impossible to agree I knew – and our respective views were grounded in a wholly different personal regard for certain things and different estimation of their value.

The fight had been long and exhausting but I saw I had won. Nadolny wound up (about 6 p.m.) by saying: 'Well, we will settle it tomorrow, we will refer the matter to Lt. Monteith on military grounds – he is the expert there & you are not – & will abide by his decision – & then if he agrees with you, you & he must sign a paper absolving us from all blame on military grounds, for the non-despatch of the men.'

That night at 11 p.m., I got a wire from Fr. Crotty he would arrive at 8.44 a.m. on Friday at Friederickshaven.

Berlin, Tuesday, 4 April 1916

Fr Strasse 8.44 to meet Fr. Crotty from Limburg. Missed him there but found him at Potsdamer Station 9.33 train for Zossen – stopped him & brought him back to hotel – gave him bath & breakfast and then told him all. He was horrified and we talked long as to best course. I told him of my idea of using Krebs perhaps to go over & try to stop the thing. I later took Krebs into our confidence – but he was not able (& rightly I think) to carry out the half thought I had had. But he remains a witness.

Fr. Crotty went on to see a certain lady and then to his Dominicans – & returned at 6.30 or 7 – & I kept him here getting him a good room.

Monteith & I went on to G.G.S. in afternoon & got all details for departure on probably Friday night from v. Haugwitz after it had been settled that only Beverley goes with us. The gun men at Zossen go on with their target practice so as not to excite suspicion if it were suddenly stopped with us both gone away.

V.[on]H.[augwitz] promised me to get poison for us. I begged him to do so – & he agreed.

We will take £100 in gold – paying German money for it – v. Haugwitz gets it for us from bank.

We are all there to go to G.G.S. at 6 or so on Friday night – I shave there – we change clothes & emerge by another door & exit (the orderlies all sent away in meantime from the corridors) to the quay by Lehrter Station & take the train to Hamburg in a reserved carriage.

Such is the plan.

Back & dinner with Fr. Crotty – & then Gaffney came and talked till 11 nearly in my room – & talked me asleep. Fr. Crotty enjoyed the change greatly I think, God bless him.

Berlin, Wednesday, 5 April 1916

Out to Zossen with Fr. Crotty. He confessed most of the men, and then I gave a short address, telling them I had to go away with Lt. Monteith for a time and begging them to go on with everything just the same. It was dreadful. I could not tell them the truth—and I had the vision before me all the time of the dreadful deception being practiced on them – and of the callous treatment they would have once we were gone and all pretence of an 'Irish Brigade' finished – God forgive me – and God protect these poor boys. I am writing the Chancellor direct about them. We (Lt. M[onteith], Fr. Crotty & I) came back to Berlin at 5.30 & I met Krebs there. He has a copy of my letter to Wedel of 30 March and a few other things – for use after the war only – & only then if I am dead.

Fr. Crotty left for Limburg at 9.17 p.m. & I came back and wrote the long 'Exposé' that follows. This I did after talk with Fr. C.[rotty]. He said to make another effort to impress the serious character of the thing on the German Govt.—& I wrote this 'Exposé' specifically for *their* eye. It will go to Noeggerath in morning.

" Eppse " April 5. 1916 87 27

Another day gone, and another last page to my Diary! Today I went to Lossen, ostensibly with the Priest who confessed the men, really to bid them goodbye. At least I have saved them! The whole thing appals me as a piece of the most ghastly folly — or rather one of the most Criminal attempts ever perpetrated. And I am debarred from saying so and taking the needed steps to prevent it by fear of incurring a personal reproach of Cowardice (already grossly implied by some of those who are handling the matter at the G.G. Staff) Am I not, perhaps a greater Coward in fearing to incur this reproach, or any reproach rather than take the wholly courageous step of protesting in the highest quarter against a Scheme that has been considered, I fear, only by underlings and is being rushed to certain failure by men of inferior intelligence at the best, and in this particular matter (Ireland) of no understan

I was still / perhaps / in presuming it but only / printing them of the arms / the critical moment.

'Exposé'

Another day gone, and another last page to my Diary! Today I went to Zossen, ostensibly with the Priest who confessed the men, really to bid them goodbye. At least I have saved them! The whole thing appals me as a piece of the most ghastly folly – or rather one of the most criminal attempts ever perpetrated. And I am debarred from saying so and taking the needed steps to prevent it by fear of incurring a personal reproach of cowardice (already grossly implied by some of those who are handling the matter at the G.G. Staff). Or worse still or perhaps, not preventing it but only depriving them of the arms at the critical moment.

Am I not, perhaps, a greater coward in fearing to incur this reproach, or any reproach rather than take the wholly courageous step of protesting in the highest quarter against a scheme that has been considered, I fear, only by underlings and is being rushed to certain failure by men of inferior intelligence at the best, and in this particular matter (Ireland) of no understanding.

How can a scheme so launched and by *such* methods as those I have had witness of the last week succeed?

On all grounds by which we may consider it, it is a scheme that can only bring failure – and probably something far worse than failure – disaster. Let us – let me put down these grounds as I perceive them. This is a record of my mind and understanding – and I want it to live after me.

1. Military

On military grounds the project is beneath contempt. To begin with it is not a military enterprise at all – but a piece of gun-running.

It has no military element about it, except poor Lt. Monteith! He, I, (and perhaps one young soldier) disguised as sailors, (each with a bottle of poison kindly supplied us!) are to invade a Kingdom – bringing with us 20,000 rifles and some cartridges.

As a gun-running enterprise or effort it might pass if attempted say by Walford & Co., of Antwerp or some other notorious firms of that character who make a living by supplying arms to *irate* savages and semi-civilized South American republics. But for the G.G.S. of the greatest military power in the world it is an astounding adventure – and as an episode in this world war it will surely be without parallel. I say nothing of the Navy because I am convinced they are doing the thing as well as it can be done and that from the naval point of view, as a 'job' entrusted to them for execution they will do everything they can to carry it through successfully.

But on all other grounds of a military character is has not been properly approached and none of the essentials to success are even being applied. I will not discuss here, tonight, these shortcomings—they must be apparent to any soldier who is given the rudiments of the proposal to consider.

On military grounds I am convinced, I could damn it before any staff college in the world. The dangers I foresee are far less from the obvious military shortcomings than due to the absence of political intelligence.

Let us consider it on political grounds.

2. Political

On political grounds, (even if the scheme were susceptible of sound military handling) it involves the gravest dangers to Germany—perhaps far greater than to Ireland.

I see dangers enough to Ireland in it at the best. The *only* reason that justifies it at all on Irish grounds is the argument put forward by John Devoy in his speech on 4-5 March in New York – viz that the Irish Volunteers were going to resist disbandment by force, and this being so their friends in America should help them. That a fight would come in any case – only a scuffle really – and it would be only chivalrous to help them to put up a better fight.

But the political dangers are so tremendous, when I put aside the natural sentiment of desire to help these young men if they do fight, that I think they far outweigh the possible gain that might come from a successful street scuffle that deferred or hindered greatly the possible recruitment of these young men.

Here are a few of those dangers. The vast bulk of Irishmen are law abiding and peace loving. They will bitterly resent bloodshed and civil strife in Ireland – forced on them as will then seem apparent by a filibustering expedition launched from Germany for that purpose. And in truth that is just what it is being sent for. Nadolny confessed quite frankly to me that what the German Staff wanted was bloodshed in Ireland – a 'diversion' there that might help Germany. The diversion may indeed come! But it will not help Germany I fancy. It may be a last straw the other way.

Once it becomes clear – as it surely will become clear – that Germany tried to incite a revolt or 'rising' in Ireland by a paltry gift of second hand rifles put in the hand of excitable young men, all that is solid and

212

respectable in Ireland will be moved to the deepest resentment – 'Pro-German' feeling of today will be changed into wrath and contempt.

The object of Asquith's visit to Rome, I believe, (or one of the objects) was to get the Pope to move the Irish clergy to an anti-German attitude. He failed I feel sure, but this 'anti-Irish attempt' of the German Govt. to embroil Irishmen on their own soil, so that Germany might reap some trifling military advantage from bloodshed in Ireland can redound only to the extreme discredit of Germany, and may easily secure from the Irish Bishops a Declaration that Mr. Asquith failed to obtain from an appeal to the Holy See.

Once the Bishops (who, with the exception of the Archbishop of Tuam, have been very fair and just) are moved to denounce a 'German plot' against the internal peace of Ireland, then we may find public feeling in Ireland change to the complete detriment of Germany and leave her with no shred of Irish goodwill. The British Recruiting Sergeant will get the reward – not the German military machine.

And certainly that machine does not deserve to get anything but a kick for the way it has tackled this problem.

The political results will not be confined to a mere increase of ill feeling in Ireland against Germany – they would I feel confident, in the end, be of a far more widespread character and would probably cross the Atlantic and sway Irish feeling in America just in the opposite way to that hoped for.

The inadequacy, the hopeless inadequacy of the means employed and the absence of any prior precautions to ensure success will convince all thinking Irishmen that the project was not inspired by goodwill to Ireland at all, but sprang solely from a desire to secure profit from any sort of blood-letting in Ireland. Anger, contempt and resentment would be aroused once the *facts* of the attempt became known, and we may trust the British government for making these very widely known with a colouring and a 'colour scheme' all their own.

Not even the 'rape' of Belgium was exploited as this attempt to stir up strife, and secure a massacre of half-armed boys in peaceful Ireland will be exploited. And the moral will be a plain one. German 'good-will' is as dangerous as that of a mad dog – it bites the friendly hand as impartially as that of its enemy. Timeo Danaos et dona ferentes.[61]

---

[61] Virgil's *Æneid* II. 49: 'I fear the Greeks, even those bearing gifts.'

If all the facts connected with the ill considered and half thought out enterprise become known – and they will become known within a very few weeks at the latest – then the fair name of Germany, or at least of the German government is tarnished before all neutral countries and chiefly in the United States. Only success could justify an enterprise of this kind – and all the elements to ensure success are wanting so far as I can see – have not, indeed, ever been invoked at all.

If my diary is ever published – as some day it may be – what a figure all these military minds or political minds of this great Empire will cut!

The excuses put forward to me that it is being undertaken *solely* at the request of Irishmen themselves and without the moral responsibility of the German government being involved at all will not hold for a moment. I, even I here, with my hands tied (as it were) and my means of communicating with my friends in Ireland or America cut off can see that this statement is only very partially true. The very methods employed to enforce my acquiescence in a project I have expressed my disapproval of convince me that these assurances are wholly insincere.

I am given no chance of a free decision – and when I seek to express the opinion of an honest man I am threatened with a wholly devilish (I can call it nothing else) charge that the blame for failure will be put entirely on me.

3. Moral

On moral grounds the thing does not bear inspection at all. As Monteith said to me, referring to how the issue effects myself – 'it is dastardly.'

How can a scheme of 'helping Ireland' that evokes such comment from a wholly unselfish and chivalrous Irishman produce happy results?

Let us look at it on 'Moral' grounds. These are closely associated with the political aspects of the affair – they cannot be dissociated from the political.

On moral grounds I think nothing *can* be said for the thing, *as it is being worked.*

Advantage is certainly being taken of me in a wholly unfair and even cowardly way – and if (the inevitable!) I am captured by the British this will be made clear.

It <u>must</u> be made clear.

Nothing I may do, or abstain from doing, can then save the character of the German Govt. Most men will charge them with putting me in a dreadful position – with running me into the hands of my enemies – some even, with deliberately handing me over to the British Government!

All the circumstances connected with the agreement the German Govt. made concerning the ill-fated 'Irish Brigade' will come to light. They are, already, fairly well known in England – and while it suits the English government today to vilify me as a 'traitor' – it will suit them far better, once I am safe in their hands, to vilify the German government for having actually betrayed me as they will say, their poor dupe, into the very hands of the Government I had defied with the concurrence and support of the German Govt.

Whatever wrong I, the individual Irish rebel, may have attempted will be swallowed up in the far graver charge of treachery the British Govt. (through its press) will bring against Germany. 'Why' – they will say – 'they couldn't be loyal even to the wretched man who had sold himself to them!'

And the world will support the charge. I, the 'traitor' of today will become the 'sacrificed dupe' of tomorrow.

The more the question, thus posed,.is inspected, the more pitiable my case will be made out – the more contemptible that of the people who launched me on the road to doom.

No one will seriously assert for a moment that the German government really believed that by sending me on a ship to Ireland, with no support, no help, no possible means of escape, even they were doing a chivalrous thing.

The 'murder of Nurse Cavell'[62] will not be in it with the 'betrayal of Sir Roger Casement.'

The English are quite capable of shutting me up in a lunatic asylum and asking the world what it thinks of the people who handled the lunatic thus!

And the world will give only one answer. My madness may be pardoned – but the cowardice of those who first took advantage of it where they thought they saw some gain, and then flung the madman to destruction,

---

[62] Nurse Edith Cavell was shot by the Germans in October 1915 for treason after helping some 200 British troops escape into the Netherlands from Belgium in violation of German military law. She became an iconic propaganda figure and her death was used by Britain to amplify German barbarism.

when they had no longer any use for him, will echo through the world as a possibly crowning example of 'Hun' methods.

I should not like to be von Falkenhayn when the British Govt., having dealt with Sir Roger Casement, turn upon those who planned this 'military aid' to Ireland!

(I much prefer to be myself in any case – with all my faults and mistakes. At least no man, or people, or country can say I sold them or gave a friend away.)

This aspect of the affair does not concern me personally – my honour and my courage cannot be questioned, however my intellect may be arraigned. I have not shirked the ordeal – and when, if ever, the facts become public of <u>how</u> I have been forced to act against my judgment in the matter then, indeed, most men will forgive me while they will despise those who put me in the fire.

I am not free here in Germany, forced by ignorance, by the dire necessities of the case (as it is presented to me) to go blindly on, to <u>dictate</u> or prescribe the necessary steps that should be taken if the attempt is to be regarded seriously.

I see what should be done – and I have said so. My clear statement in the two Memoranda I gave the General Staff has not been acted on. I am told it cannot be – for 'technical reasons.' If technical reasons prohibit the preliminary steps that are essential, from being taken then the thing should not be attempted at all. That is clear.

But I was told it must go on in spite of the absence of these essential precautions; and I am forced to assent or incur a shameful reproach. I go on – because I am fool enough, or brave enough, or coward enough – I know not which – while I know it is hopeless.

Like Francis I, I say 'all is lost but honour'.[63] The *right* thing to do even now is to stop the whole thing – to delay it, until we are quite sure of the condition of things in Ireland, of the means at the disposal of our friends there, both for resistance and for the immediate landing of arms – and until adequate steps had been taken at this end to afford sufficient help.

That is the right thing to do – obviously. I ought to insist on that. And yet I dare not. If I do – God only knows what may be the result. I am so

---

[63] This refers to the decisive defeat of the King of France, Francis I, at the battle of Pavia in 1525. In his letter to his mother after the battle Francis wrote: '… all is lost to me save honour and life …'

completely in the dark as to what is really being planned in Ireland, in America, that I dare not accept the responsibility. And no one here will accept any responsibility. They put it all on me. And threaten me in an infamous way with the responsibility of betraying my friends, if I can't fully accept what I know is a half-digested project.

I must swallow it at all costs. All I have been able to do has been to save the poor Irish lads at Zossen – and still leave even these to their fate. For, it is clear from what Nadolny said yesterday afternoon, that they are going to be treated again as prisoners of war and sent to some detention camp.

That is a gross violation of the pledge of the German Govt. – Nadolny even called them 'deserters' to my face! No wonder the English Govt. charge me with being a 'traitor'! My God – it is the most abominable position a man was ever put in. Whatever I do is wrong – is hopeless. The thing *cannot* work well, conceived in such a spirit as this – planned with a total disregard of the first essentials of military efficiency and launched with a callous indifference to the most obvious considerations of honour and sincerity it can only produce evil – of that I feel sure.

And the evil will fall on the heads of those who planned it and persisted in carrying it through in violation of all they *must* know to be right.

Whatever happens to me is a small thing – but what may happen in Ireland is a big thing – and since it *can* only be evil I feel that the evil after all, will not fall on Ireland, but on those who have ensured it.

This absurd expedition may – who knows? – produce incalculable consequences. It is Germany, I feel certain, will reap them in the end – and they will prove a sorry harvest. It may well be the turning point, with a vengeance, of German relations with America, and all the Chancellor's wise efforts to retain friendly relations with America may be wholly brought to ruin by this half thought-out scheme of soldiers who know as much of Ireland as they do of America.

[...]

Well, I can do nothing. The madness is not of my choosing, planning or design – I have done my best to preach sanity and to enforce reason and I am insulted for the effort. Fate may be using me in some inscrutable way to end the war! I sometimes think it. But how?

I who have tried to save Ireland from the horrors of the war and to be the friend of Germany may now, by the very act of the German Government become the very instrument to launch Irishmen into the war – and possibly with them the Americans too.

The whole thing is appalling – and as Saturday approaches and the irreparable step is taken, I feel like a man *already* damned. All *I* can hope for is that, later on, my part will be made clear and it will be seen how great a victim I was.

Pray God, that Germany be not the far greater victims for the sins of her military counsellors. They have usurped the place of her political advisors, in this matter at all events – and I think she will pay bitterly for the exchange.

I have no time for more than these crude fears tonight – tomorrow is already here – it is 1 a.m. – and I have much to write.

I must write Zimmermann or the Chancellor maybe on the fate of the Irish soldiers left behind at Zossen and insist that, as Wedel promised me formally in writing last June, apart from the clear terms of the agreement itself, they shall not be the victims of the G.G.S. – even as I am – but that the promises of the German Government shall be strictly and honourably filled in their regard, after I am gone. This morning when I spoke to them and pretended I was just going ahead of them on a journey to clear the way for their deployment in the East, as they think, I could scarcely refrain from crying. I felt that I was leaving them to deception and misery – they who have already sacrificed so much – to be treated as 'Deserters' – or disgraced 'prisoners of war'.

It is time I died – for if I looked them in the face again I could not say what I wrote just now – 'all is lost but honour'. I feel that *all* is indeed lost and the sooner my life is taken from me the better.

NOTE I showed *this* part of my Diary to Noeggerath. *He* saw the vital gist of the thing & went to Zimmermann who authorized him to go to G.G.S and Admiralty. I said no use going to G.G.S. but perhaps to Admiralty for submarine. He went with the result that in the end they gave the submarine – not because it ensured my safety en route so much as their own reputation. It was only that argument appealed to them! Chivalrous! But the German Admiralty is the best part of all this show – a long way the best. 8.4.16.

Berlin, Thursday, 6 April 1916

On getting up I sent for Gaffney, read him my Diary of last night with every word of which he agrees. I expressed my ever-growing anxiety as to the consequences in Ireland. He went up to Noeggerath who came down to se me; having read the Diary he went to Zimmermann, the Under Secretary of State (after having come to me) & returned to say that Zimmermann could not go to the Chancellor, who has to speak again today in Reichstag, but authorized him (Noeg.) to go to G.G.S. they were hopeless and Nadolny a low-minded intriguer but that he might go to the Admiralty.

Georg v. Haugwitz called in forenoon to say that the arrangements were as follows:

Certain articles of clothing still to be purchased by me, he supplying the rest G.G.S. [£100]? in gold ready (I to give him a cheque). Monteith to come in tomorrow to go to G.G.S. & also to see some more explosives. Sgt B[everley] (who goes with us after all) not to be told until tomorrow night, say 6 p.m., & v. Haugwitz will come too. Finally, we are all three to 'change' at G.G.S. on Saturday afternoon – when I shall change & shave (the last time was in the Hotel Prince George, coming to Germany Oct. 17. 1914!) & go off to the Station 'disguised' as sailors & in charge of the Captain of Marine who is running the show. The man I already met at Admiralty who went with me to G.G.S. ·

Noeggerath with me several times today – and dear old Krebs the faithful one. Krebs is full of fight. Monteith brought Beverley in at 11.30 or so & he went out to see the town. Noeggerath went to the Admiralty, he told me, & explained the standpoint, political standpoint—throwing a 'bombshell' in, he said. They were greatly impressed and said that they 'might have to reconsider the whole thing'.

Noeg.'s idea is that they had given no consideration to it at all – treating Ireland as a thing of no account – only a childish incident. The Chief of the Admiralty Staff was away but was to be consulted & Noeg. was told he would be informed later of the decision come to. What Noeg. chiefly impressed on them was that I should be sent to Ireland before by submarine – that it was a fearful risk for them as well as for me to send me by the steamer & they had no right to incur that risk for themselves – if they did not regard mine. Of course personal risks are not considered & cannot be in war – all go out to die – but in this case there were possible consequences (to Germany) on the lines of my Diary of last night that they had to consider and then the grave risk of being 'tarred' with responsibility for the whole thing.

This point, viz German responsibility they had none of them considered – so my Bombshell has hit the mark.

Each of the parties I have had anything to do with disclaims responsibility!

1st. The G.G.S. are 'only complying with the request of Irishmen themselves and have no responsibility in the matter – in which they were not consulted' &c. &c.

2nd. The Admiralty are 'only carrying out the work entrusted to them by the G.G.S. & have no power of decision on any point of policy' (This is all right and I agree with this – they are the only innocent parties in the business.)

3rd. The German F.O. have 'no responsibility of any kind'! – they know nothing of it as it was all arranged between the G.G.S. & 'my friends' in America! Everyone is clean handed. And yet on 29 February Assessor Meyer is kind enough to send me Robert Emmet's dying speech 'in those times'. It is quite clear they had made up their minds that although they

TRIAL OF ROBERT EMMET.

Trial of Robert Emmet: in early 1916 the German General Staff handed Casement a copy of Robert Emmet's passionate speech from the dock. Casement was well versed in the rhetoric of Irish national martyrdom, and felt somewhat slighted by the gesture. [National Library of Ireland]

had 'no responsibility', & all was between G.G.S. & America – & that America had asked to keep me out – they had decided to bring me in. My mind was to be 'prepared' by R. Emmet's speech for the proposals coming after. Now it is absurd to think that Germany had no responsibility in a matter of this supreme importance – viz – equipping (quite inadequately) a rebellion in Ireland – which is made contingent really on the arrival of arms! For it is clear 'no revolution, no rifles' is the maxim of the whole crowd here – & their fury against me is due to the fact that I am pressing home this argument & *compelling* them to shoulder some of their responsibility, & that I sent J. McG[arrity] out of the country & they fear he may call off the whole thing.

After Noeggerath had come & gone – I was in my room very unhappy until 4 p.m. when I went down to go out for a few minutes – & got in the hall an urgent letter from Wedel of Foreign Office. It was dated today (see it) and forwarded a letter from Berne of 5 April – signed by 'a friend of James Malcolms',[64] with the signs agreed on last June with J.[oseph] P.[lunkett]. This letter said that the writer was sent from Dublin *with the urgent message* from Ireland –

1st. The rising fixed for Easter Sunday night. –

2nd. The steamer with the 'large contingent' was to come to Tralee Bay not later than dawn of Easter Monday. –

3rd. German officers vitally needed. *'This is imperative'* –

4th. A submarine to be in Dublin Bay.

I wrote instantly to Noeggerath to come here before 6 & then went to the Admiralty – saw Heydell who took the letter to Chief of Staff (he said) & after 20 minutes returned to say *they would not give a submarine*. This was final! For all the other matters I was referred to the G.G.S. I said that was useless for I had the measure of their intelligence always and we saw very little in common, or eye to eye.

---

[64] 'A friend of James Malcolm' was Count George Noble Plunkett, the father of Joseph Mary Plunkett. Joseph Mary Plunkett had travelled out to Germany the previous year to negotiate for arms and officers and had agreed with Casement to use the name 'James Malcolm' in future communiqués. Count Plunkett was in Berne to finalise plans before the Rising and various messages were exchanged through the German ambassador in Berne, Gisbert von Romberg, regarding the final preparations for the Rising. Count Plunkett remained in Berne until 11 April before continuing on his way to Rome to inform Pope Benedict XV of the Rising and to seek his blessing for the republican cause.

I said even more – for I was angry – not with Heydell, but with the whole of the soulless thing.

I told Heydell some of the things I had written in my Diary as to the danger to Germany from an act of this kind – 'treachery' I called it and I wound up by saying that I had no opinion of the political intelligence of the G.G.S. and if *that* was the thing going to rule Germany '*it would send it straight to Hell!*' I don't know what Heydell thought of me – probably mad. I was for the moment & bitterly angry when I thought of Ireland, of those poor boys on Easter Sunday & Easter Monday waiting for the steamer – the 'rising' already accomplished! – & their *one* hope the ship with rifles *and* the officers – who will not be there. The utter callousness & indifference here – only seeking bloodshed in Ireland – the 'rising' is their one hope!

The guns are so timed to arrive as to ensure that the rising must precede them – '*no blood, no rifles*'.

I came back to the hotel a horrified man & telephoned at once to von Haugwitz to come & see me urgent[ly]. I wrote Wedel a brief note of thanks & said I'd reply to the Berne message tonight – *see my reply to Wedel.*

Then Noeggerath called & I showed him the letter – & Monteith who came in – & they were reading it when von Haugwitz was announced. I had to prevent him seeing Noeggerath and Monteith cleverly stopped him in nick of time & got him up to my bedroom where I showed him the letter. He said '*the officers were impossible*'. That I knew already – his reasons on military grounds, I admit at once. German officers could not go without *some* German soldiers – & to command Irish Volunteers [with] different discipline &c. &c. – I agreed on all these grounds but I pointed out then the lamentable state of the 'rising'. Here they were, some thousands of brave boys, armed very indifferently, without true cohesion, commissariat, baggage and *No Officers*, going to commit an irreparable act, & be swept down in hundreds – or perhaps thousands – & the world will always hold me responsible for the whole thing – whereas in every single particular my advice has been scorned – & I have not been consulted until too late & these wholly imperfect 'arrangements made'.

One of the things I predicted on 16 March when I was dealing with the gun running aspect of the matter alone has now come to pass – a check at the eleventh hour – all of us working in the dark – no coherent plan and no communication kept up.

How *could* a scheme so engineered with the essential preliminaries neglected be successful?

Poor young von Haugwitz, he is a gentleman – one of the very few I have met here. Heydell too, I like at the Admiralty – but the whole thing is a brazen serpent, lifted up in a wilderness of worshippers – worshippers from fear *at bottom*. This Prussian system *is* a curse. I see it clearly. It represses all the higher sentiments of humanity – they dare not exist beside it – it is the embodiment of 'soulless efficiency', in mere military things only, dominating a great people. Here in my case it is absolutely soulless – & not efficient either – because while these poor asses think they are dealing with a military problem it is a political problem of the very highest order they are assailing with such rude hands. An abortive rising in Ireland, *inadequately armed & supported by them*, yet encouraged & urged on by their promise of support – let them say what they will – is a crime they will pay for bitterly. I have now said it so plainly to them all they must be beginning to tremble. To von H.[augwitz] I said *'the ship must go* – nothing can stop her: she is bound to go – you are pledged to that – & I go too. That is all'. As regards the man at Berne, I tell him that no officers & no submarine can be given – & I will send the letter by Wedel. He said it was absolutely certain no officers could go – & if I was equally sure from the Admiralty that no submarine could go, then he agreed I might write the letter to Berne at once. I sat down and drafted what I was going to send to Berne.

Noeggerath came again & I kept him to dinner alone. We talked very much. Krebs came & squatted for a spell.

N[oeggerath] said (when Krebs was gone) that he was quite sure there were 'very serious' talks going on over the whole thing. That he hoped still for the submarine. I said yes – but they would not send me in her! 'Why?' he said.

'You know,' I answered, 'they fear my intelligence. They know how profoundly I disapprove the rising & they want it – & they fear if I get to Ireland, I may be able to stop it. It's that that they are afraid of. Their fury over my dispatch of John McGoey shows me that they meant to keep me from all communication with my friends to launch me out in the dark, & let all responsibility fall on me and others.'

There is one ray of hope – that John McGoey arrived in time & that they may listen to him. *He* knows the true character of German good-will to Ireland now. He saw how they kept their promises to the poor betrayed handful of men at Zossen & how they treated himself! No uniforms &

refusal to release him when I demanded it in February. He told me that he had sized up German militarism & he is heart and soul against it even as I am!

Later in the evening I told Noeg. that I felt an absolute conviction that the British would seize the ship & that I was praying for it, as probably the best way to avoid the greater evil. If the ship is arrested & the English Govt. *publish* the fact that they had collared a ship with rifles & Sir R.C. on board, then the mere fact of that publication will stop 'the rising' in Ireland. That is clear. Knowing that the steamer is in the enemy's hands & no relief can come they will *never* go on with it. So I pray God in His mercy to have this the solution. Anyone that saves the situation in Ireland – and saves our young people from being made the victims of this callous conspiracy. Poor Ireland! God save her indeed – only He can.

Von Haugwitz said he would bring me back the Berne letter tonight – but he did not come by midnight. That all shows that there is a very animated fight going on somewhere. Noeg. said the Admiralty people, while profoundly impressed with the gravity of the situation revealed by his views (mine of yesterday's Diary), were 'raging' at my having told him.

He said he thought they all mistrusted me – & I said I felt sure of it – and I repaid them all the compliment with a very clear comprehension of how much they deserved my mistrust.

Even Noeg. now agrees that I *must* go with the arms – that I *could* not, in honour, stay here & let the guns go, feeling as I do – but that the infamy of the thing is that the German Government does not send me in a submarine. He still hopes. So he said. I don't. He begged me not to send any reply to Berne about the submarine until he sees me again tomorrow as the naval men will let him know – I agreed.

We talked of other things till late and he left me worn out and I fell asleep at once. Here I am again.

Berlin, Friday, 7 April 1916

Tomorrow is the last day. Today there will be a last fight for the submarine. I know it is futile. Then clothes to buy – a long letter to the Chancellor about the fate of the Irish soldiers at Zossen – to see that Nadolny's infamous intentions are not executed.[65] I can only plead. I dare

---

[65] A draft copy of this letter to Bethmann Hollweg is held in NLI MS 13085 9/ix.

not threaten – it is not fair to the Chancellor either – yet I know that the machine (he hates it too I fancy) responds only to pressure and fear.

Last night among other things Noeggerath said he was convinced that S[chirmer] (who took the Findlay letters &c. over on 'Kristianisfjord' in February) has been captured!

The letters were to be in Captain's safe – I expect the British got them too! All Gaffney's doing. When I was ill to urge me as he did to send them to the Irish Convention in New York. No word from S.[chirmer] or Mary MacFadden since they sailed. They both left Berlin on Sunday 20 Feb. & were to sail on *K'fjord* on Wednesday 23rd.

The ship was held up two days (or more) we know in Kirkwall – & arrived in New York on 7th – two days after the Convention. Mary had letters to (Nina)[66] from me & S. to Cohalan – but nothing of moment save to ask them if I should try & come over as G.[affney] suggested – that I was useless here & ill & it would be far better to try and get to them.

No answer of any kind has come.

I had returned to Munich after this with G. on Sunday 27 February with fever & was in bed for a week nearly & then came Monteith on 7th & this project & everything else has paled into insignificance.

What a laugh! There in America they want me to stay here as their 'representative', thinking there is an Irish policy here & that I can influence these people – little knowing that they insult me, lie to me, break faith – & would now, for their own ends, [let me be] hanged, if it served them.

Emerson told me on 1 April when I had tea with him at Esplanade that the Turks were now completely disillusioned as to the character of German 'goodwill' to Turkey. He said when I told him of my opinion of the G.G.S. *apropos* something else – he said 'You should hear the Turks on them!'

Today is really my last day – & I shall be haunted and riven all day. It is still early.

I told that faithful splendid Monteith last night that I should be glad to go even to death on the scaffold – to an English jail to get away from Germany & these people I despise so much. He said, 'Indeed, I think I would too.' He & B[everley]. slept here last night. Latter in an old suit of mine.

---

[66] Casement's elder and only sister, Agnes Newman.

E.D. Morel: Casement's associate in the Congo Reform Association; Morel became the acting secretary of the Union of Democratic Control on the outbreak of war in 1914. He was imprisoned for a technical breach of the Defence of the Realm Act in 1917. [National Portrait Gallery]

If my papers survive and above all the Treaty and some kind friend of former years (say E. D. M[orel]) should edit them there may yet be told a strange chapter of Irish history. In any case it will be shown that I was only a fool – to trust German honour or goodwill – & never a rogue.

The picture of me in *Graphic* of February 26, 'The Voice of the Traitor' Fr. Crotty tells me was sent to many of the soldiers in Limburg.[67] The Kommandantur there asked the N.C.Os to state on oath that it was false. They refused – although Fr. Crotty says everyone knows it to be a lie.[…]

Of course, we all know that Fr. Crotty promised to contradict it in writing. I hope he may, dear soul.

I must get ready for the ordeal of this last awful day. God keep me straight and help me to go right for Ireland's sake. That is all now I can hope to do.

Monteith went out to Zossen to pay the poor boys & clear all out from bank there. He returned at 6 or so, with the balance of cash to credit of Brigade Fund – Mks 3878.30 – & handed it to me. I then told him the matter was delayed – & that the Admiralty had promised me a submarine to take him, Beverley and myself over to Ireland in time to take part in 'operations'.

At 10 I got a message from v. Haugwitz asking me to go to G.G.S. I went and found a trio – Von Hülsen, Nadolny and the young Count – he was always nice and sincere.

---

[67] *The Graphic* waged the most vociferous campaign against Casement, who eventually opened legal proceedings against the publication. See page 170.

N. produced the letter of the Delegate from Berne and we discussed it. They seemed suspicious at first – as usual – but I was able to assure them it came from the right quarter.

I telegraphed from G.G.S. as follows: – When did you leave Dublin? (2) Steamer with *so much* ammunition & rifles (stating quantities) will be off Inishtooshkert rock, N.W. on Easter Monday dawn. (3) No officers can be sent (4) No submarine going (5) When can you return to Dublin?

[…]

Nadolny was very cheery. He said it was impossible to get a submarine & he was sure this way was all right. He asked after Noeggerath, putting many questions, saying I had sent him to Z. & the Admiralty & latter were very angry & charged them (G.G.S.) with breach of faith. I said put it all on me. 'I am responsible for telling Noeg. and involving his aid to try & get a submarine since all other means had failed.' I explained how Noeg. was a confidential agent of the Foreign Office & entirely in their confidence & they might rest assured there was no danger from his being brought into my confidence.

I added I had told Gaffney a little only as I was leaving him to look after the interests of the Irish soldiers at Zossen & that I was writing to the Chancellor on that subject. They were very anxious to know if I had told anyone else – but I evaded that by talking on Gaffney's share. I was sorry to deceive them, but could not help it.

[…]

Soon after I got a phone call from Heydell asking me to go round to the Admiralty at 4 adding it was 'over the submarine'. I went & he left me with a junior nice, young Korvettenkaptain – where I stayed until 6.30 reading back numbers of English papers.

Then came Heydell in great excitement to say they had a full dress debate & the thing was settled. I was to go by submarine. Details would be arranged later. I said 'but you must promise to land me in time for any fight in good time' and he promised.

[…]

Noeggerath I had seen going into the Admiralty just before I did – but we did not greet each other.

When I got to the hotel I told Monteith in a whisper – & then came Noeg. He had been present all through the debate & it was his arguments had swayed them – but they had not told him the decision come to. He learned it only from me & was delighted. While we were talking young

Karl Liebknecht (1871–1919): leading socialist and vehement opponent of the First World War. A founder of the Spartacus League along with Rosa Luxemburg and others. [Bundesarchiv]

von Haugwitz came bringing me back my letters to the Delegate at Berne saying it was no use sending it now & he had stopped it. The telegram had gone he assured me.

I discussed what to do with the Delegate & said I'd like to get him here – or if not to send him back to Dublin post haste – but he demurred & said it was better to wait – until tomorrow at any rate. He congratulated me warmly on the change of plan & said he had been very unhappy about the steamer & that he was delighted I had got the submarine. He added 'I will bring the poison all the same.' He begged me to keep out of danger in Ireland & said many things.

Gaffney came – many times during the day – I told him only that there was a delay – no more – & that we should have more time to arrange things & talk over the proper line for him to take about the affairs of the men at Zossen after I was gone & that I was naming him in my letter to the Chancellor as my representative in their regard.

I dined with Frau Remy Barsch[68] & Krebs and turned in at 10 p.m.

[…]

Berlin, Saturday, 8 April 1916

I was to have left today – disguised as a sailor at 3 p.m. or 4 with M.[onteith] & Beverley from the G.G.S. – but yesterday's debate at the Admiralty has changed that. Now I await the fresh developments from the Admiralty at 1 p.m.

---

[68] Frau Barsch also resided in the Hotel Saxonia. She was an Egyptian married to an Austrian and became a close friend of Casement.

Gaffney called at 10. Showed me this![69]

This is awful! I don't know what they may do now. Surely there *is* a fate that hurls things on. How Liebknecht got a hold of this goodness only knows. Monteith came at my request and Zerhusen who is here to translate it. Z. has two copies he says of the Treaty; so has Hahn[70] And the soldiers had it for months—& the *Times* long ago brought out a very *fair rendering* of it.

Noeggerath just 'phoned to say he was leaving town for a few days and wished to see me – and I told him to come at once. He is coming. He came at 12.30 to bid me goodbye & to ask me to give him a letter of authority to recover the Findlay letter from the Captain of the 'Kristianiafjord'. He thinks Schirmer was arrested at Kirkwall on the outward voyage of the 'K', say 25–26 February.

S., it seems, was not on the passenger list! S. was to have handed the Findlay letter to the Captain to keep in his safe. Noeggerath thinks this was probably done & that the letter may be there, safe & sound, but the Captain does not know what to do with it, as it would have been in an unaddressed envelope. Schirmer was to have given it to D[aniel] C[ohalan] in New York – as no word has come, we presume that S. was taken off the boat.

I have written a letter authorising Noeggerath to get the letter back from the Captain, if it still is in his possession and have given N. a letter of introduction to D[aniel] C[ohalan], J.[ohn] D[evoy], and J. McG[arrity] in America.

I then went on at 1 to the Admiralty and saw Captain Stoelzel the chief of the affair & one of his under Captains. No word had yet come. Heydell had gone to Wilhelmshaven to see about the submarine – but the matter had not been settled at 1 o'clock. I was asked to call again at 3. I have just been there & saw Stoelzel & the message was there just coming by phone as I sat on this sofa. It was that a 'U Boat' would be at my service

---

[69] In a side note Casement has written 'All the papers have it. The *Preussiche Zeitung* puts asterisks for the name and omits in same way some of Herr L.'s remarks. *B. Tageblatt* and *Lokalanzeiger* has it in full. R. C.' The relevant cutting from the newspaper is no longer attached but the articles referred to a speech made by the anti-war intellectual and politician, Karl Liebknecht, the leader of the German socialist party, who had attacked Casement in the Reichstag the previous day when he read out the Treaty.

[70] Hahn was the name of the other translator attached to the Irish Brigade with Zerhusen.

from Emden on 12 April. I was to call on Heydell on Monday 10th in the forenoon and get details of departure.

We shall probably leave this for Emden on 11th April (Tuesday) night.

Monteith & Beverley are here. Latter knows nothing yet – but Monteith says he will surely go & with joy. I think M.'s real reason for taking Beverley's was this. M. was in a fearful state over my going by the steamer (I still don't know her name!) and would have done anything to save me. Seeing it was impossible to get a submarine (as we thought) & that I must go I think he meant to 'capture' me at the last moment down at Kiel or wherever the port was – with Beverley's help & tie me up and leave me behind or else, perhaps, as we were coming along the Norwegian coast (in territorial waters all the time) a chance might come to do this & put me on shore.

Old K[rebs] put the idea before me! He said M[onteith] was capable of anything to save me and that I must get on board that ship 'alive or dead'. I agreed with K[rebs] & laughed. Now since yesterday evening this 'possibility' has gone.

Zerhusen is here & buying things for Beverley 'for the journey to the East'. Z[erhusen]'s a fine chap – and his wife a good Irishwoman still. If I live I hope to see them again – but there is not much chance in this world.

Anyhow now there are three days more.

My chief trouble now is the man at Berne. They clearly want me *not* to see him or communicate with him – & I don't know what to do. I am powerless – in their hands.

[The following entries are to be found in NLI MS 17587(1)]

Berlin, Sunday, 9 April 1916

Dies non. Spent day with Gaffney and walked all night nearly to try & sleep – but none.

Berlin, Monday, 10 April 1916

Sent Monteith to G.G.S. (with Beverley) & a note to Count von Haugwitz – attached hereto and then at 11 to Reichsmarineamt and saw Captain Stoelzel and Heydell.

Former told me the 'U boat' would go either from Emden or Wilhelmshaven – not yet settled which – & we should be ready to go tomorrow night (Tuesday 11 April) at 11 p.m. from Zoological Garden station. Captain–Leut Kirchheim will accompany us. All details of departure to be arranged by G.G.S. – a coupé will be reserved.

I asked if the steamer had gone – Yes – & if there would be any chance of our meeting her & Stoelzel said that was not certain – he was not sure!!

Neither am I!

We shall start I think with sealed orders & even after the Commander of the 'U boat' has them I wonder if we three men in a boat shall ever learn our destination? I doubt it. More I think it highly probable that if the 'U Boat' find no revolution in Ireland we shall be brought back for God knows what sort of fate in Germany. If the revolution does not come off it will be put up to me and John McG[arrity]!

Monteith sent for Kavanagh today to give him some information about Quinlisk who has been saying strange things of late Monteith says – M. says it is better to know what the thing is & Kavanagh says he will not tell it save to me. [...]

My chief concern now is for the man at Berne. What a shame not to have brought him here! Just think of it – he has come all that way and I can not communicate with him or learn anything at first hand about the true state of affairs in Ireland.

I do not think for a moment they gave him my telegram comm! It was sent but probably censored by the Legation at Berne.

It looks clear to me that they don't want him to leave Berne until it is quite out of the question he should reach Dublin in time to stop 'proceedings.'

They argue possibly thus – Our people still hope for the officers and a submarine – perhaps if they were told neither was being found there would be no 'revolution' or 'revolt' I mean.

So, MacDonagh, if it indeed be he; is kicking his heels out at Berne waiting for word from me – & I am unable to send it to him.

The right thing would be to bring him here, let us talk frankly – & if he could send him, too by the submarine to Ireland!

They treat me all the time just as they think suits them & their needs – & I am really a prisoner altho' I go to an almost certain death. I tread the pavement with joy – my last day in Berlin, city of dreadful night and most 'forbidding society.' How I loathe the place!

I felt the day I arrived here 31 Oct 1914 that I had walked into a trap –
I heard the jail door close behind me – and it has indeed been my prison
and my doom.

Oh! To see the misted hills of Kerry and the coast and to tread the fair
strand of Tralee!

Monteith and Beverley back from G.G.S. with the same information
roughly as I got at the Admiralty except that they did not know the station
or hour of train departure tomorrow night. Then v. H. called bringing me
back the original telegram to Berne which clearly has not been delivered
to the messenger. (See my remarks on back of it) or else he has hurried
off again home after sending his letter to me on 5 April.

What a fearful business! They will certainly be convinced in Dublin
that the officers are coming – 'this is imperative' – & yet the scoundrels
have deliberately gone on with the enterprise, pushing those poor boys
into the fire, knowing they need officers imperatively & that none could
or would be sent.

Von Haugwitz says I must pay Mks 2010 for £75 gold – before the war
it would have been about Mks 1500.

I was with Frau Remy-Barsch & Krebs a little in afternoon – & feeling
most upset. She gave me some sleeping draught & I slept after dinner.

Berlin, Tuesday, 11 April 1916

My last day in Berlin! Thank God – tomorrow my last day in Germany
– again thank God, an English jail, or scaffold, would be better than to
dwell with these people longer. All deception – all self-interest – all 'on
the make.'

Haugwitz called at 10 – and we interviewed Beverley and put it up
to him. He comes gladly. I pointed out all the dangers & horrors & even
impossibility of it – but he said he would gladly come.

So that is settled.

[…]

Now for some clothing for the voyage – I have only one thin suit – too
cold – the suit Mr J.E. L[andy] crossed in in Oct 1914!

Gaffney several times & Krebs – & Emerson to luncheon. He & Krebs
fought or sparred. Differing types of American that is all.

I wrote a letter to the Chancellor about the Irish soldiers – also to
Count Wedel about Gaffney and the men – & a farewell to the men to be
left with Gaffney & handed to them.

Paid my bill at Saxonia – very dear – and they have swindled me over the doctor – two visits 60 mks!

These people are all swindlers.

Emerson's story of the 6 mark lunch is the best I've heard. Guests to a private house here & then the host asked them to pay for their lunch. They offered 2 marks and he said it had cost so much so they paid 6 marks.

Haugwitz says the train goes at 9.30 tonight – and we are to go to G.G. Staff before hand to get some final instructions – code for more arms etc. etc. Poison too. Haugwitz assured Beverley in my presence and M's that we should be put on shore in Ireland. Nous verrons.

We shall be 12 days I reckon in the submarine – round by Orkneys probably. It will be a dreadful voyage – confined and airless and full of oil smells I fear.

My first fear is that we shall never land – but be kept off the shore until the 'rebellion' breaks out.

[...]

PART 3
APPENDICES

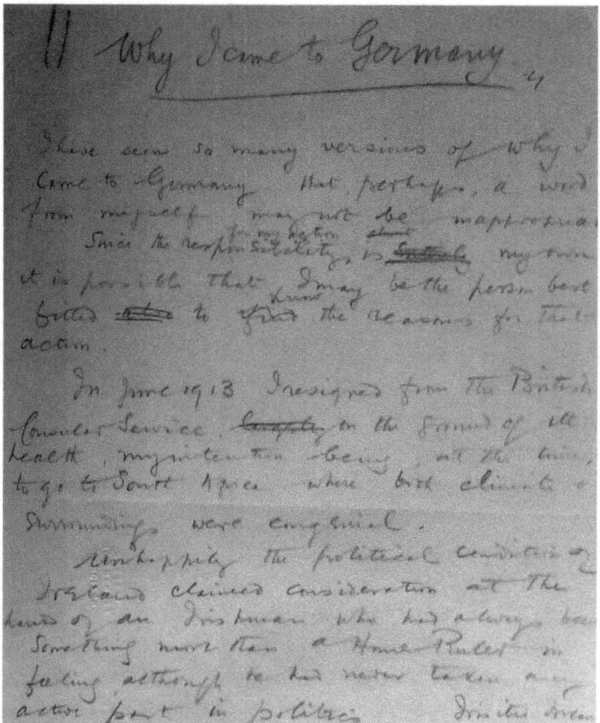

APPENDIX 1:
WHY I WENT TO GERMANY[71]

I have read so many explanations by others why I went to Germany that a word from myself may not be inappropriate. Since the responsibility for my action is my own, I am the best fitted person to tell the reasons for my action.

In June, 1913, I resigned from the British consular service on the ground of ill-health, my intention being to go to South Africa, where both climate and surroundings were congenial.

Unhappily the political conditions of Ireland claimed consideration from me as an Irishman, since I had always been something more than a Home Ruler in feeling, although I had never taken an active part in politics. My views as an Irish Nationalist of this type were well known in the British Foreign Office, and in England as much as in Ireland, for I never made any concealment of them. I had stated them openly on many occasions in the press and they were known to the British Government as fully as to my own friends.

Preparatory (as I thought) to going out to the Cape for a period of repose and quiet, within which to place on record my African and Amazon experiences in the field of tropical research,

---

[71] From the *Evening Mail* (New York), August 10th 1916. A manuscript version of the essay, with the slightly different title – *Why I came to Germany* – is held in NLI MS 13085-11 and is dated 16 December 1915.

I decided to spend the autumn of 1913 in Ireland to pay some farewell visits. As matters turned out I found it very hard to leave Ireland.

The Carson campaign in Ulster was then in full blast, and despite an innate and ever-recurring desire for retirement I found myself overborne by the solicitations of my friends to stay at home, for a time at any rate. In Ulster, where I was most at home, I tried to keep together the small band of 'scattered Protestants' there who desired friendship with our Catholic fellow countrymen, based on an equal recognition of their common Irish identity, against which the forces of intolerance and enmity were openly arrayed.

In this effort I took part throughout the autumn and close of 1913. In November of that year came the establishment of the Irish Volunteers at Dublin. The Irish Volunteers sought to do for all Ireland what the Ulster Volunteers sought for Ulster Protestantism alone – to defend the rights and liberties common to a whole people – Protestant and Catholic.

I joined Professor MacNeill and became a member of the governing body of the Volunteers, and with him addressed the first meetings held, after the inaugural Dublin meeting, in Galway and Cork in December, 1913.

An incident at this time occurred that added weight to the conviction that I already held, that no English Government whether it called itself Whig or Tory was capable of treating Ireland with justice. I refer to the abandonment of the port of Queenstown by the large Cunard vessels on the alleged ground of its dangerous character, and the subsequent action taken against the Hamburg-Amerika line, which had announced its intention of starting a line of steamships to call at Queenstown en route to Boston.

The exclusion of the ships of the Hamburg-Amerika line from Cork harbour by the action of the British authorities was an unfriendly act to Ireland and was accomplished by an underhand diplomacy that would have been unfriendly to a foreign State. How much more significant was it when the interest assailed and the people injured by this intervention were those of 'an integral' part of the realm, whose Government was supposedly that of a United Kingdom of Great Britain and Ireland, bound as much in law and honour to the service of the one island as to the other.

Here was a great Irish port doubly injured by England, first by the English company which repudiated its public contract with the support of the Government whose duty it was to compel its maintenance: next, when a great foreign shipping company undertakes to call at this Irish

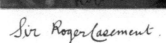

Professor Theodor Schiemann wrote a foreword to this pamphlet on *Sir Roger Casement – Irish Martyr* published in late 1916

port and perform services of great advantage to the whole of Ireland, the Government that had already connived at the breach of public contract by the Cunard Company, intervenes in a stealthy manner to prohibit the call of the Hamburg-Amerika line at the injured Irish port and succeeds in preventing the establishment of a German-Irish-American transport service.

It was clear to me that the British Government treated Ireland as a foreign State and often as a hostile State and that instead of advancing Irish interests abroad, the Department of State we maintained for that purpose worked incessantly against the development of Irish interests with foreign countries, and intrigued against our external trade just as if we had been, indeed, a part of the German Empire instead of the alleged United Kingdom.

Throughout the spring and early summer of 1914 the Volunteer movement spread. In every county thousands of men were enrolling and drilling and everywhere the cry was: 'When shall we get the rifles?'

At a personal interview with Mr. Redmond, May 7, 1914, he stated to me that the last thing he desired was that rifles should be put into the hands of the Volunteers.

I had said that the first duty of those controlling the Volunteer movement was to get arms, as had been done by the Ulster opponents of Irish nationality, and Mr. Redmond interjected that 'Rifles were the last thing to give them'.

At the same meeting it became clear to Professor MacNeill and myself that the Irish Parliamentary Party meant to capture the Volunteers and to use them as a sham army for political purposes on English party platforms.

When it became clear that all Ireland was behind the Volunteer uprisal which others had called into existence despite the efforts of the Irish Parliamentary Party to check the national enthusiasm, Mr. Redmond sought to lay hands upon it, so that it might be deflected from its original Irish purpose. A spontaneous national upheaval of Irish patriotism, designed solely for the defence of Ireland, was to be used for purposes of English political trickery to advance the interests of one English party with which Mr. Redmond had allied his political fortunes.

After making arrangements with a small band of Irish friends, whom I had gathered together in London on May 8, 1914, to get a first consignment of arms purchased on the continent and landed in Ireland, I went to America in order to complete the work of obtaining the financial support of Irish Nationalists there to get arms, just as the Ulster movement had obtained its armed support from the anti-Irish elements of England. I left Ireland in the beginning of July, 1914 (when war was not expected) and towards the end of that month I addressed meetings of Irishmen in Norfolk, Va., and in Philadelphia.

The latter meeting synchronized with the successful landing at Howth of the rifles my friends had bought abroad and landed at the points on the Irish coast I had arranged for before sailing for America – an act which led to the firing by the British garrison upon the people of Dublin on that Sunday afternoon. Were further proof needed of the unchanged and unchanging determination of all British Governments to treat Ireland as a conquered province or a hostile land held in subjection, this outrageous attack of July 26, 1914, on the inhabitants of Dublin furnished it.

At our meeting at Philadelphia on Sunday, August 2, I declared that if Irishmen did their duty by their countrymen at home, this was the last time when any British Government would dare to shoot down Irishmen and women in the streets of an Irish city.

Then came the war. On August 4th the British Government declared war on Germany, a pretext having been carefully arranged beforehand.

I had long believed that British fear and jealousy of German naval progress would bring war, and I had very frankly expressed in Government circles as elsewhere, my opinions as to the rightfulness or even sanity of English antagonism to Germany.

Germany had never injured England, much less Ireland, and it was plain that she was being attacked not for the wrong she had done to others, but from the hope those others held of doing injury to her.

Ireland was being appealed to by every agency of fear, of resentment, of misplaced chivalry, of self-interest, to send hundreds of thousands of her men to a fight that, at the best, concerned her not at all.

In return for the passage of the Home Rule Bill into 'law' but not into fact, it was being openly urged by English Ministers and by the English press that Irishmen should 'flock to the colours'.

This so-called Home Rule Bill, against which the English oligarchy (who had now declared war on Germany) had arrayed for two years all the forces of wealth, bigotry and intolerance, on the ground that even the shadow of an Irish 'Parliament' must be prevented from taking shape on Irish soil was now rushed through both Houses of Parliament in the openly avowed hope of entrapping thousands of young Irishmen into the British army, on the ground that England had at length granted 'national freedom' to Ireland.

I sought to meet this dishonest effort to betray my countrymen into the ranks of an army of aggression being massed for a dishonest attack upon a people with whom Irishmen had no just cause of quarrel, by two public letters addressed through the Irish press to Irishmen, in which I begged them to stay at home and leave England to fight her own wars of aggression.

The first of these letters reached its destination and was published in the Dublin *Irish Independent* of October 5, 1914. (The steps taken against myself by the British Government on the publication of this letter I must defer dealing with to a later period.) This first hurried letter I followed with a more carefully drafted statement of opinion written from New York, which I hoped might appear in the Irish press and might serve to keep Irishmen from enlisting in a bad cause.

My later letter, however, failed to reach the Irish press, owing to the British censorship. Soon afterwards I embarked for Germany. Letters alone, I saw, could not keep Irishmen at home or meet the numerous agencies of calumny and ill-will that were being employed to plunge them into the shambles of a war of unparalleled misery and destruction.

My object was a peaceful, not a belligerent one. Not to 'foment a rebellion in Ireland', as some of my ignorant critics have asserted, but so far as possible to keep Ireland at peace and Irishmen out of the war was my intent by placing before my countrymen a clear and authoritative statement of German aims that might go far to meet the flood of misrepresentations being steadily poured over Ireland by the British Government. I believed that if I could reach Germany and state these objects to the German Government, I could not fail to accomplish something of what I hoped to achieve.

I hoped that the German Government might be induced to make clear its peaceful intentions towards Ireland and that the effect of such a pronouncement in Ireland itself might be powerful enough to keep

Irishmen from volunteering for a war that had no claim upon their patriotism or their honour.

With this aim chiefly in view, I came to Germany in November, 1914, and I succeeded in my purpose.

The German Government declared openly its goodwill towards Ireland and in convincing terms.

APPENDIX 2:
ROGER CASEMENT'S LETTER
TO SIR EDWARD GREY

Berlin, 1 February 1915.

Sir –

I observe that some discussion has taken place in the House of Lords on the subject of the pension I voluntarily ceased to draw when I set out to learn what might be the intentions of the German Government in regard to Ireland.

In the course of that discussion I understand Lord Crewe observed that 'Sir Roger Casement's actions merited a sensible punishment.'

The question raised thus as to my action and your publicly suggested punishment of it I propose discussing here and now, since the final proof of the actual punishment you sought in secret to inflict upon me is, at length, in my possession.

It is true I was aware of your intentions from the first day I set foot in Norway three months ago; but it has taken time to compel your agent there to furnish the written proof of the conspiracy then set on foot against me by His Majesty's Government.

Let me first briefly define my action before proceeding to contrast it with your own.

The question between the British Government and myself has never been, as you are fully aware, a matter of a pension, of a reward, a decoration.

I served the British Government faithfully as long as it was possible for me to do so, and when it became impossible, I resigned. When later, it became impossible for me to use the pension assigned me by law I voluntarily abandoned that income as I had previously resigned the post from which it was derived, and as I now proceed to divest myself of the honors and distinctions that at various times have been conferred upon me by His Majesty's Government.

I came to Europe from the United States last October in order to make sure that whatever might be the course of this war, my own country, Ireland, should suffer from it the minimum of harm.

The view I held was made sufficiently clear in an open letter I wrote on the 17th of September last in New York, and sent to Ireland for public distribution among my countrymen. I append a printed copy of that letter. It defines my personal standpoint clearly enough and expresses the views I held, and hold, on an Irishman's duty to his country in this crisis of world affairs. Soon after writing that letter I set out for Europe.

To save Ireland from some of the calamities of war was worth the loss to myself of pension and honours and was even worth the commission of an act of technical 'treason.'

I decided to take all the risks and to accept all the penalties the Law might attach to my action. I did not, however, bargain for risks and penalties that lay outside the law as far as my own action lay outside the field of moral turpitude.

In other words, while I reckoned with British law and legal penalties and accepted the sacrifice of income, position and reputation as prices I must pay, I did not reckon with the British Government.

I was prepared to face charges in a Court of Law; I was not prepared to meet waylaying, kidnapping, suborning of dependents or 'knocking on the head,' in fine, all the expedients your representative in a neutral country invoked when he became aware of my presence there.

For the criminal conspiracy that Mr M. de C. Findlay, H.B.M. Minister to the Court of Norway entered into on the 30th of October last, in the British Legation at Christiania, with the Norwegian subject, my dependent, Eivind Adler Christensen, involved all these things and more. It involved not merely a lawless attack upon myself for which the British Minister promised my follower the sum of £5,000, but it involved a breach of international law as well as of common law, for which the British Minister in Norway promised this Norwegian subject full immunity.

On the 29th of October last year I landed at Christiania, coming from America. Within a few hours of my landing the man I had engaged and in whom I reposed trust was accosted by one of the secret service agents of the British Minister and carried off, in a private motor car, to the British Legation, where the first attempt was made on his honor to induce him to be false to me.

Your agent in the Legation that afternoon professed ignorance of who I was and sought, as he put it, merely to find out my identity and movements.

Failing in this the first attempt to obtain satisfaction, Adler Christensen was assailed the next day, the 30th of October, by a fresh agent and received an invitation to again visit the British Legation 'where he would hear something good.'

The second interview, held in the early forenoon, was with the Minister himself.

Mr Findlay came quickly to the point. The ignorance, assumed or actual, of the previous day, as to my identity, was now discarded. He confessed that he knew me, but that he did not know where I was going to, what I intended doing, or what might be the specific end I had in view.

It was enough for him that I was an Irish Nationalist.

He admitted that the British Government had no evidence of anything wrong done or contemplated by me that empowered them either morally or lawfully to interfere with my movements. But he was bent on doing so. Therefore he baldly invoked lawless methods, and suggested to my dependent that were I to 'disappear' it would be 'a very good thing for whoever brought it about.'

He was careful to point out that nothing could happen to the perpetrator of the crime, since my presence in Christiania was known only to the British Government and that Government would screen and provide for those responsible for my 'disappearance.'

He indicated, quite plainly, the methods to be employed, by assuring Adler Christensen that who ever 'knocked him on the head need not do any work for the rest of his life,' and proceeded to apply the moral by asking Christensen, 'I suppose you would not mind having an easy time of it for the rest of your days?'

My faithful follower concealed the anger he felt at this suggestion and continued the conversation in order to become more fully aware of the plot that might be devised against my safety. He pointed out that I had not only been very kind to him but that I 'trusted him implicitly.'

It was on this 'implicit trust' Mr. Findlay then proceeded to build the whole framework of his conspiracy against my life, my liberty, the public law of Norway and the happiness of the young man he sought to tempt by monstrous bribes to the commission of a dastardly crime against his admitted benefactor.

If I could be intercepted, cut off, 'disappear,' no one would know and no question could be asked, since there was no Government save the British Government knew of my presence in Norway and there was no authority I could appeal to for help, while that Government would shield the individual implicated and provide handsomely for his future. Such, in Mr. Findlay's words (recorded by me) was the proposition put by His Majesty's Minister before the young man who had been enticed for this purpose into the British Legation.

That this man was faithful to me and the law of his country was a triumph of Norwegian integrity over the ignoble inducement proffered him by the richest and most powerful Government in the world to be false to both.

Having thus outlined his project, Mr. Findlay invited Christensen to 'think the matter over and return at 3 o'clock if you are disposed to go on with it.'

He handed him in Norwegian paper money twenty-five *kroner* 'just to pay your taxi-cab fares,' and dismissed him.

Feeling a not unnatural interest in these proposals as to how I should be disposed of, I instructed the man it was thus sought to bribe to return to the British Legation at 3 o'clock and to seemingly fall in with the wishes, of your Envoy extraordinary.

I advised him, however, for the sake of appearance to 'sell me dear' and to secure the promise of a very respectable sum for so very disreputable an act.

Christensen, who has been a sailor and naturally has seen some strange company, assured me he was perfectly at home with His Majesty's Representative.

He returned to the Legation at 3 o'clock and remained closeted with Mr. Findlay until nearly 5 p.m.. The full record of their conversation will be laid before you, and others, in due course.

My follower pretended to fall in with the British Minister's projects, only stipulating for a good sum to be paid in return for his treachery. Mr. Findlay promised on his 'word of honor' (such was the quaint phraseology employed to guarantee this transaction), that Christensen should receive £5,000 sterling whenever he could deliver me into the hands of the British authorities.

If in the course of this kidnapping process I should come to harm or personal injury be done me, then no question would be asked and full immunity guaranteed the kidnapper.

My follower pointed out that as I was leaving that evening for Copenhagen, having already booked my compartment in the mail train, he would not have any immediate chance of executing the commission.

Mr. Findlay agreed that it would be necessary to defer the attempt until some favorable opportunity offered of decoying me down to the coast 'anywhere on the Skaggerack or North Sea' where British warships might be in waiting to seize me.

He entrusted my dependent with the further commission of purloining my correspondence with my supposed associates in America and Ireland, particularly in Ireland, so that they, too, might participate in the sensible punishment being devised for me.

He ordained a system of secret correspondence with himself Christensen should employ, and wrote out the confidential address in Christiania to which he was to communicate the results of his efforts to purloin my papers and to report on my plans.

This address in Christiania was written down by Mr. Findlay on a half sheet of Legation note paper in printed characters. This precaution was adopted he said 'so as to prevent the handwriting being traced.'

This document, along with one hundred crowns in Norwegian paper money given by Mr. Findlay as an earnest of more to follow was at once brought to me with an account of the proceedings.

As I was clearly in a position of some danger, I changed my plans and instead of proceeding to Copenhagen as I had intended doing, I decided to alter my procedure and route.

It was, then, with this secret knowledge of the full extent of the crime plotted by your Representative in Norway against me that I left Christiania on the 30th of October. The rest of the story need not take so long in the telling.

You are fully aware of most of the details, as you were in constant touch with your agent both by cable and despatch.

You are also aware of the declaration of the Imperial German Government, issued on November 20 last in reply to the enquiry I addressed to them.

The British Government, both by press reports and by direct agents had charged Germany, throughout the length and breadth of Ireland, with the commission of atrocious crimes in Belgium and had warned the Irish people that their fate would be the same, did Germany win this war.

Your Government sought to frighten Irishmen into a predatory raid upon a people who had never injured them and to persuade them by false charges that this was their duty.

I sought not only a guarantee of German goodwill to Ireland, but to relieve my countrymen from the apprehensions this campaign of calumny was designed to provoke and so far as was possible to dissuade them from embarking in an immoral conflict against a people who had never wronged Ireland. That Declaration of the German Government, issued as I know in all sincerity, is the justification for my 'treason.' *The justification of the conspiracy of the British Government and its Minister at Christiania begun before I had set foot on German soil in a country where I had a perfect right to be and conducted by means of the lowest forms of attempted bribery and corruption I leave you, sir, to discover.*

You will not discover it in the many interviews Mr. Findlay had, during the months of November and December last, at his own seeking, with my faithful follower. The correspondence between them in the cypher the Minister had arranged tells its own story.

These interviews furnished matter that in due course I shall make public. What passed between your agent and mine on these occasions you are fully aware of, as you were the directing power throughout the whole proceeding.

Your object, as Mr. Findlay frankly avowed to the man he thought he had bought, was to take my life with public indignity – mine was to expose your design and to do so through the very agent you had yourselves singled out for the purpose and had sought to corrupt to an act of singular infamy.

On one occasion in response to my follower's pretended dissatisfaction with the amount offered for betraying me you authorized your agent to increase the sum to £10,000. I have a full record of the conversations held and of the pledges proffered in your name.

On two occasions, during these prolonged bargainings your Minister gave Adler Christensen gifts of 'earnest money.' Once it was five hundred crowns in Norwegian currency; the next time a similar sum, partly in Norwegian money and partly in English gold. On one of these occasions, to be precise on the 7th of December last, Mr. Findlay handed Adler Christensen the key of the back entrance of the British Legation, so that he might go and come unobserved and at all hours.

I propose returning this key in person to the donor and along with it the various sums so anxiously bestowed upon my follower.

The stories told Mr. Findlay at these interviews should not have deceived a school boy. All the pretended evidence of my plans and intentions Adler Christensen produced, the bogus letters, fictitious maps and charts and other incitements to Mr. Findlay's appetite for the incredible were part of my necessary plan of self defence to lay bare the conspiracy you were engaged in and to secure that convincing proof of it I now hold.

It was not until the 3rd ultimo that Mr. Findlay committed himself to give my protector the duly signed and formal pledge of reward and immunity, in the name of the British Government, for the crime he was being instigated to commit, that is now in my possession.

I transmit you herewith a photograph of this document.[72]

At a date compatible with my own security against the clandestine guarantees and immunities of the British Minister in Norway I shall proceed to lay before the legitimate authorities

---

[72] This document is reproduced on page 148.

in that country the original document and the evidence in my possession that throws light on the proceedings of His Majesty's Government.

To that Government, through you, sir, I now beg to return the insignia of the Most Distinguished Order of St. Michael and St. George, the Coronation Medal of His Majesty King George V, and any other medal, honor or distinction conferred upon me by His Majesty's Government. Of which it is possible for me to divest myself.

I am, sir, your most obedient, humble servant,

(Signed) ROGER CASEMENT

The Right Honorable
Sir E. Grey, Bart., K.G., M.P.,
London.

Appendix 3:
The Treaty

Article 1: With a view to securing the national freedom of Ireland, with the moral and material assistance of the Imperial German Government, an Irish Brigade shall be formed from among the Irish soldiers, or other natives of Ireland, now prisoners of war in Germany.

Article 2: The object of the Irish Brigade shall be to fight solely in the cause of Ireland, and under no circumstances shall it be employed or directed to any German end.

Article 3: The Irish Brigade shall be formed and shall fight under the Irish flag alone.

The men shall wear a special distinctively Irish uniform.

As soon as Irishmen can be got for the purpose, either from Ireland or the United States, the Brigade shall have only Irish officers. Until such time as Irish officers can be secured German officers will be appointed with the approval of Sir Roger Casement, to have disciplinary control of the men.

But no military operation shall be ordered or conducted by the German officers of the Brigade, during such time as the men are under their control not approved of by Sir Roger Casement or not in strict conformity with Article 2.

Article 4: The Irish Brigade shall be clothed, fed and efficiently equipped with arms and munitions by the Imperial German Government on the clear understanding that these are furnished it as free gifts to aid the cause of Irish independence.

Article 5: It is distinctly understood and is hereby formally declared by the Parties to this Agreement that the Irish Brigade shall consist only of Volunteers in the cause of Irish national freedom, and as such no member of the Irish Brigade shall receive pay or monetary reward of any kind from the Imperial German Government during the period he shall bear arms in the Brigade.

Article 6: The Imperial German Government undertakes, in certain circumstances, to send the Irish Brigade to Ireland with efficient military support and with an ample supply of arms and ammunition to equip the Irish National Volunteers in Ireland who may be willing to join them in the attempt to recover Irish national freedom by force of arms.

The certain circumstances hereby understood are the following:

In the event of a German naval victory affording the means of reaching the coast of Ireland, the Imperial German Government pledges itself to dispatch the Irish Brigade and a supporting body of German officers and men, in German transports, to attempt a landing on the Irish Coast.

Article 7: The opportunity to land in Ireland can only arise if the fortune of war should grant the German Navy a victory that would open, with reasonable prospect of success, the sea-route to Ireland. Should the German Navy not succeeed in this effort the Irish Brigade shall be employed in Germany, or elsewhere, solely in such way as Sir Roger Casement may approve as being in strict conformity with Article 2.

In this event it might be possible to employ the Irish Brigade to assist the Egyptian People to recover their freedom by driving the British out of Egypt. Short of directly fighting to free Ireland from British rule a blow struck at the British invaders of Egypt, to aid Egyptian national freedom, is a blow struck for a kindred cause to that of Ireland.

Article 8: In the event of the Irish Brigade volunteering for this service the Imperial German Government undertakes to make arrangements with the Austro-Hungarian Government for its transport through that Empire to Constantinople, and to provide with the Turkish Government for the recognition and acceptance of the Irish Brigade as a Volunteers Corps attached to the Turkish Army in an effort to expel the British from Egypt.

Article 9: In the event of the war coming to an end without the object of the Irish Brigade having been effected, namely its landing in Ireland, the

Imperial German Government undertakes to send each member of the Brigade who may so desire it, to the United States of America, with the necessary means to land in that country in conformity with the United States Immigration Laws.

Article 10: In the event of the Irish Brigade landing in Ireland, and military operations in the country resulting in the overthrow of British Authority and the erection of a native Irish Government the Imperial German Government will give the Irish Government so established its fullest moral support, and both by public recognition and by general goodwill will contribute, with all sincerity, to the establishment of an independent government in Ireland.

Appendix 4:
Biographies

Bailey, Daniel Julian (aka. Beverley) (1887–1968) born in Dublin, he volunteered for the Casement Brigade and was the third man to land with Casement and Monteith at Banna Strand on 21 April 1916. He was captured and charged with treason, alongside Casement at Bow Street Magistrates' Court. He was found not guilty, and later on joined the British army.

Ballin, Albert (1857–1918) was the owner of the Hamburg-Amerika shipping line and is credited as the initiator of the idea of modern cruise ship travel. In 1913, Casement negotiated an arrangement with Ballin to bring his liners to Queenstown Harbour (Cobh) on their transatlantic voyages to and from America, thereby breaking the British transport monopoly of routes in and out of Ireland. But the plan was scuppered. In the years before the outbreak of war, Ballin tried to mediate more peaceful relations between Britain and Germany.

Bannister, Gertrude (1873–1950) Casement's faithful cousin, who he had known since his youth and holidays spent in Liverpool with her parents. She maintained a correspondence with Casement for the rest of his life. In 1916 she married Sydney Parry and went to live in Cushendun in the Glens of Antrim. Bannister donated much of Casement's archive to the National Library of Ireland.

Behncke, Paul (1869–1937) German Admiral, largely remembered for his commanding role at the Battle of Jutland. Chief of the Admiralty (1920–24). Casement met with him in January 1915.

Berckheim, Philipp von (1883–1945) a secretary at the German General Staff.

Berkessel, Johann (d.1927) Catholic priest who spent eighteen years teaching at Rockwell College. He lived about twelve miles outside Limburg, and remained supportive of Casement's efforts among the Irish POWs.

Bernstorff, Count Johann Heinrich von (1862–1939) German ambassador to the US from 1908–17. Casement met with Bernstorff before leaving New York and received a letter of introduction from him to facilitate his arrival into Berlin.

Bethmann Hollweg, Theobald von (1856–1921) was German Chancellor from 1909–17. Casement met with him privately on 18 December 1914.

Beverley, Julian, (see Bailey, Daniel, Julian)

Bittenfeld, Hans-Wolfgang Herwarth von (1871–1942) had served as German military attaché in Washington. Later, he served as a Nazi propagandist under Joseph Goebbels, where he was engaged in psychological warfare.

Blücher, Count Gebhard von (1863–1931) was the great-great grandson of the Prussian field marshal. He had known Casement since their time together in Portuguese East Africa. The Casement–Blücher correspondence, relevant to 1914–16, is held in Clare County Archives.

Blücher, Evelyn von (1876–1960), born Evelyn Stapleton-Bretherton, she married Count Gebhard von Blücher in 1907. Her memoir *An English Wife in Berlin: A Private Memoir of Events, Politics and Daily Life in Germany Throughout the War and the Social Revolution of 1918* (New York, 1920) was widely translated and included quite a substantial, and not altogether flattering, description of her meeting with Casement. After the war, Princess Blücher passed on Casement's papers, which had been left in her custody, to British intelligence.

Blunt, Wilfrid Scawen (1840–1922) poet, writer and anti-imperialist, he developed a strong sympathy with the struggle for Irish independence. He was known to Casement through Irish circles, and the two men met in 1914.

Boehm, Captain Hans W.L. (1873–1959) assigned by the German High Command to assist Roger Casement while he was in Germany to raise a brigade among Irish prisoners-of-war to return to Ireland, and assist the fight for independence. While Casement spoke no German, Boehm was married to an American and had several Irish friends. He assisted Casement significantly until he was sent on a mission, possibly to the US, in September 1915. He was arrested in British waters off Falmouth in 1917 and interned. The correspondence between Casement and Boehm is held in the UCD archives.

Cheetham, Milne (1869–1938) career diplomat; he had served with Casement at the British Embassy in Brazil, before being sent to Cairo in 1910. He was appointed acting High Commissioner following the declaration of a British protectorate over Egypt in 1914.

Childers, Robert Erskine (1870–1922) author of the best-selling spy novel, *The Riddle of the Sands*, he collaborated with Casement and Alice Stopford Green on a gun-running operation into Ireland in July 1914. Casement admired his book *The Framework for Home Rule* (1911); his copy with annotations is held in the National Library of Ireland.

Christensen, Eivind Adler (1890–?) born in Moss, Norway. Migrated to the US in 1909 and settled in Pennsylvania where he married in 1911; a child was born later that year. In 1914 he was employed by Casement as his manservant, and together they collaborated in a dangerous conspiracy against the British Foreign Office.

Clarke, Tom (1858–1916) Clarke dedicated his life to Irish liberation, was imprisoned for long spells and worked in the shadows of various republican organisations, through his newsagents shop in central Dublin. He was the main advocate for sending Monteith to Germany. A signatory of the Proclamation of the Irish Republic, he was executed in May 1916.

Cockran, William Bourke (1854–1923) born in County Sligo and educated in France, a noted orator and politician.

Cohalan, Daniel F. (1867–1946) US lawyer and senior figure within Clan na Gael circles, and close friend of John Devoy. Cohalan had worked closely in the preparations to send Casement to Germany. Later on he was active in the *Friends of Irish Freedom*.

Colum, Padraic (1881–1972) versatile writer, folklorist and leading light of the Irish Literary Revival. Casement met him through literary connections in London and contributed to his magazine *The Irish Review*. In 1914 Colum travelled with his wife Mary to New York and saw Casement quite regularly.

Conan Doyle, Sir Arthur (1859–1930) physician and novelist, Conan Doyle developed a relationship with Casement over several years, and supported both his Congo and Putumayo campaigns as well as the Morel testimonial of 1911. The two fell out over the First World War.

Crewe, 1st Marquess of (1858–1945) son-in-law of Lord Rosebery. From 1892–95 he served as Lord Lieutenant of Ireland and Secretary of State for the Colonies 1908–1910.

Crotty, Father Thomas (1867–1930) born in New Ross to a family with a prosperous bakery business in Kilkenny. He joined the Dominicans in 1884. In November 1914, Crotty was sent by the Vatican to Germany and began to work as a special envoy to Irish POWs, first in Limburg and then Zossen. He developed a strong bond with Casement and appears to have influenced Casement's own spiritual shift towards Catholicism. The correspondence between Crotty and Casement is held in NLI MS 13085/20.

Curry, Charles (d. 1935) a resident of Riderau near Munich, where Casement resided in the summer and autumn of 1915, Curry became a critical figure in Casement's last weeks in Berlin and was left detailed instructions by Casement as to the dispersal and publication of his papers, including his diaries. After the war, Curry edited the first edition of Casement's war-time diaries, which was also translated into German.

Curzon, George, 1st Marquess Curzon of Kiddleston (1859–1925). He had worked with Casement while Under-Secretary of State for Foreign Affairs from 1895–98, and was then appointed Viceroy of India (1899–1905). His second wife Grace was the widow of the Irish Argentine diplomat, Alfredo Huberto Duggan. Her three children from this marriage (Alfred, Hubert and Grace) were brought up by Curzon.

Dernburg, Bernhard (1865–1937) German banker and politician; headed the Imperial Colonial Office from 1907–1910; active in the US during the war, organising anti-British propaganda.

Devoy, John (1842–1928) born in Kill, County Kildare, after a brief spell in the French Foreign Legion, Devoy submerged himself in the Fenian movement. Exiled to the US, he earned a living from journalism. By 1914 Devoy was the most active Irish-American involved in revolutionary circles and with his own newspaper: *The Gaelic American*. He communicated closely with the Germany embassy, and supported Casement's diplomatic mission (with some reservations). However, the shared aspiration of Casement and Devoy for a united and independent Ireland was compromised by their different views on how that end might be achieved. By early 1916, Devoy had apparently lost confidence in Casement. He was particularly concerned about indiscreet talk, and those he was prepared to allow into his confidence.

Donnersmarck, Guido Henckel von (1830–1916) mining and steel magnate.

Dowling, Joseph Patrick (1886–1932) a carpenter by trade, he joined the British army in 1904 and was called up in 1914. Captured at the battle of Mons in September 1914, he joined the Irish Brigade in March 1915.

Egan, Patrick (1841–1919) nationalist and agitator, born Ballymahon, County Longford, early member of the IRB, instrumental in exposing the Piggott forgeries.

Emerson, Edwin (1869–1959) journalist, secret agent and a graduate of Harvard University. Emerson served as Theodore Roosevelt's clerk during the Spanish-American war. He later worked as a mercenary in South America, and as a journalist for various US publications. Sympathetic to Germany, on the outbreak of war in 1914 he was involved in editing the English language propaganda newspaper *The Continental Times*; Casement regularly contributed to the paper during 1915. After the war, he was expelled from various countries for subversive activities, before setting up the *Society of American Friends of Germany* in 1933.

Exner, Paul, (d.1927) a major-general and commandant of the Limburg prison camp.

Falkenhayn, Erich von (1861–1922) chief of the German General Staff during the First World War. After taking over as chief of the general staff in 1914, Falkenhayn responded positively to Casement's plan.

Findlay, Mansfeldt de Cardonnel (1861–1932) British Minister at Christiania, he conspired to have Casement captured or 'disappeared'. Findlay had previously been involved in the notorious Denshawai affair, an incident in Egypt between British military officials and local Egyptians, which led to the hanging of seven men. Despite his somewhat nefarious activities on behalf of the British Foreign Office, he was later knighted for his services to the Crown.

Freeman, George, editor of the *Gaelic American*. Freeman was actively engaged in Indian national independence, and was closely involved in seditious activities linking Irish republicans and Indian anti-colonial nationalists. Casement met with him in New York City in 1914.

Fromme, Franz (1880–1960) linguist and author. Fromme translated many of Casement's essays into German, published in *Sir Roger Casement: Irland, Deutschland & Die Freiheit der Meere & Andere Aufsätze* (Munich, 1916). He later wrote on Ireland's independence struggle in light of the rise of Nazism, in *Irlands Kampf um die Freiheit,* (1933).

Gaffney, Thomas St John (1864–1945) born in Limerick, Gaffney was the US consul general in Dresden (1905–12) and then Munich (1914). His pro-German and pro-Irish sympathies eventually led to his dismissal by US President Wilson. Gaffney was part of Casement's revolutionary circle in Germany. He enjoyed Casement's confidence most of the time. He was entrusted with the care of the Irish Brigade in April 1916. His volume of memoirs – *Breaking the Silence: England, Ireland, Wilson and the War* (New York: Horace Liveright: 1930) – contained quite extensive chapters on Casement and revealed sensitive aspects of the war on truth.

Gardiner, A.G. (1865–1946) Editor of the *Daily News* (1902–19). He had supported Casement's Putumayo campaign.

Gasquet, Cardinal Francis Aidan (1846–1929) Benedictine monk and historian of the late-medieval and early-modern period. Ordained a cardinal in 1914, he was appointed as head archivist of the *Archivum Secretum Apostolicum Vaticanum* (Vatican Secret Archives) in 1917. His sympathies lay with Britain and not with Irish nationalism.

Graaf, General de, according to Casement, a former friend of King Edward VII, and native of Wiesbaden.

Green, Alice Stopford (1848–1929) historian, Irish nationalist and founding secretary of the African Society, Alice Stopford Green acted as a mentor and friend to Roger Casement. Their friendship from 1904–16 was critical to the intellectual formation of Irish independence, and in defining Ireland's anti-colonial dimension in the build-up to the Easter Rising. Her extensive network of friends rallied behind Casement's work in both the Congo and the Amazon. It was in Stopford Green's house on Grosvenor Road that the decision was made to run guns into Ireland in 1914. During Casement's trial, Stopford Green worked tirelessly for his defence. In 1922 she was elected as one of the first four women senators.

Gregory, J.D., joined the British Foreign Office in 1902, and grew close to Sir Edward Grey. He worked closely with Casement over the Putumayo Mission Fund 1912–13. Fiercely anti-Bolshevik, he worked as a press liaison officer after the war, and his name was associated with the publication of the Zinoviev Letter. In 1927 he was dismissed from office for improper speculation in foreign currency. He later wrote a volume of memoirs *On the Edge of Diplomacy: Rambles and Reflections 1902–28* (1929)

Grey, Sir Edward (1862–1933) served as British Foreign Secretary from 1905 to 1916. Casement returned to the foreign service in 1906 on a personal request from Grey, and the two cooperated closely on Congo reform and the revelation of the Putumayo atrocities. As Casement became more intolerant of the betrayal of Gladstonian Liberal ideals by the Liberal Imperialism of Grey, the respect between the two men declined. Casement never forgave Grey for taking Britain into the war. In 1915, Casement wrote a blistering attack on Grey, published in *The Continental Times* (18 October 1915) and the *Gaelic American* (20 November 1915). Casement was executed in 1916 on the anniversary of Grey's epoch-making speech to the House of Commons on 3 August 1914.

Hahn, Countess Theresa, an intimate friend of Casement's during his time in Berlin. The two regularly dined together.

Haugwitz-Hardenberg-Reventlow, Count Curt Ludvig Heinrich Georg Max Erdman (1885–1963) was a member of the Politik-Berlin of the German General Staff, and worked as a liaison officer between the German F.O. and the Emperor's Military HQ. Von Haugwitz was in charge of organising the shipment of arms to Ireland. Later, he wrote a brief account of Casement's time in Germany describing an unrealised plan to return with Casement to Ireland in a memoir presented to Éamon de Valera in 1947. The document is held in NLI MS 13774.

Heydel(l), Eberhard, Imperial German naval officer, who liaised with Casement in the weeks before his departure. Casement wrote a letter to Heydel, while on board the U-19, shortly before landing in Ireland.

Hobson, Bulmer (1883–1969) activist and republican. The friendship between Roger Casement and Bulmer Hobson was vital to preparations for the 1916 Rising. Hobson was a tireless grassroots campaigner, and organised various republican initiatives including the Dungannon Clubs, Na Fianna Éireann and edited newspapers such as *The Irish Peasant* and *Irish Freedom*. He was instrumental in the pick up of guns from Howth harbour in July 1914. In the days before the Easter Rising, Hobson did his best to call off manoeuvres and implement Eoin MacNeill's countermanding order. To prevent this, he was held in a house in Phibsboro.

Howard, Sir Henry (1843–1921) British career diplomat, in December 1914 he became the first envoy to the Vatican for over 350 years.

Hülsen Bernhard von (1865–1950) a German general who formed a paramilitary group after the war heavily involved in the suppression of the Spartacus League.

Isendahl, Walter (1872–1945) directed German Naval intelligence or 'N' (Nachrichten-Abteilung) for much of the war.

Jagow, Gottlieb von (1863–1935) diplomat and the German foreign minister from 1913–16, he played a key part in international negotiations before and after the outbreak of war.

Kavanagh, Sean Francis (1890–1965) joined South Irish Horse and captured early on in the war. He was an early recruit to the Irish Brigade. In 1922, he wrote a volume of memoirs of his experiences in Germany *The Betrayal of Roger Casement and the Irish Brigade* (Unpublished).

Kelly, Bryan, a student in Germany when the war broke out, Kelly was imprisoned and then released. He helped Casement with recruiting, and was later dispatched back to Ireland.

Kenny, John (1847–1924) President of Clan na Gael, using his status as a businessman, Kenny served as an intermediary in the brokering of the deal over the organising of the German arms for the rising.

Keogh, Michael (1891–1964) born in Tullow, County Carlow. He met Casement for the first time in New York in early 1912. He joined the Royal Irish Regiment, and was captured in the opening weeks of the war. He became a senior NCO in the Irish Brigade. He would later write a volume of embellished memoirs *With Casement's Irish Brigade* (2010).

Kiliani, Richard (1861–1927) jurist and diplomat; on the outbreak of war he was deployed to oversee the press department in the German Foreign Office.

Krebs, Franz Hugo (1868–1950) a graduate of Harvard Law School, Krebs worked as a pro-German journalist during the war for, among other newspapers, the *New York Times*. He arranged Casement's meeting with the cinematographer, Albert K. Dawson.

Larkin, James (1876–1947) socialist and trade union organiser, who founded the Irish Labour Party and the Irish Transport and General Workers' Union. He played a critical role in the Dublin Lockout of 1913. From 1914–23 he located to the US and continued his activism.

Lay, Julius G. (1872–1939) US diplomat, served as consul general in Berlin during the war. He met with Casement on several occasions.

Leiningen, Emich, fifth Prince of (1866–1939) born in Osborne house, Isle of Wight. His paternal grandfather was the half-brother of Queen Victoria. He accompanied Casement during his visits to Limburg in late 1914.

Lersner, Kurt von (1883–1954) German diplomat and politician; he became a close friend of Franklin D. Roosevelt when stationed at the German embassy in Washington in 1913/14. Casement met with von Lersner in New York before journeying to Germany and was one of the officials he met on his visit to the German Headquarters of the Foreign Office at Charleville.

Leyds W.J. (1859–1940) Dutch lawyer. During the South African war (1899–1902) he became special envoy to the South African Republic and Minister Plenipotentiary in Brussels and met with many of the pro-Boer Irish, including Maud Gonne.

Lichnowsky, Karl Max, Prince (1860–1928) German ambassador in London in 1914. He took a highly critical view of German diplomacy during the July crisis.

Lüttichau, Count Graf von,(1853–1939) descended from an old Prussian family, who were counts of the Holy Roman Empire, he accompanied Casement on his journey to Charleville in November 1914.

MacDonnell, Antony (1844–1925) Irish-born civil servant and supporter of Irish Home Rule, he served for many years in the Indian Civil Service. He was a close friend of Alice Stopford Green, through whom he met Casement.

McGarrity, Joseph (1874–1940) born in County Tyrone, he came from a strong Irish nationalist tradition. McGarrity emigrated to the US in 1892, and became a leading figure in Clan na Gael. He provided support for many causes in the build up to 1916, including Casement's fund-raising tour among Irish-America sympathisers. Casement stayed with him during his trip to the US in 1914. He was deeply implicated in the Hindu–German conspiracy, and organised and paid for the *Annie Larsen* arms purchase. He steadfastly opposed the Treaty of 1921. He spent considerable time and money trying to salvage Casement's reputation from the propaganda conflict of the post-war years. Unlike Devoy, his belief in Casement never wavered.

McGoey, John (1883–1924) Scottish-born to Irish parents, he emigrated to Canada and US in 1903. In late 1915 he was sent by McGarrity to assist Casement and joined the Irish Brigade at Zossen.

McMurrough, Francis (c.1887-?) enrolled in the Leinster regiment and was an early recruit to the Irish Brigade, although he backed out after discovering it was a voluntary organisation.

MacNeill, Eoin (1867–1945) born in Glenarm, County Antrim, MacNeill founded the Gaelic League. In 1908 he was appointed professor of Irish History at UCD and became first Chief-of-Staff of the Irish Volunteers in 1913. MacNeill and Casement collaborated closely in Irish Volunteer recruitment rallies in late 1913 and early 1914.

Macran, Henry S., Hegelian philosopher and a Fellow of Trinity College, Dublin 1892–1937.

Meyer, Eduard (1855–1930) brother of Kuno Meyer, a distinguished German historian of mainly ancient history, he held various posts in Germany, mainly at Leipzig and Berlin, and lectured at Harvard in 1909. In 1916 he published *England, its political organization and development, and the war against Germany*. He received honorary degrees from Oxford, Chicago and St Andrews.

Meyer, Kuno (1858–1919) the eminent Celtic philologist, founded the School of Irish Learning in Dublin and edited the journal *Ériu*. Kuno

Meyer was a key link in Casement's German network, and a close friend of Theodore Schiemann. Casement met Meyer frequently in the weeks after his arrival in Berlin. In November 1914, Meyer left for the US and made a series of anti-British speeches mainly to Irish-American audiences.

Meyer, Richard, served as Casement's liaison officer with the German Foreign Office, and was one of the few Jews on the permanent staff. Almost all communication to and from Casement during his time in Germany passed across Meyer's desk, and the two cooperated closely on the formation of the Irish Brigade and the preparations for Casement's return to Ireland in April 1916. Meyer was involved in various covert operations on other fronts, and went on to direct the Political Division of the Foreign Office. He was denied citizenship by Hitler in 1936. However, because of his many years of public service, he was allowed to 'escape' to Sweden in 1939.

Monteith, Robert (1879–1956) was born in Newtownmountkennedy, County Wicklow. He saw action in India and South Africa and served for sixteen years in the British Army, before throwing in his lot with James Connolly and the Irish Workers' movement. He was one of the first recruits to the Irish Volunteers in November 1913, and elected as Captain of A Company of the First Battalion of the Dublin Brigade, Irish Republican Army. He began to openly drill both the Citizen Army and Volunteers in Dublin. After the outbreak of war, he was forced to leave his house at 6 Palmerston Place (now the editorial office of *History Ireland*) and settled in Limerick to instruct the Volunteers. In October 1915, he left the US for Germany where, on Casement's insistence, he took over command of the Irish Brigade at the end of November 1915, although he felt he was not up to the job. He maintained a diary during his time in Germany that was later reproduced in F.M. Lynch, *The Mystery Man of Banna Strand* (New York, 1959)

Montgelas, Count Max Von (1860–1938) Bavarian general, diplomat and historian. He was a prominent figure in the negotiations at the Paris Peace conference. In 1925 he published his controversial *The Case for the Central Powers: An Impeachment of the Versailles Verdict*. He was co-editor of the Karl Kautsky documents on the outbreak of the FWW.

Morel, E.D (1873–1924) journalist and activist; in 1904 he founded the Congo Reform Association with Casement. On the declaration of war, he helped to set up the pressure group the Union of Democratic Control, and his sympathies shifted towards the International Labour Party. In 1917 he was imprisoned for a technical violation of the Defence of the Realm Act. He defeated Winston Churchill in a bitterly fought election for Dundee in 1922. Casement's extensive correspondence with Morel is held in the London School of Economics.

Morten, Richard (d.1930) Casement's closest friend, who often had him to stay at his Elizabethan manor house, The Savoy, on the outskirts of London. It was there in 1911 that Casement wrote his reports on the Putumayo. The following year Casement travelled with Morten through Germany by motor car.

Nadolny, Rudolf (1873–1953) born in Poland. After holding various diplomatic posts in Russia, Persia and Albania he was given a post in Abteilung IIIb, where he created an independent political operation known as 'P' (Politik) and became a spymaster, directing covert support for various anti-government groups in Russia, Ireland and elsewhere. Nadolny's negotiations with Casement turned increasingly bitter. After the war, Nadolny became a singular advocate of the German–Soviet alliance.

Noeggerath, J.E. (1877–1936) a German-American electrical engineer with extensive connections in Berlin. Noeggerath was closely involved with German secret services. In 1914, he published a brief *The Truth about the War* (Munich, 1914). He proved indispensable in early April 1916, helping Casement to obtain the submarine.

Nordenflycht, Ferdinand von (1850–1931) career diplomat, who befriended Casement during his time as German Minister in Brazil. Married Adelheid Mühlig (1863–1933) and had two sons and two daughters, the younger Augusta, nicknamed Gussy, who appears as the 'Baroness Gussie' in the diary. Casement spent time convalescing with the Nordenflychts in the spring of 1915.

O'Connor, T.P. (1848–1929) journalist and politician, he served for almost fifty years as a backbench member of parliament.

265

O'Gorman, Canice (1872–1941) Augustinian priest sent from Rome to attend to the spiritual needs of the Irish prisoners. He stayed in Limburg during the later months of 1914 and returned to Rome in early 1915.

O'Laughlin, John Callan (1873–1949) US journalist. He served as US Secretary of State in 1909.

Oppersdorff, Hans Georg von (1866–1948) from an old Silesian family, he was a leading German Catholic.

O'Riordan, Michael (1857–1919) rector of the Irish College, Rome, born in Kilmurray, County Limerick, he was a keen supporter of Irish language movement and with his friend, Bishop Edward O'Dwyer, pushed a strong nationalist agenda in Rome. He wrote widely on ecclesiastical affairs for the *Catholic Bulletin* and, though opposed to the rising, he supported the aims of the rebels.

Papen, Franz von (1879-1969) Diplomat and German Chancellor; as the German military attaché in Washington in 1914, von Papen collaborated closely with Casement and other Irish revolutionaries to destabilise the Anglo-American alliance. Important communications between von Papen and the IRB were stolen from a German embassy office on Wall Street, which contained revealing information about international aspects of Irish revolutionary activity. Von Papen later wrote the foreword to the second edition of Robert Monteith's *Casement's Last Adventure* (Dublin, 1953).

Pasha, Enver (1881–1922) Ottoman military leader and leader of the Young Turk revolution. In December 1915, Casement intended visiting Constantinople in order to discuss the deployment of the Irish Brigade 'in the Eastern warfield' with the object of assisting the Ottoman forces expel the British from Egypt.

Plunkett, Joseph Mary (1887–1916) born of a wealthy Dublin family, his father was a papal count. He joined IRB and was sent in 1915 by that organisation to negotiate with the Germans on their behalf. In Berlin he collaborated with Casement on the 'Ireland Report', setting out how Germany might contribute towards an Irish rebellion (NLI MS 13085-5).

Plunkett was later a key committee member in the organisation of the Easter Rising; a signatory of the Proclamation of the Republic, he was one of the sixteen executed leaders.

Pokorny, Julius (1887–1970) Celtic scholar, in 1920 he succeeded Kuno Meyer as Professor of Celtic Philology in Berlin. He met and photographed Casement in Hamburg in February 1915, and later published a small appreciation of Casement in the German Irish publication *Irische Blätter* 'Meine Erinnerungen an Sir Roger Casement', v.1, 93–96.

Purser, Sarah (1848–1943) portrait painter, stained-glass artist and national activist. Her portrait of Sir Roger Casement, the property of the National Gallery of Ireland, hangs in Dáil Eireann.

Puttkamer, Jesco von (1855–1917) German military official, he was selected to serve as Governor of Cameroon on nine different occasions between 1887 and 1906. Casement had dealings with Puttkamer during his earliest official posting to the British consulate in the Niger Coast Protectorate.

Quinlisk, Timothy (1895–1920) joined Royal Irish Regiment in 1911, he arrived in France in August 1914, was captured in October and imprisoned in Limburg where he volunteered as one of the first recruits into the Irish Brigade. After the war, due to a failed attempt to find favour with Michael Collins, he turned informer and was shot dead by the IRA in February 1920.

Quinn, John (1870–1924) Irish-American corporate lawyer who patronised leading literary modernists including Joseph Conrad, W.B. Yeats and James Joyce; his collection of post-impressionist and modern art was unrivalled in the US. Casement stayed with Quinn during his time in New York City in 1914, and his correspondence with Quinn is held in the New York Public Library. Quinn wrote a moving elegy about Casement after his execution.

Redmond, John (1856–1918) Irish nationalist MP and leader of the Irish Parliamentary Party from 1900–18. Casement met with Redmond in May 1914 to discuss the fate of the Irish Volunteers, but their relations were civil at best. Casement never forgave Redmond for committing Irishmen to the defence of the British Empire.

Reuss of Greiz, Hermine (1887–1947) born of a sovereign house, in 1922 she married the exiled Kaiser Wilhelm II; they were fifth cousins through their common descent from King George II.

Roeder, Baron von, courtier and confidant to Kaiser Wilhelm; married to an English woman. They had two sons who fought on different sides in the FWW.

Stumm, Wilhelm August von (1869–1935) was Director of the Political Department at the German Foreign Office, with tremendous influence at the highest level of German imperial power. In 1916 he became under-secretary of state for foreign affairs. Casement met von Stumm in Charleville, and it is likely that von Stumm's approval was vital to the acceptance of Casement's plan for the Irish Brigade.

Schiemann, Theodor von (1847–1921) historian, archivist and policy expert on Germany's Eastern Front; he was a key intellectual ally of Casement and a close friend of the Kaiser. Schiemann was collaborating with anti-British elements in the Irish republican movement from as early as 1906. He visited Britain just before the outbreak of war to consider the deepening political crisis in Ireland. His report on the imminent outbreak of civil war in Ireland influenced Germany's urging Austria to go to war with Serbia, based on his view that internal conflict in Britain would prevent involvement in any European conflict. In 1915, he published *Die Achillesferse Englands* (England's Achilles Heel) containing his translation of excerpts from Casement's essays published in *The Crime against Ireland* (1914). After Casement's execution he wrote a foreword to Antonie Meyer, *Der Casement-Prozess und seine Ursachen / Sir Roger Casement: ein Irischer Märthrer* (Berlin, 1916).

Schröder, Kurt von (1889–1966) member of the German banking dynasty with established financial operations in both the City of London and Wall Street. He is widely remembered for his part in financing and facilitating Hitler's rise to power.

Solf, Wilhelm Heinrich (1862–1936) scholar, statesman and diplomat, Solf served as secretary of the German Colonial Office until 1918. He met with Casement on 12 December 1914.

Stanhope, Aubrey, journalist with extensive contacts and a close friend of the U.S. newspaper proprietor, James Gordon Bennett; he worked as a special correspondent for the *New York Herald* for twenty-five years. This included a long stint in London. He published a volume of memoirs *On the Track of the Great: Recollections of a Special Correspondent* (1914). As editor of the anti-British, Berlin paper, *The Continental Times*, he helped Casement in his propaganda offensive against the British Foreign Office in 1915.

Tirpitz, Alfred von (1849–1930) during his time as Secretary of State for the German Imperial Navy, he built the German navy into a formidable power. His support for submarine warfare antagonised the US and in 1916 he was dismissed from his post.

Tyrrell, William (1866–1947) permanent official in the Foreign Office, he served as Sir Edward Grey's private secretary from 1907–15. Casement had a friendship with Tyrrell going back many years, however, it would not survive beyond 1914.

Vollmöller, Karl (1878–1948) German playwright and screen writer; he is best known for writing *The Blue Angel*, the film that made Marlene Dietrich a star.

Wedel, Count George von (1862–1943) was one of the notable diplomats in the Kaiser's service. He had served as an attaché in Tokyo, Vienna, Cairo and Rome before taking on the direction of the English Department at the German Foreign Office (Auswärtiges Amt). Von Wedel arranged with the German secret police for Casement to be granted diplomatic immunity on his arrival in Berlin. Von Wedel and Casement remained in close contact until the departure for Ireland in April 1916.

Wiegand, Karl (1874–1961) German-born journalist and war correspondent, he worked for *United Press* and the Hearst newspaper empire. His published interview *Current Misconceptions about the War*, containing an interview with Frederick Wilhelm, Crown Prince of Germany, gave credence to the view that the war had been forced upon Germany.

Wiegand, Theodor (1864–1936) German archaeologist and founder of the Pergamon Museum in Berlin. He had journeyed to the archaeological ruins of Troy with Alice Stopford Green.

Zerhusen, Joseph (1880–?) worked in the timber trade before the war and was located in Liverpool, where he was briefly a partner of the West African Mahogany Syndicate. He married Ellen Hand in 1914. In 1915 he was assigned to serve as one of the translators of the Irish Brigade. NLI MS 43 570/1–2 contains a ninety-eight-page typescript of Zerhusen's recollections about the Irish Brigade from 1915–18, with a particularly good description of the camp at Zossen.

Zimmermann, Arthur (1864–1940) was Undersecretary of State at the German Foreign Office, succeeding Gottlieb von Jagow in November 1916. He met with Casement the day after his arrival in Berlin in November 1914 to discuss the various aspects of his mission to Germany.

SELECT BIBLIOGRAPHY

Editions of writing by Roger Casement:

Sir Roger Casement: Irland, Deutschland & Die Freiheit der Meere & Andere Aufsätze (Munich: Jos Hubers, 1916).

Sir Roger Casement, Le Crime contre l'Europe (Brussels: Veritas, 1916)

Roger Casement: The Crime against Europe with The Crime against Ireland (Belfast: Athol Books, 2003)

Diaries of Sir Roger Casement: His Mission to Germany and the Findlay Affair (Munich: Arche Publishing, 1922)

Sir Roger Casement: Meine Mission Deutschland während des Krieges und die Findlay-Affaire (Altenburg/Thüringen, 1925)

Casement in Germany: A Guide to the Roger Casement papers in Clare County Archives (Ennis, Clare County Council, 2005).

Angus Mitchell (ed.), *The Amazon Journal of Roger Casement* (London and Dublin: Anaconda Editions & Lilliput Press, 1997)

Angus Mitchell (ed.), *Sir Roger Casement's Heart of Darkness: The 1911 Documents* (Dublin: Irish Manuscripts Commission, 2003)

Memoirs & Contemporary Sources:

Blücher, Princess Evelyn, *An English Wife in Berlin: A Private Memoir of Events, Politics and Daily Life in Germany Throughout the War and the Social Revolution of 1918* (London: John Murray, 1932)

Blücher, Princess Evelyn and Chapman-Huston, D., *Memoirs of Prince Blücher: A Moving Record of Anglo-German friendship 1865–1931* (London: John Murray, 1932)

Colum, Mary, *Life and the Dream* (New York: Macmillan & Co, 1928)

Devoy, John, 'Sir Roger Casement and the Irish Brigade in Germany', *The Gaelic American*, 28 June, 1924.

John Devoy, *Recollections of an Irish Rebel* (New York: Charles P. Young, 1929)

Gaffney, Thomas St John, *Breaking the Silence: England, Ireland, Wilson and the War* (New York: Horace Liveright: 1930)

Gerard, James W., *My Four Years in Germany* (London, 1917)

Gregory, J.D., *On the edge of Diplomacy; Rambles and Reflections 1902–1928* (London: Hutchinson, 1929)

Keogh, M., *With Casement's Irish Brigade* (Drogheda: Privately Published, 2010); originally published in the *Catholic Bulletin*, January–December 1928.

McGuire, J.K., *The King, the Kaiser and Irish Freedom* (New York: The Devin Adair Company, 1915)

Meyer, Eduard, *England: its political organization and development and the war against Germany* (Boston: Ritter and Company, 1916)

Monteith, Robert, *Casement's Last Adventure* (Chicago: Privately Printed, 1932)

Quinlisk, T. 'The German Irish Brigade: diary of Casement's lieutenant', in *Land and Water* (6 November 1919).

------------, 'The German-Irish Brigade: An Inside Story from one of Sir Roger Casement's chief Lieutenants showing how the Kaiser tricked men he made traitors', *South Bend News-Times*, 25 January 1920.

Rothenfelder, Franz, *Casement in Deutschland* (Augsburg: Verlag Gebrüder Reichel, 1917)

Schiemann, Theodor von, *Die Achillesferse Englands* (Berlin: Verlag von Georg Reimer, 1915)

Spindler, Karl *The Mystery of the Casement Ship [with authentic documents]* (Berlin: Kribe-Verlag, 1931).

Secondary sources:

Clayton, Xander, *Aud* (Plymouth: G.A.C. Books, 2007)

Doerries, Reinhard R., 'Die Mission Sir Roger Casements im Deutschen Reich 1914–16', *Historische Zeitschrift*, Bd. 222, H.3, (Jun., 1976), 578–625.

----------------, *Prelude to the Easter Rising: Sir Roger Casement in Imperial Germany* (London: Frank Cass, 2000).

----------------, 'Hopeless Mission: Sir Roger Casement in Imperial Germany', *The Journal of Intelligence History* 6 (Summer 2006).

Dopperen, Ron van and Graham, Cooper C., 'Film flashes of the European front: the war diary of Albert K. Dawson, 1915–16', *Film History*, 23, 2011, 20–37.

Horne, John and Kramer, Alan, *German Atrocities, 1914: A history of Denial* (New Haven: Yale, 2001).

Hünssler, Wolfgang, *Das Deutsche Kaiserreich und die Irische Frage 1900–14* (Frankfurt am Main: Peter Lang, 1978).

Kluge, Hans-Dieter, *Irland in der deutschen Geschichtswissenschaft, Politik und Propaganda vor 1914 und im Ersten Weltkrieg* (Frankfurt am Main: Peter Lang, 1985)

Lerchenmueller, Joachim, '"The wretched lot"—a brief history of the Irish Brigade in Germany, 1914–1919', *Yearbook of the Centre for Irish-German Studies* (University of Limerick, 1998-99), 95–113.

McGrath, Andrew, 'Just war Theory in Roger Casement's *The Crime against Europe*', *Field Day Review* 10 (2014), 90–98.

McHugh, Roger 'Casement and German help', in F.X. Martin (ed.), *Leaders and Men of the Easter Rising: Dublin 1916* (London: Methuen, 1967).

Meyer, Antonie, *Der Casement-Prozess und seine Ursachen / Sir Roger Casement: ein Irischer Märthrer* (Berlin: Berlag Karl Curtius, 1916)

--------, *Dublin 1916* (London: Arlington Books, 1966).

Mitchell, Angus, *Roger Casement* (Dublin: The O'Brien Press, 2013).

Mitchell, Angus, 'Phases of a Dishonourable Phantasy', *Field Day Review*, 8, 84–125.

Mitchell, Donald, *The Politics of Dissent – A Biography of E.D. Morel* (Bristol: Silverwood, 2014)

Monteith, Lynch, Florence *The Mystery Man of Banna Strand: The Life and Death of Captain Robert Monteith* (New York: Vantage Press, 1959).

O'Brien, Anthony, 'The Celtic Cross at Limburg an der Lahn, Germany: a sentimental journey', *The Irish Sword*, 24, Summer 2005, 241–276.

Ó Lúing, Seán, *Kuno Meyer: A Biography* (Dublin: Geography Publications, 1991)

Ó Síocháin, Séamas, *Roger Casement: imperialist, rebel, revolutionary* (Dublin: The Lilliput Press, 2008),

Roth, Andreas, 'The German soldier is not Tactful: Sir Roger Casement and the Irish Brigade in Germany during the First World War', *The Irish Sword* 19, 1995, 315.

Ryan, Des, 'Thomas St. John Gaffney: United States Consul General in Germany 1905–1915', *The Old Limerick Journal*, 47 (2013), 33–38.

Sloan, Geoffrey, 'The British State and the Irish Rebellion of 1916: An Intelligence Failure or a Failure of Response?', *Journal of Strategic Security*, Vol. 6:5, Fall 2013, 328–357.

Wiel, Jérôme aan de, *The Irish Factor 1899–1919: Ireland's Strategic and Diplomatic importance for Foreign Powers* (Dublin, Irish Academic Press, 2008)

-------- '1914: What will the British Do? The Irish Home Rule Crisis in the July Crisis', *The International History Review* (2014), 1–25.

Wolf, Karin, *Sir Roger Casement und die deutsch-irischen Beziehungen* (Berlin: Dunker und Humblot, 1972).

INDEX